AA

ORDNANCE SURVEY
LEISURE GUIDE

FOREST OF DEAN AND WYE VALLEY

Produced jointly by the Publishing Division of the Automobile Association and the Ordnance Survey

Cover: view from Yat Rock
Title page: Ross-on-Wye
Contents page: swan on River Wye
Introductory page: Forest of Dean in spring

Editor: Rebecca Snelling

Copy editor: Virginia Langer

Art editor: Glyn Barlow

Design assistants: KAG Design

Editorial contributors: David Bick FSA (Industrial Archaeology); Heather and Jon Hurley (Walks); Douglas McLean (The River Wye, Myths and Legends, Gazetteer box features); Martin Morris (The Story of Dean and the Wye); David Mullin (An Ancient Forest); Mike Pratt (Wildlife of Forest and Valley); Peter Wenham (Gazetteer)

Picture researcher: Wyn Voysey

Original photography: Harry Williams

Typeset by Avonset, Midsomer Norton, Bath
Printed in Great Britain by Chorley & Pickersgill Ltd, Leeds

Maps extracted from the Ordnance Survey's 1:625 000 Routeplanner map, 1:250 000 Routemaster Series and 1:25 000 Pathfinder and Outdoor Leisure Map Series, with the permission of Her Majesty's Stationery Office. Crown Copyright reserved.

Additions to the maps by the Cartographic Dept of the Automobile Association and the Ordnance Survey.

Produced by the Publishing Division of the Automobile Association.

Distributed in the United Kingdom by the Ordnance Survey, Southampton, and the Publishing Division of the Automobile Association, Fanum House, Basingstoke, Hampshire RG21 2EA.

AA ISBN 0 86145 669 6 (hardback)
AA ISBN 0 86145 659 9 (softback)
OS ISBN 0 31900140 7 (hardback)
OS ISBN 0 31900139 3 (softback)

Published by the Automobile Association and the Ordnance Survey.

AA Reference: 55521 (hardback)
AA Reference: 55518 (softback)

FOREST OF DEAN AND WYE VALLEY

Contents

Using this Book

The entries in the Gazetteer have been carefully selected although for reasons of space it has not been possible to include every community in the region. A number of small villages are described under the entry for a larger neighbour, and these can be found by using the index.

Each entry in the A to Z Gazetteer has the atlas page number on which the place can be found and its National Grid reference included under the heading. An explanation of how to use the National Grid is given on page 80.

Beneath many of the entries in the Gazetteer are listed AA-recommended hotels, restaurants, garages, guesthouses, campsites and self-catering accommodation in the immediate vicinity of the place described.

For reasons of space the AA-recommended establishments under some entries are a selection only. For full details see the AA range of annual guides and the AA *Members' Handbook*.

HOTELS

1-star — Good hotels and inns, generally of small scale and with acceptable facilities and furnishing.

2-star — Hotels offering a higher standard of accommodation, with some private bathrooms/showers; lavatories on all floors; wider choice of food.

3-star — Well-appointed hotels; a good proportion of bedrooms with private bathrooms/showers.

4-star — Exceptionally well-appointed hotels offering a high standard of comfort and service, the majority of bedrooms should have private bathrooms/showers.

5-star — Luxury hotels offering the highest international standards.

Hotels often satisfy some of the requirements for higher classifications than that awarded.

Red-star — Red stars denote hotels which are considered to be of outstanding merit within their classification.

Country House Hotel — A hotel where a relaxed informal atmosphere prevails. Some of the facilities may differ from those at urban hotels of the same classification.

RESTAURANTS

1-fork — Modest but good restaurant.

2-fork — Restaurant offering a higher standard of comfort than above.

3-fork — Well-appointed restaurant.

4-fork — Exceptionally well-appointed restaurant.

5-fork — Luxury restaurant.

1-rosette — Hotel or restaurant where the cuisine is considered to be of a higher standard than is expected in an establishment within its classification.

2-rosette — Hotel or restaurant offering very much above average food irrespective of the classification.

3-rosette — Hotel or restaurant offering outstanding food, irrespective of classification.

GUESTHOUSES

These are different from, but not necessarily inferior to, AA-appointed hotels, and they offer an alternative for those who prefer inexpensive and not too elaborate accommodation. They all provide clean, comfortable accommodation in homely surroundings. Each establishment must usually offer at least six bedrooms and there should be a general bathroom and a general toilet for every six bedrooms without private facilities.

SELF CATERING

These establishments, which are all inspected on a regular basis, have to meet minimum standards in accommodation, furniture, fixtures and fittings, services and linen.

CAMPSITES

1-pennant — Site licence; 10% of pitches for touring units; site density not more than 30 per acre; 2 separate toilets for each sex per 30 pitches; good quality tapwater; efficient waste disposal; regular cleaning of ablutions block; fire precautions; well-drained ground.

2-pennant — All one-pennant facilities plus: 2 washbasins with hot and cold water for each sex per 30 pitches in separate washrooms; warden available at certain times of the day.

3-pennant — All two-pennant facilities plus: one shower or bath for each sex per 30 pitches, with hot and cold water; electric shaver points and mirrors; all-night lighting of toilet blocks; deep sinks for washing clothes; facilities for buying milk, bread and gas; warden in attendance by day, on call by night.

4-pennant — All three-pennant facilities plus: a higher degree of organisation than one–three-pennant sites; attention to landscaping; reception office; late-arrivals enclosure; first aid hut; shop; routes to essential facilities lit after dark; play area; bad weather shelter; hard standing for touring vans.

5-pennant — A comprehensive range of services and equipment; careful landscaping; automatic laundry; public telephone; indoor play facilities for children; extra facilities for recreation; warden in attendance 24 hours per day.

Quiet forest glades and cider-apple orchards, romantic gorges, medieval castles, ruined abbeys and peaceful hamlets all contribute to the beauty of Dean and the Wye.
Packed with information on where to go and what to see – plus colour photographs, motor tours and walks – this book provides a splendid introduction to a region rich in history, legend and interest.
Written by people who know and love the area and backed by the AA's research expertise and the Ordnance Survey's mapping, this guide will appeal as much to the first-time visitor to this area as to those who already know it well.

The Story of Dean and the Wye

The fast road from the Midlands to South Wales carries an unending stream of cars and lorries past Ross-on-Wye. Yet much of the Forest of Dean and Wye Valley stays remote from the late 20th century. Still, silent woodland covers vast tracts, and in the Golden Valley on the road to Hay and in the parallel valleys of the Escley and Olchon the motorist drives through mile after mile of sparsely populated rural England.

Traces of ancient times

Remote too is King Arthur's Cave on the Great Doward towering above the Wye near Symonds Yat, which is not easy to find among the labyrinth of lanes and footpaths sprawling over the limestone hill. It is most unlikely that Arthur was ever here, but aeons before his rule man made his home in this shelter – 60,000 years ago when most of Britain was encased in the Ice Age. With the exception of Kent's Cavern in Devon, no other cave in Britain has a longer sequence of occupational phases. Men of the Old Stone Age were here, followed 40,000 years later by those of the Creswellian Age. To the cave came the men of the Middle Stone Age of 10,000 years ago, and successively those of the New Stone Age, the Bronze Age, and right up to the arrival of the Roman legions as they thrust deeper and deeper towards Wales.

Long before the Roman invasion there was strife in this rugged border country where to this day the hills show evidence of old fortifications. The Silures, who made their home here, fought the

Celts until making an alliance with the Goidelic Celts in the struggle against the Brythonic Celts. All three tribes united under the leadership of Caractacus in their resistance to the Romans. There are several places along the Marches of Wales where Caractacus is reputed to have made his final stand – one is among the rock faces at Symonds Yat. It is not a strong claim, although there is evidence of extensive defensive emplacements.

Wherever that last stand was made, the vanquisher of Caractacus in AD50 was Ostorius Scapula, who may have given his name to Caplar Hill where a double entrenched camp commands a loop of the Wye. Inside the next loop, at Kings Caple, is a tumulus opposite the church rising some 15ft. But this old burial ground is now seeing happier times, and is a gathering place for villagers at times of national celebration – and every year on bonfire night.

Conflict and change

The Romans took over the Silurian settlement of Venta Silurum and renamed it Caerwent. Monmouth is believed to be on the site of Blestium, but there were no habitations at the present Hereford and Ross. At Kenchester, six miles north west of the city was Magna Castra, one of the smallest of all Roman walled towns, extending to only 25 acres. A major town was Ariconium, now buried beneath the fields near Weston-under-Penyard, built just over half a mile from a site at present-day Linton, where flint and stone tools had been manufactured. It was obviously found opportune to move production to a place with easy access to the iron-ore of the Forest of Dean where smelting was carried out, and the iron was forged into objects of domestic as well as military use.

Excavations 25 years ago at Huntsham, within the Yat loop of the Wye, revealed a considerable Roman villa. It has since been covered in again, but on land belonging to the same farm is the Queen

View of the Wye from Yat Rock. Insets: a Roman coin found during excavations beneath Monmouth School, and King Arthur's Cave, where Stone Age men sheltered

Engraving of Goodrich Castle – guardian of a strategic crossing of the Wye

Stone, an erect block of Old Red conglomerate some 7½ft high. The stone bears no geological relation to the alluvial plain on which it stands and must have been tossed there by some prehistoric convulsion. Its name probably comes from its shape and the impression of the folds of a regal dress given by 13 near-vertical groovings, carved by some primeval stream.

The departure of the Romans in the 5th century allowed the Welsh to take command of western Herefordshire up to the Wye as it cuts a wide arc through the county. This has had a lasting influence, for to the west of the river Welsh place-names abound – Llangarron, Llandinabo and a host of others – but there are virtually none to the east. Even in the Middle Ages Welsh was as common a language as English in the streets of Hereford, and as late as 1830 services in Welsh were conducted regularly in the church at Walterstone.

It was the King of Mercia, Offa (757–96), who incorporated Herefordshire into an English kingdom and made the boundary of Wales very much what it is today. To define the boundary and to strengthen his position, Offa ordered the building of the dyke that 1,200 years later still bears his name. It ran from Chepstow to Prestatyn and was mainly of earthworks, though below Monmouth stretches of the Wye were considered to be sufficient defence without man-made additions.

Within Mercia and well to the east of the Dyke was the tiny kingdom of Archenfield, enclosed by the rivers Wye, Monnow and Worm. The population of Silurians held allegiance to Offa but maintained their ancient customs and rights. They were brave warriors and among the earliest Christians in these islands, with their own saints whose names are still remembered by the dedication of several local churches – Deinst, Denys, Tysilio, and, most famous of all, Dubricius. Legend says he had a miraculous birth when his mother Eurdil was consigned to be burnt at the stake, and he grew up to crown King Arthur at Cirencester.

Archenfield was within the see of Hereford, one of the oldest in Britain. As early as AD601 a bishop of Hereford was one of the seven British prelates summoned by Augustine of Canterbury to an ecclesiastical convention. The cathedral is dedicated to St Mary and St Ethelbert; the latter was the king of East Anglia whom Offa had murdered while he was entertaining him in his palace near the city. This treacherous deed aroused such abhorrence and remorse that Ethelbert's name was perpetuated in many ways, including Ethelbert's Fair.

The cathedral was destroyed in 1055 by Elfgar, Earl of Mercia who, on being outlawed by Edward the Confessor, collected an army in Ireland and brought an invasion fleet of 18 vessels to Wales. In an alliance with King Griffin he led an army of Welsh, Irish, and Danes on a march of destruction to Hereford. The following year Harold, son of Earl Godwin and destined to become king for a few months before being killed at Hastings, attempted to exact vengeance by taking an expedition into Wales. It was not a success, for Bishop Leofgar and several other dignitaries were killed in combat near Glasbury.

Monuments to power

William the Conqueror appointed his friend, William Fitz Osbern, to the earldom of Hereford and charged him to be 'diligent in the work of castle building'. This he was, for in the five years before he was killed fighting in Flanders he started a programme of building which was to dominate life in the Marches for centuries. His first castle was at the mouth of the Wye at Chepstow, and he was the reputed builder of the castles at Monmouth and Hereford. Those at Goodrich, Wilton, Raglan and St Briavels were all started within 70 years of the Conquest, and the trio of Skenfrith, Grosmont and White Castle followed in the 13th century. There were several other castles of lesser importance. The exact number has never been established, but Herefordshire is reputed to be second only to Northumberland in its profusion of ancient castles.

The architecture of Hereford Cathedral, begun in the 12th century, spans seven centuries

providing a colourful ceremony at the start of Hereford's May (St Ethelbert's) Fair when he receives a bushel of corn as a token of his dues. At Ross, the bishops were lords of the manor from the 11th century until Elizabeth I seized it for herself.

The final act in the warfare with the Welsh was in 1405 when 18-year-old Prince Henry (who was born at Monmouth, spent some of his childhood at Courtfield and later became Henry V) crushed Owen Glendower at Grosmont. The might of the castles was now on the wane and many fell into disuse after the Wars of the Roses. A decisive battle of these wars took place in Herefordshire at Mortimer's Cross in 1461. Edward IV routed the Lancastrian army and Owen Tudor, second

Below: White Castle, one of three which protected the Monnow Valley in the 13th century

Hereford Cathedral remained desolate for over 20 years until it was rebuilt by Bishop Robert Losinga (1079–96). The second quarter of the 12th century brought the building of three abbeys by the Cistercian order. The most glorious was that at Tintern, founded in 1131 by Walter Fitz Richard, lord of Lower Gwent. It was set in a remote place – a deliberate policy of the Cistercians. Flaxley Abbey was built on the spot where Milo of Gloucester, Constable of Gloucester Castle, was accidentally pierced by an arrow while hunting deer on Christmas Eve, 1143. The third Cistercian abbey was that at Abbey Dore founded by Robert of Ewyas, grandson of the Conqueror and the monks of Herefordshire are credited with establishing the county's breed of sheep, the Ryeland. A historian of the time of Elizabeth I described the wool as 'the equivalent of the golden fleece of the ancients, and poets compared it for its fineness to the web of the silkworm and for its softness to the cheek of a maiden'.

Just as the governors of the castles imposed their will upon the people under their protection, so did the bishops' power extend beyond the spiritual life of their charges. They held manorial rights, demanding tolls from markets and rents from tenants – recalled in recent years by the bishop

husband of Henry V's Queen Katherine, was captured. He and others were taken to Hereford and beheaded in public, but only 24 years later, his grandson, Henry VII, was to found the Tudor royal line.

Civil War to serene fields

The Civil War brought no major battles in the Valley or Forest, but those years were packed with incident. Monmouth, which both sides regarded as the key to South Wales, fell to the Parliamentarians through the treachery of Colonel Robert Kyrle, a kinsman of John Kyrle, who was to gain some renown as the Man of Ross (see page 60). As was not uncommon at that troubled time, the colonel had switched his allegiance. While with the King's forces at Monmouth, he took a patrol out of town and fell into the hands of Roundhead Colonel Massey. Fearful that retribution might be wrought upon him for previous change of heart, he did a deal to lead the enemy into Monmouth. The unsuspecting guard let down the drawbridge on seeing Kyrle, and the town was seized with scarcely a shot being fired. In the same year, 1645, a Scots army besieged Hereford for six weeks before withdrawing on the approach of Charles I from Raglan. The Scots fled to Gloucester and, on their way, ravenous after weeks in the field, subjected Ross to a night of pillage and terror.

For the very last time the border castles were used for conflict. Raglan Castle suffered severe damage by siege and bombardment, and its surrender to Fairfax was regarded as the final act of the first Civil War. Castles at Monmouth and Hereford were dismantled, and that at Goodrich was destroyed in a six-week bombardment by a locally cast mortar known as Roaring Meg.

Thus, after many centuries, the turbulence of war was stilled in field and forest. The age of the castle gave way to that of the country mansion whose denizens continued to direct and influence the lives of those living on their estates. To a slight degree this lingers on in a more democratic age, though staffing problems in and after World War II have resulted in many country seats being converted into hotels and schools. Some have disappeared altogether – demolition squads have been active. Most prominent of these was Goodrich Court, built as a 'mock castle' by Sir Samuel Rush Meyrick in 1828 and, after a stately life of little more than a century, reduced to rubble in 1949.

Excavations have shown that prehistoric man in King Arthur's Cave was a hunter, but on the river plain cultivation of the rich red soil must soon have become of greater concern. Seventeenth-century historian John Speed wrote, 'The climate of Herefordshire is most healthful and the soyle so fertile for corn and cattle that no place in England yieldeth more or better conditions.' Rye, beans and vetches were the most common crops on the feudal system of scattered strips of land. With the land enclosures wheat and oats became the main crops, and this century has seen increasing acreage given over to malting barley to meet the needs of the breweries. Another dramatic increase in production was that of sugar beet, when in the 1920s it became the first commodity to be blessed with a guaranteed price.

Products that have made the area world famous are cider (see page 47) and cattle. The first reference to the white-faced Hereford cattle is dated to London's Smithfield Show in 1799, and 30 years later William Cobbett in his *Rural Rides* described them as the 'finest and most beautiful of all horned cattle'. Hereford bulls have been exported to many parts of the world, but now, sadly, in their native county the cattle are being replaced by the Continental breeds of Charolais, Simmental and Limousin to meet the demands of the housewife for leaner beef and smaller cuts.

The second half of the 20th century has seen an acceleration of trends for farms to become fewer and larger. They now extend up to 1,200 acres, more than twice as large as 20 years ago. It is symptomatic of a people who, while having roots deep into the past, are forever looking to the needs of the future.

Archaeological excavations of King Arthur's Cave in 1871 were assisted by the use of dynamite!

A prize bull of Herefordshire's own breed

Industrial Archaeology

The Wye Valley is best known for its natural beauty, but the equally picturesque Forest of Dean, dividing the gorge-like lower Wye from the Vale of Severn, conceals a very different history. It is difficult to believe that this densely wooded upland district was long a centre of heavy industry, or that as recently as 1945 coal-mining gave employment to half its male population. Nowadays, though the physical testimony has been in great measure swept away in the name of environmental improvement, plenty remains of the legacy bequeathed by mineral wealth and the sundry other activities which developed.

Thus the industrial archaeologist will find much to detain him, whether an 18th-century iron-works, an old tram-road or canal, a ruined lime-kiln, or a private coal-mine still at work, or perhaps an ancient cider-mill annually resuscitated to provide a farmer with his drink. Old practices die hard, and how pleasing it is to discover that in this backwater of England, some have not died yet.

Coal-mining

The pennant sandstones of Dean are interspersed with numerous coal seams, of which the Coleford High Delph is the most important. Coal was worked by the Romans, and mining had become firmly established before 1300. By the 18th century it was flourishing, and the local habit of christening pits with imaginative names was indulged in to the full – *Rainproof, Farmer's Folly, Strip and At It,* and *Work or Die* are but a few.

The industry was regulated by the Court of Mine Law attended by the Gaveller, who was responsible for leasing parcels of land known as gales, on behalf of the Crown. Eventually, a chaotic situation arose due to a profusion of pits, often in close proximity to each other. An Act of Parliament settled the problem in 1838, and aided by 'foreign' capital plus a network of tram-roads to carry the coal, the industry grew rapidly. However, associated evils were not far behind. In 1842 a Government report referred to boys dragging coal-tubs day after day in wet seams scarcely 2ft high; according to a witness, their hands and knees became 'perfectly hoofed' by the continual wear and pressure. Fathers took sons of six or seven down with them to earn an extra penny or two. Conditions in the iron-mines were better, and a visitor could always tell one form of miner from the other, one being black and the other red, from the colour of the ore.

In 1880, 63 collieries yielded 800,000 tons between them, the biggest being Foxes Bridge, near Cinderford. Near by, Lightmoor Colliery also rose to prominence. It was owned by the Crawshays of South Wales and did not close until 1940. Like many others, it employed big Cornish pumping-engines, and a beam-engine for winding is now displayed at the Dean Heritage Centre (see page 65).

The gales were grouped into seven large areas in 1904 and the deeper seams supplied steam coal. Total output rarely fell below 1,000,000 tons per year, but after World War II a decline set in and the last big pit, Northern United, closed in 1965. Since then indiscriminate landscaping has left few

Lightmoor Colliery was one of several developed by Henry Crawshay, 'the Iron King of the Forest of Dean', and his brother William. The beam engine (inset) is a prime exhibit at the Dean Heritage Centre

traces behind, except for volcano-like tips clothed in conifers towering above their forest neighbours. Spared only by their enormous bulk, they are indeed fitting monuments, and one, at New Fancy, has been adapted as a public look-out point with fine views of the district.

Finally, the small and long-abandoned Newent Coalfield is worth a mention. It is of great geological interest and complexity, and was once promising enough to bring the Hereford and Gloucester Canal to its centre.

Though the all-pervading sulphureous smell has gone, old traditions are sustained by the Free Miners (see page 71), who by ancient rights still work on their own account. Such activities are part of Dean, and deserve to continue.

Below: sinking pits at the turn of the century. Water was a major hindrance to miners here at Cannop

Iron-mining and smelting

Geologically, the Forest of Dean is an oval bowl of Carboniferous limestone, stretching about 10 miles from north to south beneath which were large deposits of iron-ore, extending across the Wye into Herefordshire. This, and ample timber for charcoal, provided the basis for an important iron industry, and gave the Romans the incentive to move their iron production there from the Sussex Weald in the 2nd century.

Originally ores were smelted in bloomeries, or small furnaces, yielding only a few pounds of spongy iron at a time which needed refining in forges. Huge waste-tips rich in iron accumulated over the centuries, and laid the foundations for a great revival when the far more efficient charcoal blast-furnace was introduced. The Earl of Shrewsbury erected a furnace near Goodrich before 1575, and the right to construct furnaces in the Royal Desmesne of Dean was granted to William Herbert in 1612, with the authority to remove 12,000 cords of wood for charcoal every year.

The Forest had a high reputation for good quality iron, and in about 1620 Sir Basil Brooke, 'the great steel-maker', is supposed to have had a forge in Gloucestershire – perhaps at Linton near Ross, where the name 'Steelworks Farm' survives to this day. At Newent a furnace was built to exploit nearby ores and cinders, bringing the total number of furnaces in the area to about 20. One has recently been restored in the Angiddy Valley west of Tintern. After 1650 the Foley family dominated the industry, and shipped great quantities of pig-iron up the Severn to their forges in the West Midlands. This monopoly lasted for a century and one of their furnaces still survives, though in an altered and decrepit state, at Gunn's Mill, near Flaxley.

Partly due to the poor coking qualities of Forest coal, the coke furnace came late in Dean, and its ultimate success owed more to practical men than to the metallurgist David Mushet of Coleford, who failed in the attempt. Ironically, Whitecliff Furnace (*c.* 1800), the scene of his endeavours, is now a listed building and an important industrial monument.

In 1826 coke furnaces were erected at Cinderford and Parkend, where a 50ft-diameter waterwheel powered the blast. Two big storage ponds were constructed a mile or two away, at Cannop, and are now a much-frequented beauty spot. In 1864 Parkend produced nearly 300 tons of iron weekly, and a magnificent engine-house still marks the site, having been converted for other uses. Traditionally, the ore was brought to the surface in baskets on the backs of boys, but later, large pumping and winding engines were erected, total output reaching almost 200,000 tons in 1871. However, before the end of the century all smelting had ceased due to failing ores and competition and although mining lingered on, it did not survive World War II.

With their mysterious grotto-like caverns topped by venerable yews, the ancient surface-workings, or scowles, have long been a tourist attraction. One, at Puzzle Wood near Coleford, is open to the public, and takes about an hour to explore. For those wishing to taste the life and tribulations of the miner in a more practical manner, the subterranean workings at Clearwell Caves (see page 36) are not to be missed.

Dean's Free Miners jealously guard their ancient rights

A common Forest scene – a disused mine near Cannop

Stone and lime

The building stones of the region are extensive and diverse. They include the lovely pale orange Downton Castle sandstone of Gorsley and Newent, the grey and blue pennant sandstones and limestones of Dean, and the red and grey Old Red sandstones which occur over a wide area bordering the Wye Valley. Quarries in Dean were once numbered in their hundreds, and several at Bixslade near Coleford remain active thanks to a rising demand for restoration and new buildings. Pennant stone is very hard-wearing and resistant, and was exported as far as London and Belfast. Eastnor Castle near Ledbury was built of Forest stone, carried pannier-fashion across country on the backs of donkeys. It is a tragedy that such sources are now seldom exploited, so that over the years the architectural flavour of rural areas must inevitably become diluted, if not entirely lost.

Stone was also much in demand for fashioning into grindstones, mills and vessels of various kinds. In the Wye Valley gorge below Monmouth red sandstone conglomerate was worked into millstones, probably as early as Roman times. Cider-mills were another important product. The task was laborious and sometimes ended in disaster, as is evident from great wheel-like specimens in the quarries, abandoned where they broke, or in the river where they fell while being loaded on to boats. These old mills and stone water-troughs are now prized as garden ornaments.

Another ancient industry was lime-burning for agricultural and building purposes. The main areas of production were the Forest of Dean, the Woolhope and May Hill districts, and Gorsley Common where the remnants of a battery of five kilns still survive. Another source of limestone were the cornstones of the Old Red sandstone in Monmouthshire and Herefordshire. With their gaping tunnel-like façades, often crumbling and covered in ivy, many disused kilns still exist, as on the roadside at Symonds Yat.

Another early activity in the area was glassmaking. Four hundred years ago there were glassworks near May Hill, and examples (somewhat crude in execution) are displayed in Gloucester Museum. The local pub is still called The Glasshouse. There were similar works at Newnham and St Weonards, near Ross.

Wireworks were established in the Wye Valley prior to 1565 and cable-making began in the area before World War I. Chemical factories also flourished by distilling wood into acids and alcohols. The last works justified a branch railway, and were a well-known landmark at Cannop Crossroads until about 15 years ago.

Even gold-mining was tried in the Forest of Dean in 1906 but the venture proved uneconomic. The old entrance to the workings, the Bailey Level, is still open, near the side of the road between Drybrook and Lea. It was latterly used as a water supply. Trials for the precious metal were made at Taynton in the 1680s, and traces have recently been found by panning.

At Chepstow, Lydney, Newnham and Broadoak on the banks of the Severn, shipbuilding was carried on for centuries, and at Broadoak boats were actually launched across the turnpike road into the water. Some of the little pills and creeks were also the sites of building and are well worth exploring, though the sound of sawing and hammering has not been heard for generations.

Forest iron miners ready for work in about 1860

Transport – water, road and rail

The Severn has always been England's greatest waterway, and carried an enormous amount of traffic before the age of the railway. The Wye was much less important, mainly because of the difficulties imposed by shallows and rapids. Even so, it was an artery for coal, stone, iron and other heavy goods until the Hereford and Gloucester Canal opened in 1845.

Roman roads radiated from Gloucester via Dymock to Kentchester (near Hereford), towards Mitcheldean and via Chepstow to Caerwent. The kerbed and paved way of the well-known Dean Road, from Mitcheldean to Lydney, is exposed at Blackpool Bridge near Blakeney; whether or not it is indeed Roman, its antiquity is without doubt. After the Roman occupation, roads lapsed into a deplorable state before turnpike roads were built. When a witness at an 18th-century commission was asked about Herefordshire roads he replied, 'Roads, we have no roads. We travel in ditches.'

Horse-drawn railways came to the Forest before 1800, and the Severn and Wye Railway, between Lydbrook and Lydney, opened in 1813. It carried much mineral traffic, which numerous branches to quarries and mines soon augmented. The little Bullo Pill dock on the Severn below Newnham was the terminus of one such line. Another important horse-railway was from Hereford to Abergavenny, and the Tram Inn near Much Dewchurch is a legacy of its route. Higher up the Wye Valley, the Hay to Brecon tram-road was opened in 1816.

Most of these primitive lines were eventually converted to modern railways, which in their turn have largely succumbed to the motor vehicle. A notable survivor is part of the old Severn and Wye, from Lydney to Parkend, and now in the care of the Dean Forest Railway Preservation Society. Fine relics of early tram-roads also survive, including a road bridge at Redbrook and a long line of stone sleeper-blocks in the Bixslade Valley, Coleford.

The only substantial canal was the Hereford and Gloucester, begun in the 1790s but not completed for 50 years. A railway from Ledbury to Gloucester destroyed much of its course in the 1880s, but plenty still remains including the 1¼-mile Oxenhall Tunnel at Newent and the Ashperton Tunnel beyond Ledbury. Features of the canal are being restored by a preservation society, and we may yet see a narrow boat on its waters once more.

In steam on the Dean Forest Railway. There are train rides on 'Steam Days', and restored locomotives, railway buildings, relics and rolling stock can be seen at the Norchard Steam Centre near Lydney

Wildlife of Forest and Valley

The geology of any area has a fundamental influence on its natural history, and the Forest of Dean and Wye Valley are no exception.

At the heart of the Forest is a small, isolated coal basin of Carboniferous rocks – poor in nutrients and on the whole supporting a limited flora. A belt of older Carboniferous limestones surround this core, and there is an outer ring of older still Devonian red sandstones and conglomerates. Uplift and differential erosion have formed an upland forest area in Dean, with the flat Severn plain to the east and the limestone gorge of the Wye Valley to the west. Harder sandstones form a series of ridges between the valleys within the Forest.

From the top of these wooded ridges, views stretch across miles and miles of trees, a rare sight in a country now so poorly wooded. A closer look at the woods of the Wye and Forest, which seem to blend together, reveals that they have different stories to tell, stories which are etched into their structure and composition. Man's part is not to be underestimated either, as his interaction with the landscape forms the fabric of this area's intriguing natural mosaic of wildlife habitats.

But woodland only forms part of the pattern. Two important rivers – the Wye and Severn – define the area, offering diverse wildlife havens. There are also open glades, rides, cliffs and the remnants of old industry which contribute to this overall diversity.

Valley woodland

Six thousand years ago lowland Britain was covered in a temperate jungle of deciduous trees, a wild mixture of oak and lime, elm, ash, birch, willow and other species which colonised the country after the last Ice Age. This was the home to wild boar, wolf and beaver, truly natural woods existing in harmony with their associated wildlife, and slowly replacing themselves as necessary.

Most of our surviving woods bear little resemblance to this wildwood condition. Few can claim any real link with their past, having been felled and re-planted, but the steeply wooded sides of the Wye Valley remain relatively untouched. However, the hand of man is still recognisable in trees coppiced in a time when the woods were managed as a self-renewing resource. Thus some trees, mostly lime and hazel here, were cut in rotation to provide a regular crop from the same parent stool. Now unmanaged, these trees once again form full crowns, but often appear to have many trunks growing from their wide bases. The woods still reflect the natural dominance of small-leaved lime, and there is also the rare large-leaved lime. Of secondary importance are various mixtures of oak, cherry, ash, hazel and elm, much of which have died off, but those surviving are still important for the white-letter hairstreak butterfly.

The yellow-necked mouse forages for food on the woodland floor, and often up into the lower branches

Wildwood plants and animals

Rare and unusual indigenous trees and plants indicate the woods' long pedigree. Indeed the whole plant community growing on light limestone soils is incredibly diverse and rich, indicating how little it has been interfered with.

Seen here is the curious herb paris sanicle and goldilocks buttercup (characteristically with one or more yellow petals missing), and yellow archangel grows on the woodland floor. Among these the more common spring flowers – wood anemone, celandine, sorrel, dog's mercury, primrose and violet – all try to bloom before the overhead foliage thickens. In April these are joined by seas of bluebells, wild garlic (or ramsons) and early purple orchids. One can actually smell the change! Summer often reveals specialities such as the broadleaved helleborine, or bird's-nest orchid. Also watch for the flesh-coloured parasitic toothwort growing on the roots of hazel in spring. Country folk nicknamed this unearthly flower the corpse flower, believing it only to grow on graves.

Other floral surprises include hybrids of whitebeam and wild service trees (itself an indicator of an ancient woodland), which often show quite baffling leaf characteristics. In the Tintern area one can also find the 'Turk's hat' or martagon lily, a familiar garden plant but growing naturally here.

The ungrazed parts of these woods are truly wild, consisting of multi-storeyed habitats with mixed shrub and field layers beneath the canopy of tall mature trees – often all connected by intertwining briars, honeysuckle and traveller's joy. This is very evident in Lady Park Wood, an ecological reserve set up by the Forestry Commission to study unmanaged woodland. Such areas provide thick cover for the dormouse and yellow-necked wood mouse, and birds such as the 'scrub warblers', the blackcap and garden warbler. Woodpeckers take advantage of old rotting trees and dead elms for drumming out their territories and drilling out their nest holes.

The sheer limestone cliffs of the Wye Valley provide ideal nest sites for corvids and raptors, and jackdaws and kestrels commonly breed here. The peregrine falcon has returned to its traditional breeding site at Coldwell Rocks now that its numbers have recovered from the effects of pesticide poisoning in the 1960s. The RSPB protect the site and wardens are usually on hand to point out the birds.

Visitors to the famous Symonds Yat Rock viewpoint gaze across the Wye into Herefordshire and the long brownish form of Coppet Hill. This rather incongruous hillside is the nearest thing to moor and heath in the Forest and Wye Valley, and is extremely interesting. Buzzards often wheel overhead, and heathland birds such as lesser whitethroat and meadow pipit may be seen.

The ancient earthwork of Offa's Dyke, together with the Wye Valley Walk, provide an ideal way of seeing these ancient woods and its wildlife. An evening walk can be particularly rewarding, as badgers have dug their setts into many parts of the Dyke, almost as if it were made for them. The badger has been here as long as the woods themselves, and is an important part of the complex web of life. He is a wild animal in the truest sense of the word, and is fascinating to watch and study.

Forest woodland

The Forest of Dean differs markedly from the Wye Valley in many ways. It is much more varied in its woodland types due to a chequered history of management, each phase of which has left its mark on the natural history of the area. Virgin woodland lasted here until the 12th century, so it can still claim close connections with its ancient origins, but much of it has been felled and replanted. It now consists of a series of intermixed plantations of different ages, and both native and exotic species.

This is a Royal Forest, once the hunting reserve of Norman kings. Wild beasts, including the unusually common wild boar, native red, roe and fallow deer (introduced by the Romans) and their natural predator the wolf, were almost all hunted to extinction. The fallow deer is our only surviving living reminder of this important phase in the history of the Forest of Dean. Two main herds now inhabit the areas of Highmeadow Woods around Staunton, and the Speech House. These are timid creatures, but a quiet approach upwind of them at dawn or dusk may offer an opportunity to see the two different colour types, one dark chocolate brown and the other sandy red.

Oaks, birds and butterflies

Napoleonic oak plantations which were never actually needed for naval shipbuilding now stand as an important wildlife legacy. Dating mostly from the early 19th century, they are best seen in the Nagshead (now an RSPB reserve) and Cannop Valley areas. Scattered among them are a few enormous oaks dating from the 1600s, such as the Charkes Oak near Churchill Lodge.

These individual trees, with their enormous spreading crowns of perhaps 10 million leaves, can support up to 300 different insects alone, and their old, hollow, rattling branches and trunks have been home to generations of tawny owls and woodpeckers. The associated bird life is typical of mature oak woods, with five species of tits, all three woodpecker species, nuthatch, tree-creeper, jay and sparrowhawk. In spring migrant birds return to breed from their African wintering grounds. The more open heavily grazed areas are favoured by the tree pipit and redstart, while pied flycatchers and willow warblers prefer at least a patchy shrub layer.

Wood warblers are also found here singing in the tree tops and nesting low down, and can also be found in the mature beech woods of the Forest. The elusive hawfinch prefers more mixed plantations, which support hornbeam, cherry and yew. Birds such as the pied flycatcher have benefited from nestboxes erected originally to encourage more tits to breed, and help rid the oaks of the defoliating oakleaf roller moth caterpillar. A pilot scheme, the first in the world of its type, was launched in 1942 by the Forestry Commission. There are now nearly 400 nestboxes on the RSPB reserve, and many more elsewhere in the Forest.

Wood warblers haunt the beeches and oaks of the Forest in summertime

Bluebells beneath coppiced ash, sycamore and hazel. Insets: the speckled wood, one of 11 species of brown butterflies characterised by 'false eye' markings, and the martagon lily – or Turk's hat

A walk on a warm summer day along various Forest rides and paths can reveal over 20 different butterflies. These man-made glades have rich herbaceous and bramble-strewn borders attractive to many species. In the mixed deciduous areas the purple hairstreak can be found on oak. Two startlingly large butterflies, the white admiral and the silver-washed fritillary can be found in midsummer – often feeding on bramble blossom, and spring is heralded by the bright yellow brimstone and the orange tip. More easily found is the speckled wood, which patrols its territory along a stretch of path or in pools of sunlight penetrating the thick leafy canopy.

Birds of the conifers

Straight, fast-growing and easy to extract, conifers make excellent timber trees and are an important economic resource. Many were brought in from overseas in the 19th century and early parts of this century, including Norway spruce, European and Japanese larch and Douglas fir and western red cedar from North America, and these now make up half of the Forest's woodlands.

Although they have left much of their dependent wildlife in their country of origin, these trees still have their value. Tall, mature Douglas firs which have been regularly thinned often have an understorey of deciduous woodland and wood warblers can be heard trilling out their territories from the tall tree tops while nesting in the shrubs beneath. Foraging parties of goldcrests, coal tits, redpolls and siskins frequent the conifer plantations in winter but there are also conifer specialists such as the crossbill, which feeds exclusively on conifer seeds, extracting them from the cones with its tweezer-like bill.

Our summer night hawk, the nightjar, is also found associated with young to middle-aged conifers which resemble its more usual heath scrub habitat. It can be seen hawking over the young trees for insects and heard 'churring' its rather tropical song in late evening.

Freshwater life

The Wye and Severn and other smaller waterways and pools in the Forest of Dean and Wye Valley support important freshwater communities, adding an exciting variety to the wildlife of this thickly wooded landscape. The importance of the unpolluted nutrient-rich waters of the Wye and its underwater life is recognised in the fact that it is designated a Site of Special Scientific Interest along its entire length.

Within its clear waters there is a balanced assortment of freshwater plants, duckweeds, crowfoots and algae which are the start of complex food webs. The shoals of minnow are the bread and butter of the river, feeding on algae and other plant matter and in turn taken by a variety of larger fish such as the chub and eel. These are then eaten by fishing herons and mink, or even the cormorant, seen occasionally on the Wye and Severn in winter. The otter is a rarity nowadays, another victim of the 1960s pesticide poisoning, but there are some signs of it making a come-back.

Woorgreens Lake – one of Dean's wildlife havens

Much of this underwater world goes by undetected except for the occasional glimpse of a fish or a large eel near the surface. Eels can live up to 30 years on the bottom of a river, but curiously always return to the Sargasso Sea in the mid Atlantic to breed. The young eels, or elvers, are a special feature of the Wye and Severn, along with the salmon which use the rivers as water-highways to their traditional spawning grounds. However, numbers of both have dwindled in recent years.

The River Wye and ditches and pools within the woods are important for over 20 species of the brightly-coloured dragonfly and their smaller relatives the damselflies, which rest with their wings closed. The green and black club-tailed dragonfly can often be seen resting on the iris and bur reeds at the side of the Wye. Watch the surface of Forest ponds carefully for the large common and southern hawkers and the emperor, as they patrol the sides for their insect prey – superb aerial predators of the insect world. The broad-bodied chaser, a robust smaller species with a hesitant, staccato flight pattern can be approached closely as it rests on a waterside reed stem. In midsummer the waterways are covered in mists of small common red and blue damselflies as well as smaller numbers of the strikingly beautiful demoiselle.

The Wye and the Forest streams are frequented by the dipper and the grey wagtail, a bird particularly fond of old mill races such as the one at the Dean Heritage Centre, where it nests in the walls of an old corn mill. The kingfisher, although seen occasionally, is suprisingly uncommon. Dabchicks, little grebe, moorhen, coots and tufted duck frequent the ponds at Cannop and Soudley.

For wildfowl the Severn Estuary can hardly be beaten. The home of the Wildfowl Trust is across the river at Slimbridge, but the Forest side is also interesting. There are large flocks of wigeon, teal, shelduck and waders including curlew, whimbrel, dunlin and snipe in winter at Guscar Rocks near Woolaston. Up to 100 Bewick swans gather at Walmore Common near Minsterworth in January.

Diverse coexistence

Along Severnside and among Forest villages are many old orchards with rare and local fruit trees including Blakeney pear, Blaisdon red plum and Severn bank apple. They are a favourite haunt of the green woodpecker, which feeds mostly on ants on the ground among the old trees. Wildlife takes full advantage of the remains of the area's industrial past. Old hammer ponds, mill-races and coal workings are now home to Forest amphibians and their reptile predators, the adder and grass snake. Woorgreens Lake, which has been created as a nature reserve near the Speech House, was once an opencast coal-mine, but is now a nationally important dragonfly and damselfly site and haven for winter wildfowl. Also, the old iron-mines, or scowles, in the Forest and disused stone railway tunnels and furnaces form important roosts for bats, including the lesser and greater horseshoe bat.

The Forest of Dean and Wye Valley area supports a great diversity of wildlife habitats. It can do so due to sensitive management by the Forestry Commission and their close liaison with conservation bodies. There are many potential conflicts between conservation and recreation in this modern working forest, but despite this the whole area remains a fascinating natural wonderland. Much of the woods retains a real sense of wilderness, and perhaps nowhere else do the ancient and modern coexist so imperceptibly.

Whimbrels are mainly migrant birds, visiting the Severn Estuary in spring or late summer

An Ancient Forest

Wedged between the River Severn and Wye Gorge is the mysterious Forest of Dean. Geographically isolated and traditionally neither England or Wales, it has a character all of its own. The Forest is an area of contradiction and contrast. In turns it has been a wildwood, a royal hunting ground, a naval timber preserve and an industrial centre. Now known and valued for its natural beauty and wildlife, the past is inextricably interwoven with the present.

Dean actually covers over 120,000 acres, but much of this land is farmed and the woodland area now only consists of about 27,000 acres at the heart. This is Crown Land, vested in the Forestry Commission, and constitutes most people's idea of a forest. Substantial parts of it consist of native trees, particularly English oak, which perhaps gives rise to the widespread belief that the broadleaved woods of Dean have not changed since ancient times. The truth is otherwise: all things change and the Forest – very much the work of man – is no exception.

Early settlement

As the last Ice Age ended trees advanced into Britain from Europe and 53 species colonised the country to become our native trees. Together they formed the wildwood, ancestor of the modern Forest of Dean in which lived many creatures, including man. The process of man-made change began in about 4000BC when the New Stone Age people (the first farmers) displaced the Middle-Stone Age hunter-gatherers who had made very little demand on their environment. These new settlers kept sheep, goats, pigs and cattle for meat, milk, skins, wool and other products. To grow crops they tilled the soil with imported tools of flint and other hard-wearing, workable stones. Hunting diminished in importance. The land became a resource whose value outweighed that of the vegetation and wild creatures it supported. Woodland clearance – necessary for arable crops and enclosed pasture – began by burning and felling with stone axes, and the remaining woods formed (as they still do) an extensive pasture in which livestock could browse and forage.

Farming communities were in some measure settled, and used wood from their immediate surroundings for many purposes. Wood of small cross-section was easily felled and convenient for most uses ranging from firewood to house building. Many native trees coppice; that is, when cut they do not die, but produce new shoots from the base and it is likely that prehistoric people secured an indefinitely renewable supply of small wood by coppicing. However, much of the wildwood was probably still relatively undisturbed because the massive timbers were only occasionally required.

Early industry

This survival of extensive tree cover began to distinguish Dean from surrounding areas but here the Iron Age was to have profound implications. Development thus far had relied on imported stone and bronze tools, but beneath Dean lay iron ore, which outcrops in an irregular arc from Lydney to Staunton in the south and west, and from Wigpool to Ruspidge in the north and east. Outcrop mining left a fantastic landscape of pits, rifts, tunnels and rock pinnacles and as the land was rendered useless for agriculture, many scowles, or ancient surface workings, still survive. They are invariably well-wooded and colonised with lime-loving plants but nevertheless indicate the scale of the early iron industry in Dean.

Looking into woodland of the Serridge Inclosure, west of Cinderford. Below: ancient Forest traditions have survived to the present – hauling timber near Lydney

A step-by-step guide to making charcoal from Diderot's Encyclopaedia, 1762 . . .

. . . And today, the centuries-old tradition continues, with the dome of cord wood around the flue

For 2,000 years charcoal fuelled this industry. In Dean charcoal-making began before the Romans and continued, using traditional methods, into this century. Coppice stools were cut to give cord wood (4ft lengths about the thickness of a man's arm), which was stacked in a dome-shaped pile, about 15ft in diameter around a central flue. This was then covered with earth and set alight. The mound was allowed to burn slowly, for several days, during which it needed constant attention. The charcoal-burners led a nomadic life moving from one wood to the next as the cord wood was used up. They lived for months at a time, alone or with their families, in simple conical huts secluded in the woods. Today many hundreds of level, circular charcoal hearths can still be seen throughout the Forest.

Charcoal-burning thus increased the value of coppice woodland which prevented further clearance for farmland and encouraged the coppicing of more woods, resulting in fewer standard timber trees.

Vert and venison

The first real check to the farmers, charcoal-burners and iron-makers in Dean came with the Norman Conquest. Dean was made a Royal Forest – a game reserve where special laws protected wild beasts ('venison') and the trees which gave them food and shelter ('vert'). Much of Dean became Crown land, but Forest law applied equally to private land which was within the boundary of the Forest and a complex system of officials and courts was set up to administer these laws. In Dean the court of Attachment — known as the Verderers' or Speech Court — survives to the present day.

Originally the Court was held every 40 days but although it now meets less frequently, it is still held at the Speech House — built for the purpose in the reign of Charles II. The Speech House – now an hotel – stands in the centre of the Forest and replaces an earlier court house, Kensley Lodge, which stood close by.

The Norman kings' passion for hunting was only one reason for the creation of Forests. At a time when meat was difficult to preserve the Forest was an immense living larder. Many records survive of deer and boar from Dean being ordered for the royal household.

Although living in a Royal Forest, the inhabitants of Dean were not dispossessed or forcibly removed. Their actions in regard to the beasts and trees were constrained, but otherwise life in the forests was much the same as elsewhere. Rights of common became established in respect of wood for fuel and house repairs, and the pasture of pigs and some other livestock in the Forest. This did not include sheep, which were held to make wood pasture unpalatable to the deer.

The grazing of sheep in the Forest in modern times is a custom with uncertain legal status. It may have arisen after medieval times when lax administration of the Forest allowed it to become established and it is still a source of some controversy. In the past keepers of sheep (known as 'ship badgers') used their flocks to supplement the low wages of the mines. But whatever the origins of grazing in the Forest, the custom has been guarded by the ship badgers, with strong opposition over hundreds of years to any attempt to restrict or fence out animals. Today the Forestry Commission has agreed a limit on the number of breeding ewes with the Commoners' Association – the modern organisation of ship badgers – and grazing sheep are a common sight throughout Dean as they have been for centuries.

Other activities such as iron-mining and charcoal-making continued both legally and illegally. It is likely that the unique Free Mining system which still survives has its origin in medieval times. The Crown owned the mineral rights within the Forest. Mining of iron ore and probably a little coal was carried out by Free Miners — who claimed the sole right to mine in Dean under a complex series of customs. These were administered partly by Crown officials (the Gaveller and Constable of St Briavels Castle) and partly by the miners themselves in their own Court of Mine law.

The effect of forest law is difficult to gauge. It did not prevent wild boar being hunted to extinction and the deer being greatly reduced in numbers by the beginning of the 14th century. Poaching certainly went on, but the Forest could simply not sustain the level of legal hunting. For example in 1254 Henry III ordered 100 boars and sows from Dean for his Christmas feasting!

In Dean, forest law may have led to the survival of pockets of primeval woodland longer than anywhere else in Britain. Between 1241 and 1254, 71 oaks were granted from Dean for the construction of Blackfriars Priory in Gloucester providing the main timbers of the roof which survive to this day. The trees from which these timbers were cut were of exceptional girth and length, described by Arthur Rackham as the last remains of the wildwood above ground in England.

The Forest in disarray

As the importance of forests to the Crown for hunting declined, their importance as a source of revenue grew. The harsh penalties of death or maiming for harming the forest were commuted to fines, and in time the fines were no longer exacted as a punishment, but became a form of rent. Forest law ceased to control assarting (conversion of woods to farmland), over-grazing and the demand of the iron industry for charcoal.

This situation became very much worse with the introduction of new iron-making technology. In 1595 the first of many charcoal blast-furnaces was built in Dean. These had an infinitely greater capacity to produce iron than the bloomery furnaces which preceded them.

They required immense quantities of charcoal, and worse still, the iron they produced was brittle – unlike that of the bloomeries. For most purposes it could not be used direct from the furnace; it had to be refined, and the refineries used yet more charcoal. With Forest administration in decay timber trees were felled for charcoal and the coppice woodlands were also unprotected from over-grazing – a disastrous combination for Dean as a woodland.

The response of the Crown was equivocal. With the growing importance of Naval power the trees became valuable for shipbuilding. But the iron industry was also important as it produced armaments and was a source of revenue to the Crown. So Henry VIII passed laws to protect coppice woods by enclosing them against livestock after felling, and 12 timber trees were to be grown on each acre of coppice woodland. In the 17th century the Crown attempted to have the best of both worlds. James I permitted the building of four furnaces and forges (known as the King's iron-works) in Dean at Soudley, Parkend, Cannop and Lydbrook, which were then leased – along with rights to coppice woodlands for charcoal – to local iron masters. Charles I went even further and granted all of the Forest to Sir John De Winter. De Winter was an iron master of Lydney, and he set about converting the Forest to charcoal. Had not the Civil War intervened it is likely that the noblemen's woodcutters and commoners' livestock would have destroyed the woodland completely.

In 1653 the Commonwealth Council attempted to protect the woodland. Major John Wade was appointed administrator to 'preserve the timber from waste and embezzlement and to preserve its growth'. Before this, Forest trees had been renewed by enclosure to allow natural regeneration. Major Wade's actions were a new departure: he made enclosures and within them planted acorns (for which he paid one shilling a bushel) and seedling oak trees (for which he paid nine pence a thousand). This, in 1657, was the first deliberate planting of trees in Dean. But the commoners resented having their livestock fenced out of part of the Forest and in 1659 they rioted, destroyed the

Only two herds of fallow deer now inhabit the Forest – once the hunting reserve of Norman kings

enclosures and let in their livestock: as a result Major Wade resigned.

Shortly afterwards the monarchy was restored and Sir John De Winter found favour with Charles II. Twice more the Forest of Dean was granted to him by the King, but opposition from residents in Dean and from Parliament was too great and the grants were revoked.

Trees for the Navy

In 1668 The Dean Forest (Reafforestation) Act was passed, legislating to preserve trees. A new administration followed whereby 11,000 acres of the Forest could be enclosed as nurseries for naval shipbuilding timber, and the commoners lost all rights in the enclosures. The Speech House was built to house the revived Verderers' Courts, the gaol at St Briavels Castle was renovated, and in 1674 the iron-works in the Forest were demolished by order of the Crown. Thus the needs of the Navy had triumphed over those of the commoners and iron-masters, and Dean survived both as a Royal Forest and as a woodland.

The 18th century was less dramatic as far as the Forest was concerned, but there was one notable departure from the Crown policy of replanting with oak. In 1781 Weymouth pine were planted in Sallowvallets enclosure near Cannop – the first conifers planted in Dean. By the end of the century the Forest was again in need of reform to meet changing times when war against Napoleonic France once more increased the need for timber.

Nelson visited Dean in 1803 and criticised the state of the Forest; only 676 of the 11,000 acres permitted by the Act of 1668 were in fact enclosed.

The expansion of mining – particularly the growth of coal-mining – had made inroads into the timber reserves, with Free Miners claiming the right to help themselves to any timber they needed for pit props in their coal mines. More people had been drawn into Dean to work in the mines and other industries which grew up, and many of these built cottages encroaching on the Forest. The vastly increased scale of mines, with the introduction of steam engines and horse-drawn tramways destroyed timber, and the legitimate passage of miners to and from the pits through the enclosures made policing of the naval timber reserves impossible.

The modern Forest

An Act of 1808 echoed many of the provisions of the 1668 Act, and within 10 years all 11,000 acres allowed were enclosed. Nearly 900,000 trees of ash, elm, sweet chestnut, Scots pine and Norway spruce were planted. (Norway spruce was new to the Forest, but Scots pine was a re-introduction – it had been part of the wildwood in Dean, and may have become extinct locally as a result of felling by Neolithic man.) Over four million oak trees were planted and subsequently nurtured through both natural and man-made disasters. In 1813 a plague of mice and voles destroyed 200,000 trees and 100,000 vermin were trapped, and in 1831 rioters destroyed hundreds of miles of enclosure fences and let in their livestock.

In 1838 the Free Miners' rights were for the first time recognised in law, but in return they were compelled to pay for all the timber which they needed and their freedom to sink pits wherever they chose was restricted. In 1850 the remaining fallow deer were hunted down, so that the inhabitants of Dean would not be tempted into poaching, and – once engaged in crime – steal or destroy the growing naval timber.

The oakwoods of Dean which we enjoy are a 19th-century creation. They are almost exclusively English oak, whereas the wildwood in Dean probably contained a high proportion of sessile oak. Ironically, their value as shipbuilding timber was destroyed before they were half grown. In the American Civil War ironclad warships proved their superiority over wooden hulled vessels and almost overnight the wooden warship was rendered obsolete. After this many more conifers, particularly larch for pit props, were planted in Dean, and with the setting up of the first forestry school in the country in 1904 at Coleford and then Parkend, Dean became a training ground for foresters.

World War I saw the woodlands ravaged to provide timber for the war effort, and as a consequence the Forestry Commission was established in 1919 to ensure a strategic reserve of timber in Britain's forests. Dean was extensively replanted and the recreational use of the Forest increased. On the eve of World War II measures were in hand to designate Dean the first National Forest Park. During this war Dean once again supplied great quantities of timber, and afterwards much replanting was necessary. Since then iron-mining has ceased, the large coal-mines have all closed and new industries, not dependent on local resources, have come to the Forest. Nevertheless, remnants of the old traditions survive. Verderers still meet at the Speech House, Free Miners still work small coal levels, and ship badgers pasture their flocks in the woods. With change and increased recreational use, understanding of the unique history of the Forest has grown.

The Forest has a wealth of trails and footpaths clearly waymarked by the Forestry Commission and the Ramblers' Association

The River Wye

The Upper Wye at Erwood, where drovers used to cross their sheep en route to England. Inset: a scene from the past – a barge and trow at Brockweir

In remotest mid Wales the double crown of Plynlimmon overlooks the rugged beauty of the surrounding hills. Here the Wye and Severn are born almost within hailing distance of each other and begin their long meandering journeys, each following its own path of adventure to meet finally in the Severn Estuary at Cheptow. The Wye is known as Britain's most beautiful and unspoilt river, for unlike her sister Severn, her route is away from areas of industrial development and large towns and cities.

Virtual freedom from pollution has conserved a wide range of plant and animal life and consequently the river has been designated a Site of Special Scientific Interest. The vegetation that clothes the steep sides of the Wye Valley below Ross-on-Wye includes a remarkable 65 species of native trees and shrubs. The alkaline limestone and acidic sandstone soils support a wide variation of flora which attracts many different species of native and migratory birds, and scenery here is some of the finest in Europe.

Origins of the Wye

This wonderful scenery owes much to the geological history of the area. It was 400 million years ago that the mountain rivers of northern and mid Wales drained south-eastward creating a vast river delta and depositing sandstones and siltstones, and half a million years later the area became a clear warm sea and the shells of billions of sea creatures were deposited to become the limestones. Two million years ago the Wye began to meander over these rocks, cutting downwards as the sea level fell. Today, the Old Red sandstones form most of the gentler sloping wooded valley flanks, while the Carboniferous limestones were eroded to form the spectacular cliffs of Yat Rocks, Devil's Pulpit and Wintours Leap. The lower parts of the limestone are abundant with fossils of sea lily stems (crinoids) and mollusc shells (brachiopods).

The geography of the Wye, with fast tributary streams which could power waterwheels, attracted early industry to the lower Wye, and river traffic became more important. In the mid 17th century there were various schemes to establish the Wye as a regular commercial waterway – the deepening of the river, the construction of locks and weirs and the provision of towpaths, but few of the schemes were acceptable or feasible. The river traffic continued to increase but had to depend on the tides and the amount of water in the river. More weirs were built, causing upset between the industrialists who wanted the weirs to power their machinery, and the merchants who wanted the river kept clear for navigation.

In the 18th and 19th centuries Severn trows, wooden sailing vessels specially evolved for navigating the tidal Severn and lower Wye, were able to sail from Chepstow eight miles up river to Brockweir. At Brockweir, the limit of the tidal Wye, the trows were unloaded and their 40 to 60 tons of merchandise transferred on to barges, which continued the journey to Ross and Hereford. The opening of towpaths after 1809 improved matters more, especially for the transportation of Forest of Dean coal from Lydbrook. The trows and barges were mostly built locally and there were boatbuilding yards at many of the riverside towns and villages. There are signs today of bygone river navigation – pub names like the Sloop at Llandogo, the Boat Inn at Redbrook and the Hope and Anchor Inns at Lydbrook and Ross.

New Weir in 1797. When the Wye Tourers travelled along here an iron forge polluted the atmosphere of the valley

The Wye Tour

In 1782 William Gilpin published his book *Observations on the River Wye and Several Points in South Wales.* It was important in its day as the first guide to publicise the growing fashion among the well-to-do to experience the Wye Tour, a boat trip down the lower Wye Valley, usually from Ross-on-Wye to Chepstow, with an overnight stop at Monmouth. The tourers were cult followers in search of the 'picturesque', that is, scenery that should be beautiful as well as complying with complex rules of feature, form, proportion, foreground, background and colour. A magnificent view could not be considered 'picturesque' if a single tree or rock was out of place or the wrong colour.

Gilpin, who was considered a 'high priest of the picturesque', illustrates these strange prejudices when describing the view to Goodrich Castle which '. . . is one of the grandest on the river'. However, he goes on to say, 'I should not scruple to call *correctly picturesque*: which is seldom the character of a purely natural scene. Nature is always great in design; but unequal in composition. She is an admirable colourist; and can harmonise her tints with infinite variety, and inimitable beauty; but is seldom so correct in composition as to produce a harmonious whole. . . . Hence therefore, the painter, who adheres strictly to the *composition* of nature, will rarely make a good picture. His picture must contain *a whole*; his archetype is but *a part*.'

Preparing to launch in about 1900 from William Hurd's boatyard – the last in Chepstow to build wooden ships

The Wye Tour became more and more fashionable and, thanks to Gilpin, was considered an indispensable experience to the 'man of taste'. Many eminent writers and artists were attracted to the scenes. It was in 1798 that William Wordsworth, who loved the Wye Valley, stayed at Llandogo and wrote his evocative *Lines Composed a Few Miles Above Tintern Abbey.*

From 1866 salmon netting was restricted, licences issued and ladders constructed on the weirs. Below: the massive 800ft limestone Wyndcliff towers above the river as it curves around the Lancaut Peninsula

Five years have past; five summers with the length
Of five long winters! and again I hear
These waters, rolling from their mountain springs
With a soft inland murmur, – Once again
Do I behold these steep and lofty cliffs,
That on a wild secluded scene impress
Thoughts of more deep seclusion; and connect
The landscape with the quiet of the sky.
The day is come when I again repose
Here, under this dark sycamore, and view
These plots of cottage-ground, these orchard-tufts,
Which at this season, with their unripe fruits,
Are clad in one green hue, and lose themselves
'Mid groves and copses. Once again I see
These hedge-rows, hardly hedge-rows little lines
Of sportive wood run wild; these pastoral farms,
Green to the very door; and wreaths of smoke
Sent up, in silence, from among the trees!
With some uncertain notice, as might seem
Of vagrant dwellers in the houseless woods.
Or of some Hermit's cave, where by his fire
The Hermit sits alone.

By 1827 eight rowboats a day were leaving Ross carrying from two to six oarsmen, depending upon the size of the party. The Wye Tourers were looked after in style; protected from the weather by an awning, they sat at a central table which, when not being used for writing and sketching, was laden with the best food and wine.

Prize salmon

The River Wye is well known to the anglers of both game and coarse fishing as a unique and superlative fishing water, but perhaps it is best famed as one of Britain's greatest salmon rivers. The cleanliness of the river and frequent flushing and oxygenation by its tributaries makes the Wye an attractive environment for the salmon. They can swim up river during spates and rest in the deep pools when it falls, and then head for the upper reaches where gravel beds are ideal for spawning. The excellence of Wye salmon has led to many disputes over the centuries. When selling land at Monmouth, Elizabeth I specifically retained 'the tithes of salmon and other fish to be taken in the waters and rivers within the parish of Monmouth'. But the lower reaches of the Wye were also ideal for the development of early industry, and the indiscriminate building of weirs to provide water power restricted the movements of the salmon, and made them easy prey for netsmen or even boys with sharpened sticks.

By about 1860 through ignorance and greed, the river was almost empty of salmon. In 1862 a small group of men tried to save the situation by forming the Wye Preservation Society. Their object was to protect the fishing during spawning, and they made some progress, but they failed to tackle the real problem of netting, so the decline of the salmon continued. In 1866 the Duke of Bedford took charge and reformed the group as the Wye Board of Conservators. But it was not until 1906 when netting was restricted to tidal waters only that the salmon stocks began to improve.

Now over one and a half million pounds are spent on the River Wye each year, much coming from the salmon rod fishermen who spend large sums for the privilege of fishing the prestigious beats. The Wye is famous for its large fish – in 1923 a monster 59½lb rod-caught salmon measuring 52½in was recorded. But this could not compare with a dead salmon found in the river by a poacher a few years earlier measuring just half an inch less than five feet, which could have weighed up to 80lb according to experts at the time. In recent years the average weight of rod-caught fish has been around 12½ to 13lb, and there are regular catches of fish weighing over 30lb.

Chub, dace and elvers

The Wye is also excellent for coarse fishing, and the river has a fine reputation for big chub which, along with dace, are the most frequently caught. The river is also known for grayling, perch, pike, roach and shad. Shad, belonging to the herring family, is rare in all British Rivers except the Severn and the Wye. It arrives in from the sea in spring and will sometimes travel as far as Builth to spawn. Trout are mainly confined to the upper reaches of the river, and its tributaries such as the Monnow and the Lugg.

Each spring huge shoals of elvers, finger-sized young eels, enter the Severn and the Wye estuaries to live out seven years of their life cycle in the rivers and streams before returning once more to the sea. Their appearance is heralded by fishermen on the river banks with curious scoop-shaped nets on poles, patiently awaiting the elvers' arrival. Elvers are usually cooked in the same way as whitebait or, boiled and pressed into a mould, they can be sliced and fried. Recently the elver has become a prized delicacy, and their netting has become such a lucrative business that they are in serious danger of becoming overfished.

The valley today

Today, the old Wye Tour by water is no more. But thousands now come to view the wonders of the Wye. They can discover for themselves the valley's varied landscape and impressive 'picturesque' by donning stout footwear to follow as much or as little as they wish of the Wye Valley Walk. Its course, a clearly waymarked and well maintained path, runs from Hereford to Chepstow. A useful guide to this 52-mile path is the *Wye Valley Map Pack*, available from information centres and bookshops. It contains six Ordnance Survey route cards and a guide to places along the way.

Canoe touring is becoming increasingly popular and is now the only way to follow the full course of the Wye Tourers. Since the 16th century the whole length of the river below Hay-on-Wye is subject to 'free navigation' which means that canoeists enjoy the right to travel the Wye from Hay to Chepstow and the Severn Estuary. The right of navigation, however, does not give the right of access to the river bank and in most places permission must be sought for launching and landing canoes. There are several official access points for canoes and several places along the river where canoes can be hired.

Canoeing on the Wye should not be undertaken by the inexperienced or by poor swimmers, and must never be done alone. The Wye is fast flooding and after heavy rain can rise at over a foot an hour; flood warnings are given and should be heeded. The Welsh Water Authority has produced the useful *Canoeists Guide to the River Wye,* which includes maps and itineraries and is available at bookshops and information centres.

However today's Wye Tourer chooses to travel, whether by boat, car, or on foot, the valley has a great deal to offer. Sport and recreation opportunities abound, and the scenery, though not up to William Gilpin's standards, will not fail to impress the most discerning modern visitor.

Fishing for salmon on the upper reaches of the Wye at Erwood. Inset: canoeists enjoy an outing farther downstream at Lower Lydbrook

Myths and Legends

The pastoral landscapes of Herefordshire and the contrasting sylvan hills and vales of the Forest of Dean and Gwent borderlands seem to have only the winding River Wye in common. This belies the fact that for thousands of years before the Romans, the whole area was inhabited by the Celts, a close-knit mysterious people who were among the first inhabitants of the lower Wye Valley. As a race they mistrusted written language, so the spoken word and the oral tradition were the main means of communication and learning, and the art of story-telling was considered a very important part of their culture. Here and there throughout the region can be found menhirs, or standing stones, which remain as a legacy of these ancient Britons, but another heritage continues with the abundance of folk tales and legends – of dragons, witches, strange happenings and ancient spirits. Many of the traditional tales may well have been passed down through folklore directly from the Celts, while others may have more modern origins. As to the real beginnings, the answers are lost in the mists of time, but the traditions of story-telling were certainly founded by the Celtic Druids and bards.

The legend of the Buck Stone

In a lofty spot above the Dean village of Staunton rests the massive Buck Stone which, until vandalised just over a century ago, would rock on its own axis. In 1885 six men joined forces to tip the huge stone from its plinth, causing it to shatter into pieces in a field below. The public outcry was such that the Crown authorities soon undertook to repair and replace the stone in its rightful resting place – where it remains today. But alas, the Buck Stone no longer rocks. Local belief is that it was once a sacred Druid site, and that a hollowed stone close by was for sacrifices. It is said that any person who walks three times around the Buck Stone as the sun rises may be granted a wish.

During the Roman invasion of Britain when the Celts fought so fiercely against their military superiors, a young bard resting from the wars is supposed to have been strangely drawn to the Buck Stone to seek solace and tranquillity for a while. He sat and rested against the rock to contemplate the wonderful panorama of the Wye Valley, and so taken was he by the beauty of the scene that he was unaware of the approaching silent procession of Druid priests. Startled, the bard leapt to his feet, but on recognising the Druids as friends he smiled a welcome. However, instead of returning his welcome the priests greeted him in sorrow and dismay. The archdruid stepped forward and explained that in a dream he had been told to come to the rock where an important sacrifice would be waiting. Both he and the bard knew that the dream had to be fulfilled, so the bard submitted himself to the sacrificial altar. The sun rose to its height, shadows were cast over the stone and the moment came for the plunge of the ceremonial blade to end the life of the young bard. But at the very moment the archdruid raised the knife, a magnificent stag burst into the clearing and fell panting beside the altar. With joy the Druids knew that here was the real sacrifice, and that the young bard's life would be spared. Moreover, the gods had given the bard an opportunity to prove his heroism and worth by showing his willingness to offer his life for the sake of his people.

An old engraving of the Buck Stone, then so perfectly balanced that even a strong gust of wind could set it gently rocking. Inset: the restored Buck Stone today

The Mordiford dragon

A few hundred yards from where the River Lugg meets the Wye stands the village of Mordiford. Until about 1811 the village church had a large green serpentine dragon painted on its west end and tradition says that it represented a dragon which once inhabited the woods near the village.

The story goes that long ago a young girl was wandering through the fields when she chanced upon a small green creature which she picked up and took back to her home to keep as a pet. Her father recognised the animal as a young dragon and wanted to kill it, but the girl would not hear of this, and sobbed and pleaded for its life to be spared. The father reluctantly gave in to his daughter, but fearing that he might still attempt to kill the dragon she took it away to a secret spot where she secretly fed it on milk. The creature quickly grew, and its appetite turned to ducks, then geese, sheep, cows and finally, to people. But it never once harmed its young keeper. The villagers were terrified but no one was courageous enough to kill the beast, nor indeed knew how. One day a man who had nothing to lose and everything to gain spoke out and volunteered to tackle the monster. He was a condemned criminal named Garson, and was offered a free pardon if he could put the Mordiford dragon to death.

Every day the dragon went down to drink where the Lugg joins the Wye and Garson placed a large cider barrel close to its route and hid inside. As the dragon passed by he shot a fatal arrow into its heart through a hole in the barrel. Sadly, however, Garson was never to enjoy his reward, for in its dying gasp, Herefordshire's last dragon incinerated the barrel and its unfortunate occupant.

The Staunton Longstone

By the side of the main road which leads from the village of Staunton to the town of Coleford, there is a relic of the ancients in the form of a menhir, or standing stone. According to local folklore, if it is pricked with a pin at exactly midnight, it will bleed.

The Staunton Longstone, one of several isolated standing stones in the area which date from the Bronze Age

Jack o' Kent

There are probably more stories about the mythical character Jack o' Kent than any other in the Wye Valley, and it is likely that they are very ancient in origin. Jack was a wizard in league with the Devil. In his boyhood he sold his soul in exchange for supernatural powers, and when he died he was buried inside the walls of the church so that he should be 'neither in nor out'.

There is a tale that the bridge over the River Monnow between Kentchurch and Grosmont was built by Jack and the Devil in a single night. The bridge had to be complete before daylight, otherwise it would fall down. Jack agreed that the first living thing to cross the bridge would belong to the Devil. But Jack, who loved to outwit the 'Old Un', threw a bone across which was chased by an unfortunate dog. The dog was all the Devil had for his pains.

Jack's supernatural powers were such that at will he could become a huge giant – 'Why, one day he jumped off the Sugar Loaf mountain right on to the Skirrid, and there's his heel mark to this day, an' when he got there he began playing quoits. He pecked (pitched) three stones as far as Trelleck, great big ones, as tall as three men (and there they still stand in a field), and he threw another but that did not go quite far enough, and it lay on the Trelleck road, just behind the five trees, till a little while ago, when it was moved so a field might be ploughed, and this stone, in memory of Jack, was always called the Pecked Stone.' (*Folklore of Herefordshire,* 1912)

Jack once went from Kentchurch in Herefordshire to London carrying a hot mince pie for the king. He started at daybreak and arrived at the palace in time for breakfast with the pie still hot. However, on the way he lost a garter which was later found on top of a church spire, having caught in the weathercock as he flew over.

One of the remaining forests of its kind in Britain, this secret woodland is rich in superstition and tales of strange happenings
Left: the 'haunted' ruined towers of Goodrich Castle

The legend of Goodrich Castle
More recently, in the time of the English Civil War, Alice Birch and Charles Clifford fell very much in love and wanted to marry. The opposition from their families was great, for the Birches were strong supporters of the Parliamentarian cause and the Cliffords were Royalists. The lovers saw no alternative but to elope, and their first night together was within the refuge of Goodrich Castle. But tragedy struck when the castle was laid siege by Parliamentarian troops under the command of none other than Colonel Birch, Alice's uncle. The young couple fled, and gathering his sweetheart up behind him Charles rode on horseback to the Wye in a desperate bid to escape to the opposite bank. He urged his steed into the storm-swollen river, but halfway across all three were swept under and drowned.

It is said that to this day the spirits of Alice and Clifford haunt the ruined towers of Goodrich, and are heard during every storm, shrieking from the waters of the Wye.

Forest cottages
Much of the unique charm of the Forest of Dean lies in the seemingly disordered scattering of a few old houses throughout the woods. At one time Foresters believed that it was their right to build a house anywhere in the forest without purchase or permission, as long as smoke rose from the chimney before sunset on the day building work began. It most cases this meant that the fence was put up and the chimney only was built in a single day, the rest of the dwelling being built around it at leisure.

The enchanted Forest
The Forest of Dean has a magical atmosphere all of its own. Some find it daunting, others find the enchantment of the ancient woodlands comforting. There is a legend that centuries ago there was a secret enchanted glade where a weary hunter could seek refuge. Provided he entered the clearing alone, he had only to say the words 'I thirst', and a boy dressed in green would appear with a golden drinking horn brimming with a wonderfully reviving mead.

One day, a duke and a visiting knight had just finished a long day's hunt when the duke initiated his friend into the mysteries of the magic grove. A few days later the knight urged the duke to take him again to the grove so that he might drink once more from the golden horn. But the knight was dishonest, and contriving to be the last to enter the grove, he hid the precious horn under his cloak. Unfortunately, it was not well enough concealed, and the brightness of the gold was spotted by one of the duke's men while he was riding back through the forest. The alarm was raised and the knight took flight, but he was soon brought down by the troops. For his sins the knight was tried and put to death in Gloucester and the magic horn was taken back to the enchanted grove to be reclaimed by the boy in green. But it was never reclaimed, and no more hunters found refuge in the grove.

The Devil's Pulpit

Across the Wye from Tintern Abbey there is a wonderful viewpoint high up on the rocks called the Devil's Pulpit. It was from this spot that 'Old Nick' himself is said to have preached to the monks, urging them again and again to give up their life of reverence and devotion and sell their souls to him. Needless to say, Satan's evil demands were unheeded.

The Slaughter

Downstream from Symonds Yat on the east side of the River Wye, there is an area marked on the map as The Slaughter. There are at least three explanations as to how this dramatic name originated: from a Civil War battle, from a Viking skirmish, and from a fight between the invading Roman army and the Celts. There is no reason why all three could not be true, but perhaps the most vivid is the story of the Vikings of Symonds Yat.

About the year 910, Eric the Bloody Axe, with a full complement of marauding Vikings, sailed up the Severn Estuary to land at Beachley near Chepstow. The army plundered their way across the Forest of Dean and finally set up camp on Symonds Yat where they could survey the yet unpillaged meadowlands of Archenfield, west of Ross-on-Wye. In the meantime the shires of Hereford and Gloucester had secretly joined forces to assemble a massive army of troops and volunteers who surrounded the unwelcome visitors. Seeing the troops advancing towards them, the Viking horde retreated down the rock towards the river where they could escape to the strategically superior Great Doward. But their action was foreseen. An ambush lay in wait, and the bloody outcome was such that the site of the ambush is still called The Slaughter.

The fairy changeling

Once, long ago, there lived in Herefordshire a widow with two sons – the elder already a soldier when the younger was born. The elder son went off to war, and when he came back years later he saw that his 'brother' was still a baby, although his face was hairy and strange. After watching the baby the soldier said to his mother 'That's not my brother.' 'It is, it is!' said the mother. 'We'll see about that,' he said. And with that he took an egg from the kitchen and, carefully making a hole in one end, drained away the contents. Then he filled the egg with malt and hops and began to brew the mixture over the fire. At this a cackle came from the cradle and for the first time the baby spoke. 'I am old, I am old, ever so old,' said the changeling, 'but I never saw a soldier brewing beer in an egg shell before.' With a terrible shriek, the creature leapt out of its cradle, whereby the soldier chased it round and round the room with a whip. At last the changeling ran out through the door and vanished. When the widow and her son ran after him, they were met by a handsome, healthy young man. The fairies had exchanged him for the creature when he was new-born. He said he had had a wonderful life with the fairies, but when his mother called he had to come home. And, as in the best legends, they all lived happily ever after.

The Devil's Pulpit above Tintern, stance of 'Old Nick'

FOREST OF DEAN AND WYE VALLEY

Gazetteer

Each entry in this Gazetteer has the atlas page number on which the place can be found and its National Grid reference included under the heading. An explanation of how to use the National Grid is given on page 80.

Above: Eardisland

Abbey Dore

Map Ref: 84SO3830

Abbey Dore lies at the southern end of the peaceful and beautiful Golden Valley, close to the Black Mountains. One of the finest Cistercian abbeys was founded here in the 12th century, a good example of the relaxation of previously austere styles of architecture. Its presbytery contains three particularly beautiful bays, behind which are the remains of the usual five chapels of Cistercian design. Building was not completed until the 1260s. The abbey was suppressed in 1535 and soon fell into ruins.

In the middle of the 17th century, John, first Viscount Scudamore, commissioned John Abel (assisted by David Addams of Ross) to repair the church, and though his motives have sometimes been questioned the result is one of the outstanding churches in all England. What makes Abbey Dore exceptional is its contrasting and unexpected blend of superbly simple Early English architecture with Abel's heavily impressive wooden work – a roof of Herefordshire oak and a remarkable screen which he carved himself. Among other delights are some very fine 17th-century stained-glass lancet windows.

John Hoskyns, who was imprisoned in the Tower of London at the same time as Sir Walter Raleigh and helped to revise his *History of the World*, is buried in the south chapel. He is said to have been the organiser of Bacton's famous Morris Dance (see Bacton). The gardens of Abbey Dore Court are open regularly in summer. The River Dore runs through the grounds, which include a pond and rock garden, a walled kitchen garden and a circular herb garden.

AA recommends:
Self Catering: Kerrys Gate Farmhouse, *tel.* (0981) 240281
Poplar Cottage, *tel.* (0981) 240281

Aconbury

Map Ref: 85SO5133

Aconbury, once a thriving community, consists of just the church and a few farm buildings. A priory for Augustinian nuns was founded in this quiet valley, possibly by the wife of William de Lacy, but today the church, with the scant remains of the priory cloisters, is no longer in use and is usually locked. The site is reputedly haunted by a monk – not as surprising as might at first appear, since most priories were under the control of a monastery. There are many examples of rare plants being found near religious houses or sites and Aconbury is no exception. Danewort, probably used for purging, and elecampane, which was introduced from Europe, are both found here although uncommon in the surrounding area.

From the massive Iron Age hillfort on Aconbury Hill above the church there are fine views into Wales, and because of its strategic value the site has been regularly occupied over the centuries, most recently during the Civil War. Roman pottery has been found on the site and it seems likely that the Romans established a camp here after forcibly evicting the local population.

Below: Abel's oak roof and chancel screen inside Abbey Dore. Right: Charles I's coat of arms atop the screen

Bacton

Map Ref: 84SO3732

This pretty village is the birthplace of Blanche Parry, who attended the three-year-old future Queen Elizabeth I, and was her lady-in-waiting until she died in 1589, dedicating her life entirely to Elizabeth's service and never marrying. Blanche is buried in London, but her heart is in the tomb she had prepared at Bacton church – even in death her alabaster effigy curtsies to her queen.

The church has an ancient rood beam and staircase, which once led to the now demolished rood loft. Bacton church probably suffered from the effects of war in the Middle Ages; it was exempted from paying the King's Aid in 1406 and was considerably altered during the 15th century. The elaborately worked altar frontal is supposed to have been embroidered by Blanche Parry.

In 1609 the villagers, under the direction of John Hoskyns (see Abbey Dore), arranged a Morris Dance with a difference for the visiting James I. It was performed by nonagenarians and centenarians – the oldest was Meg Goodwin at 120, six were well over 100 and the total of their ages was said to be 1,000 years! They vowed that

'Herefordshire for a Morris Dance, puts down, not onely all Kent but verie near . . . three quarters of Christendome'. There is a story that one of the gallant band collapsed during the dance – whether from drink or exhaustion is not recorded.

In a nearby field, St Margaret's Church appears to offer little, but inside there are recently restored wall texts – the one beside the door urging the visitor to 'Go and sin no more' – and a Norman chancel arch. Even more important is the outstanding pre-Reformation rood screen and loft.

Brobury Gardens descend to the Wye

Bishopstone

Map Ref: 84SO4143

A Roman mosaic pavement was found when the rectory at Bishopstone was built during the last century, but no trace of it now remains. Urns containing coins were also uncovered, and since Magnis (*Kenchester*, see page 50) is nearby, it seems certain that this was the site of a Roman villa. Wordsworth visited the site when staying at Brinsop (see page 34) and wrote, in the sonnet *Roman Antiquities Discovered at Bishopstone*, 'Fresh and clear . . . as if its hues were the passing years, Comes this time-buried pavement'.

Bishopstone Church and Court are all that remain of the old village. The 13th-century church, set in a pretty churchyard, has a broad nave under a fine Jacobean roof; the painted reredos is also Jacobean. To the north is Bishopstone Court – a moated house with a ruined early 17th-century gateway.

On Garnons Hill to the west of Bishopstone Court there are some earthworks, all that remains of a hamlet of 10 houses known to be here in 1886. It seems likely that displaced villagers settled on the hill, finally drifting away during a period of agricultural depression early in this century.

Kilvert's memorial at St Andrew's Church, Bredwardine

Bredwardine

Map Ref: 84SO3344

This peaceful village, beautifully set on the west bank of the Wye, is famous principally because the Victorian diarist, Francis Kilvert, was rector here. He lived in the vicarage for two years before dying from peritonitis in 1879, just five weeks after his marriage. Kilvert is buried in the churchyard, his grave marked by a cross in white marble with the inscription 'He being dead – yet speaketh.' There is a stone seat to his memory just inside the churchyard gate in front of a sharply leaning old yew tree.

The late Norman church, partly built in tufa (a porous rock) stands on a knoll above the Wye. The exterior is lopsided but attractive; the interior contains two fine effigies, one believed to be of Walter Baskerville and the other of Sir Roger Vaughan, killed at Agincourt. Both were members of families who owned Bredwardine Castle which has almost entirely disappeared, although the remains of the oblong bailey may be seen on the banks of the Wye below the church, beside a footpath to Moccas Court (see page 54). Built as one of many castles to protect the Welsh border in the 11th century, it had declined by the 15th century.

There is a fine 18th-century six-arched bridge over the Wye in Bredwardine, survivor of the flood of 1795 which demolished all the other bridges in the area. Kilvert had to cross this bridge to reach his kitchen garden, half a mile away. His diary shows him as a good host, entertaining on a grand scale. Near the bridge is an attractive, unrestored medieval stone house, Old Court, and a toll cottage.

Bredwardine means 'the place on the slope of the hill', and behind the village is Bredwardine Hill, over 1,000ft high, with the Golden Valley beyond. On the way to Arthur's Stone (see Dorstone) are the remains of the hamlet of Crafta Webb, thriving in Kilvert's time, but deserted by the early 1900s. The road to Crafta Webb starts beside the Red Lion Inn, a late 17th-century red brick building.

The little hamlet of Brobury has a long history; after the Norman Conquest it belonged to the son of one of William I's followers, and later owners included the Seymour family, who held the manor in Tudor times. There is no record of a church in Domesday Book, but one certainly existed in the early 1300s. By the time Francis Kilvert came to Bredwardine, however, Brobury had been absorbed into the larger village, its church converted to a mortuary chapel.

AA recommends:
Guesthouses: Bredwardine Hall, *tel.* (09817) 596
Red Lion (inn), *tel.* (09817) 303

Bridstow and Wilton

Map Ref: 87SO5824

One of a cluster of villages around Ross-on-Wye, Bridstow's church was founded by King Harold, and it traces its incumbents back to 1277. The Perpendicular tower, Norman chancel arch and Early English chapel have all survived a Victorian rebuilding and, pleasantly light, it has scissor-beam vaulting and an ornate stone pulpit. The church lies in a hollow just off the Ross to Hereford road.

The six-arched Wilton Bridge was built in 1597 and, though strengthened and widened in this century, it retains an inscribed 18th-century sundial. Views of Wilton Castle and, in particular, of Ross on its knoll attract a steady stream of summer visitors; the bridge is also a popular launching place for canoeists exploring the Wye both up and downstream from Ross.

Wilton Castle is a picturesque ruin on the banks of the river beside the bridge (in the grounds of a hotel, not open to the public). The remains of several red sandstone towers and walls date from the 13th century but there has been a fortification on the site at least since the reign of Stephen. The de Greys owned the castle from the 13th to the 16th century, when it passed to the Brydges, and the Royalists destroyed it during the Civil War as an inducement to the dithering owner to declare which side he supported. Not surprisingly he opted for the opposition! The ruins were later purchased by Thomas Guy, benefactor of the London hospital which bears his name.

AA recommends:
Self Catering: The Lodge (cottage), *tel.* (0989) 62880
Pear Tree & Wysteria (flats), *tel.* (0989) 62880

The old west tower dominates the Church of St Bridget, Bridstow

Interior of St George's Church Brinsop, with its 14th-century rood screen. Inset: the William Wordsworth window

Brinsop

Map Ref: 84SO4344

Set among old orchards near a stream, the charming 14th-century church at Brinsop has excellent examples of the Herefordshire School of Carving (see page 52), including a Norman tympanum depicting St George and the Dragon. There is some fine stained glass – medieval and modern – the latter commemorating William Wordsworth and his family, and there are several memorials to the Daunsey family, owners of the manor house for 400 years.

William and Dorothy Wordsworth often visited Brinsop, staying with William's brother-in-law who owned the lovely moated stone-built manor of Brinsop Court. The house retains its 14th-century Great Hall; it has a crown-post roof, uncommon in Herefordshire – the architect was probably copying examples of similar building he had seen in the eastern counties. Kilvert admired the 'grand old manor house' and saw the cedar planted in the grounds by Wordsworth. Roman pottery was found in a well at Brinsop in the 19th century and there are some earthworks, possibly also Roman and connected with Magnis – the Roman *Kenchester* (see page 50).

Just to the north-west is Mansell Lacy, well worth a detour from the A480. The much photographed, half-timbered post office with its dove loft is only one of several delightful houses in the village representing different periods. The brick manor house is 18th-century; the church has an excellent 14th-century east window with typical ball-flower decoration. There are lovely views from Merryhill Wood, and the whole of the little valley of the Yazor Brook is delightful.

Brockhampton

Map Ref: 85SO5932

The village of Brockhampton – sometimes called 'by Ross' to distinguish it from Brockhampton by Bromyard – is remarkably remote considering its nearness to Ross and Hereford. It is remarkable too for its modern church and the pleasing similarity of many of its dwellings. The well-maintained cottage gardens complete a picture of rural charm.

The old Church of Holy Trinity at Brockhampton stands in the grounds of Brockhampton Court, a 19th-century Elizabethan-style house. This church is a roofless ruin in which one service is held each year, and was replaced in 1902 by a new church which many have hailed as the architectural masterpiece of the Arts and Crafts movement. Inside, its pews are beautifully carved with wild flowers and there is a tapestry woven by the William Morris Company from a design by Burne-Jones. Externally, All Saints uses both wood and stone and has a thatched roof and lych gate.

Capler Camp is near by, on top of 600ft Capler Hill. The Wye Valley Walk passes close to the summit where this well preserved Iron Age hillfort commands a magnificent strategic position over the Wye. On its western side, Capler Hill descends steeply to the river from the large, oval fort which was designed to take full advantage of this natural feature. It was defended by a single rampart on the west and north but had extra ramparts and ditches on the south and east. A pond in the south ditch allowed rainwater and dew to collect, compensating for the lack of a natural water supply.

There is a view from Capler Cottage (below the camp, on the road from Brockhampton to Fownhope) which many believe to be unsurpassed, even by Symonds Yat. Trees frame a view of the serpentine Wye, gentle riverside pastures and the distant Black Mountains. There is parking for one or two cars on the grass opposite the cottage.

Brockweir

Map Ref: 87SO5401

With its pleasant group of white painted houses on the banks of the Wye, Brockweir invokes memories of some Cornish villages. Until 1904, when the present bridge was built, the village was reached from the Monmouthshire bank by a ferry. Some of the houses are Tudor, and there is an interesting Moravian chapel with Gothic windows, art nouveau glass and a bell-cote. The riverside road, the Quayside, forms part of the Offa's Dyke Long Distance Footpath.

The scant remains of wharves and quays act as a reminder that this was one of the major boat building ports on the lower reaches of the river. A further reminder appeared in 1967 with the discovery of *La Belle Hélène*, a small steamer, still moored to Brockweir Quay, but totally submerged in mud. Until 1824 only small boats (up to 100 tons) were built on the Wye; in that year the larger *Duchess of Beaufort* was constructed at Monmouth and fitted out at Brockweir – and from then on boats of up to 500 tons were regularly built here. At one time Brockweir had some 16 pubs serving the shipbuilders – they and the workers went with the coming of the railways.

Another trade the railways affected was the barge trade – for many years teams of men pulled heavy coal or iron barges upstream as far as Hereford and even Hay. It was desperate work – from Brockweir in 1847 it took 32 men, harnessed eight at a time in relays, to haul a barge as far as Monmouth – and various ideas including a towpath and a canal were introduced before the railways came to the area and solved the problem.

For fishermen Brockweir has a special significance. Until the 1920s the netting of salmon was permitted along the whole length of the Wye and stocks steadily declined. Due almost entirely to the efforts of one man – Frank Buckland – netting is now prohibited above the village and is strictly controlled below it.

AA recommends:
Guesthouse: Sylvia (farmhouse), Brockweir Common, *tel.* (02918) 514

Caerwent

Map Ref: 87ST4690

Caerwent, or *Venta Silurum*, was built by the Romans in about AD75 to complement the military establishment at nearby Caerleon. It was the second largest civilian settlement in south-west Britain (Bath was larger) and the only civilian town the Romans built in Wales.

Excavations carried out since 1855 have revealed the remains of a forum, baths, a temple and dwelling houses; recently a row of Roman shops has been discovered. The site is still surrounded by walls – some as high as 15ft. Most of the excavated sites have been covered to preserve their excellent condition, but the remains of a combined house and shop are open to visitors.

Venta Silurum was in decline by the 4th century, as the Roman Empire crumbled. By the end of the 5th century life in Caerwent was centred around a small Celtic monastery founded by the Irish St Tathan. The church was originally dedicated to St Tathan, but was re-dedicated to St Stephen some 200 years later. The list of incumbents goes back to the Abbots of St Tathan's monastery. Much of the interior is 13th-century; it has a chancel built of Roman material, a Roman mosaic floor and other relics. Outside, the double lych gate is a memorial to Thomas Walker who helped to build the Severn Tunnel and the Manchester Ship Canal.

There are extensive remains of the Roman wall at Caerwent

Revellers step into the past at a medieval banquet in Caldicot Castle

Clearwell Caves

The caves are a well-known complex of ancient iron ore mines that were worked for over 2,500 years. Apart from these mines there is evidence near by of even earlier 'open cut' workings known locally as 'scowles'. Spectacular examples of these can be seen at Puzzle Wood (see page 76).

Clearwell Caves are a natural system that filled with deposits of iron ore during a geological period which started approximately 270 million years ago and lasted some 50 million years, when the sands and shales of the newly formed local coal measures were subject to massive erosion. It was during this period that rocks rich in iron were layered on the land surface. Thousands of years of rainwater and glacial meltwater, which had become acidic from the sulphur in the coal measures, dissolved the weaker parts of the underlying Carboniferous limestone, enlarging cracks and fissures and forming underground stream passages and rivers. But the waters were also rich with iron minerals which were gradually deposited around the walls and caverns, rather like the furring of a kettle. The passages became choked with ore and lay waiting for Iron Age man to make his first scratchings where the ore outcropped to the surface. But it was the Romans who really developed the mining industry in Dean. They traded with the Ancient British iron miners who by now had begun to venture underground and the industry grew.

Between 1832 and 1880 524,299 tons of iron ore were extracted from these mines. The last iron ore raised commercially was in 1945 from workings 600ft deep. Today we are left with a complex system of caverns and many miles of passages honeycombing an area covering over 600 acres.

Eight large caverns are open to the public and caving trips are also available by appointment

Caldicot Castle

Map Ref: 87ST4888

Caldicot, now more of a modern town than a village, has a restored castle and an unspoiled medieval church with some fine window tracery and an interesting porch. The castle is a 19th-century restoration of a 12th-century building, retaining much that is original. The idea of a round keep was probably introduced from Germany in the late 12th or early 13th century, and the keep at Caldicot is believed to be one of the earliest to survive. There is an impressive 14th-century gatehouse, state chambers and bedrooms.

Caldicot has a fascinating history. Among the owners of the castle have been Milo Fitz-Walter, first Earl of Hereford and the powerful de Bohun family from whom it passed by marriage to the Plantaganets in 1381. Thomas of Woodstock, sixth son of Edward III, improved and completed the castle; the gatehouse is one of his additions.

Henry VII was born here and the Earls of Pembroke owned the castle briefly, but after their departure it fell into ruin; a large amount of its stone was used for building houses in the village. It was subsequently let to various people including the Somersets, owners of Raglan Castle. Joseph Cobb bought the castle in 1885 and restored it, and the Cobbs owned it until 1963, when the local council opened it to the public. Medieval banquets are held regularly here and there is a museum and an art gallery on the premises as well.

Chepstow

Map Ref: 87ST5393

The commanding Norman castle, towering above the town, was one of the first to be built on the Welsh border. It was begun in 1067 by William Fitz Osbern, acting as regent in the absence of William, protecting his interests in Normandy. Fitz Osbern was responsible for commissioning at least seven of the castles of the period but he can rarely have been presented with a better site – a perfect strategic position on limestone cliffs high above the River Wye. In the 11th century most castles were built of earth and wood, but Chepstow was built from the outset in stone, consisting of a great tower (the oldest still surviving) and basic defensive system. The additions which produced the massive structure still apparent today were mainly made during the 13th and 16th centuries.

In the Civil War Chepstow was held for the king, but in 1645 the foundations were undermined, and the garrison surrendered. The castle declared for the king during the Second Civil War and, after a long and bitter siege during which Cromwell came in person to demand surrender from the defender, Sir Nicholas Kemeys, whom he considered to be a turncoat, the walls were breached. The castle continued to be garrisoned and later became a prison, housing the regicide Henry Marten who, strangely, appeared to be given every consideration in the tower now named after him. The garrison was withdrawn in 1695, and the castle slowly lapsed into ruin.

The town still retains a good part of its 13th-century wall and Town Gate, spanning the main road. Medieval streets twist through the town from the river – a 19th century port and shipbuilding centre.

In spite of development in the town there are still many fine buildings of different periods; particularly noteworthy are two sets of almshouses near the Church of St Mary. The interior of the church is vast – the nave was part of the Benedictine priory suppressed at the Dissolution. By contrast, the museum is small, but it houses an excellent exhibition on the history of Chepstow.

AA recommends:
Hotels: Beaufort, St Mary Street, 2-star, *tel.* (02912) 2497
Castle View, 16 Bridge St, 2-star, *tel.* (02912) 70349
George, Moor St, 2-star, *tel.* (02912) 5363
Guesthouse: First Hurdle Hotel, 9 Upper Church St, *tel.* (02912) 2189
Campsites: Chepstow (TRAX) Caravan Club Site, Chepstow Racecourse, St Arvans, 3-pennants, *tel.* (02912) 3710
Howick Farm, Howick (1¾m NW on B4293), Venture Site, *tel.* (02912) 2590

Powerful towers and Great Gatehouse of Chepstow Castle. Left: a peaceful Mounton Valley scene

Cinderford – see Soudley Valley

Clearwell

Map Ref: 87SO5708

A few miles south of Coleford is Clearwell, where the neo-Gothic Clearwell Castle has had a long and very varied history. Claimed to have been a home since Roman times, the present building is a painstaking restoration of a house first built in the 1720s, gutted by fire in the 1920s, rebuilt and lived in until 1947, then deserted and vandalised in the 1950s and finally purchased by the son of the former gardener to the estate. Clearwell is now a hotel with a veteran cycle museum and a variety of other attractions including a lake and bird garden. Close by are the old mines forming Clearwell Caves (see panel).

AA recommends:
Guesthouses: Tudor Farm, *tel.* (0594) 33046
Wyndham Arms (inn), *tel.* (0594) 33666

Clehonger

Map Ref: 84SO4638

'Clunger' is the local name for Clehonger, one of several villages in some danger of becoming satellites of Hereford. The main attraction here is the church, with its effigies, including the 14th-century altar tombs believed to be of Sir Richard Pembrugge, founder Knight of the Order of the Garter, and his wife.

A mile or so away is Belmont Abbey, one of the dozen or so monasteries, mostly Benedictine, which survive in this country. Belmont was founded fairly recently, with its great Victorian church dedicated to St Michael. A cathedral from 1855 to 1920, it now incorporates the monastery and a school; Belmont House, at the other end of the estate, is 18th-century with Gothic additions. This, and a Queen Anne house in Breinton, across the river, belong to the Wegg-Prosser family, builders of St Michael's. The church here, not easily reached, is Victorian but retains a small Norman window. Beside it is Breinton Camp on the site of a deserted medieval village – long thought to be of great antiquity but proved by excavations to be a 12th-century homestead enclosure. It is in the care of the National Trust.

Clifford

Map Ref: 84SO2445

'Clifford' was a borough at the time of Domesday Book, and the site of the most westerly of the castles built by William Fitz Osbern. It was originally a simple motte-and-bailey castle where Jane de Clifford was born – mistress of Henry II and better known as *Rosa Mundi* or Fair Rosamund. The castle followed the usual Norman pattern of development and, by the 13th century, had become a massive structure occupying some three and a half acres. Although the castle was destroyed by Owen Glendower in 1402, its size can be gauged from what remains – the keep, hall and twin towers of the gatehouse.

The parish church, enclosed by trees, stands about half a mile from the village, and contains one of only two surviving wooden effigies in the county. The 13th-century oak carving is of a priest, probably a Rector of Clifford.

Clifford is an attractive, if scattered, village with several good 17th-century houses, and the scant remains of a Cluniac priory are incorporated into buildings at Priory Farm, south of the church. Within the parish are the remains of two other castles, one at Upper Castleton, and another fine motte-and-bailey example at Newton Tump – one of the dozen or more undocumented motte-and-bailey castles in this part of Herefordshire.

Clyro

Map Ref: 84SO2143

Clyro is an attractive village, little more than a mile from Hay-on-Wye yet very different; charming whitewashed stone cottages cluster round the church, huddling for shelter against Clyro Hill. Only the A438, noisily bypassing the village, disturbs this peaceful scene.

For hundreds of visitors each year Clyro is an important place of pilgrimage although, ironically, the man whose fame brings them here disliked tourists – especially British tourists. Francis Kilvert was curate at Clyro for seven years between 1865 and 1872, and rector of Bredwardine from 1877 until his tragically early death in 1879. From 1870 Kilvert kept a remarkably frank diary of his daily activities and thoughts as he moved among the parishioners of these remote districts. It is a record of suffering and hardship, fun and laughter, a succession of young women with whom the susceptible Francis fell madly in love – and always a sustaining faith. The world may have changed greatly since he wrote his diary, yet part of its charm is that people and places, like Clyro, are much as they ever were.

Kilvert is commemorated by a plain plaque inside the church, and the Kilvert Society has erected a sundial to his memory in the churchyard. Sadly, the church suffered extensive 19th-century rebuilding which almost obliterated signs of its 13th-century origins, with little to interest the 'pilgrim'.

The mound of a Norman castle is visible beside the road from Hay, but more significant is the Roman fort near Boatside Farm (frequently mentioned in Kilvert's diary). Excavations suggest that this was one of several camps set up by the Roman general, Ostorius Scapula, and that it became, for a short time, one of the largest forts on the border.

Coleford

Map Ref: 87SO5710

Originally a mining centre, Coleford has attracted alternative industry in recent years and is a lively, vital centre of the Forest of Dean. The town received a Royal Charter from Charles I in recognition of its loyalty to his father.

Most important of its former inhabitants are probably the Mushets, father and son, who were responsible for many developments in the iron and steel industry. Robert, the son, lost all his patents through his failure to pay stamp duty; as he had anticipated the work of Sir Henry Bessemer, who discovered a process of turning molten pig iron directly into steel, the loss was incalculable. The dedication of the isolated church

A wintery Golden Valley from Snodhill. Left: Clyro village and church, where Kilvert was curate, and the plaque on his Clyro home
Right: Arthur's Stone – its original earth mound may have been 84ft long

tower in the square recalls the World War I hero, Angus Buchanan, VC.

Speech House is three miles east of the town. Built in 1676 as a hunting lodge for Charles II and now a hotel, it has played a major role in local history as the courthouse of the Verderers of the Forest of Dean (see page 20).

AA recommends:
Hotels: Speech House, Forest of Dean, 2-star, *tel.* (0594) 22607
Lambsquay, 1-star, country house hotel, *tel.* (0594) 33127
Campsites: Christchurch Forest Park Camping Ground, Braceland Drive, Berryhill, 2-pennants, *tel.* (0594) 33057
Blackthorne Farm, Hillersland, Venture Site, *tel.* (0594) 32062

Dorstone

Map Ref: 84SO3141

The little River Dore runs through the centre of this pretty, sleepy village clustered round the green. Pandy Inn looks just as a village inn should, and it has a history covering at least 500 years. The Court House is one of many attractive buildings, and the store does not seem to have changed in years – it lies behind white painted iron railings and carries old-fashioned advertisements for popular teas in its windows.

The church dates from 1889, but incorporates stone work from a church originally built, probably on a pre-Conquest site, during the 13th century. Traditionally said to have been built by Richard de Brito, one of Becket's murderers, it seems more likely that a descendant fulfilled a promise made by de Brito. The church contains a rare 13th-century sepulchral chalice and paten, discovered in a tomb during rebuilding.

The motte-and-bailey remains of Dorstone Castle lie some 300yds south-west of the church, but the major monument of the parish is Arthur's Stone on Dorstone Hill above the village, the object of much speculation over the centuries. A Neolithic tomb with a single capstone more than 20ft long covering the burial chamber, it commands fine views over the Golden Valley.

Dymock

Map Ref: 85SO7031

For a quiet place in the relatively remote area of north-west Gloucestershire, Dymock has a remarkable history. Extensive research in recent years has pointed to the existence of a small Roman town – believed by some to be the 'lost' town of *Macatonium*. During the Norman and Plantagenet period the manor was held by some of the most famous and important families in the land, and in the early years of this century Dymock attracted a group of influential figures of the 'Georgian' literary period (see page 41).

The centre of Dymock is lovely and full of attractive vernacular buildings, but in this scattered parish there are many other good houses worth seeking out along quiet lanes. The Church of St Mary the Virgin dominates the village centre, lying back from the road behind an attractive green and framed by fine chestnut trees, while a massive old yew shelters the lych gate. An alternative entrance, from a tiny car park set between some very attractive cottages along a side road, is just as pleasant.

The church is basically Norman, with a richly sculptured Norman doorway representing the work of the Dymock School of Sculpture. The tympanum depicting the tree of life is probably the work of the same mason as that at Kempley. Inside, a great sense of size is created by the combined length of the nave, tower and chancel. A 13th-century stone coffin lid, a 17th-century turned oak font and some good modern glass by Kempe are just a few of the treasures in the church. None the less, many visitors to the church, and indeed the parish, will concentrate on the corner of the church dedicated to the Dymock Poets.

One of Eardisley's pretty cottages.
Left: The font in Eardisley church, with its dramatic bold frieze

Eardisley

Map Ref: 84SO3149

Unusually for Herefordshire, Eardisley has a long main street – many beautiful houses run north from the church and castle remains. Timber-framed houses, cruck cottages, weather-boarding and Victorian brick exist side by side in harmony. The Forge is of cruck construction, as is a tiny, two-bay gem of a cottage; a nine-bay timber-framed barn, perhaps once a longhouse, has been sensitively converted into four cottages. At the end of the street is Upper House Farm, an example of the many fine larger buildings around the parish.

The unpopular though efficient 13th-century Bishop of Hereford, Peter de Aquablanca, was 'closely confined' in Eardisley Castle for three months during the Barons' War. Generally considered to have abused his power to enrich himself and his master, Henry III, it must be conceded that he also did much for the cathedral, including rebuilding the north transept. It can still be seen and enjoyed, but only the mound of the castle now remains; the bailey site is occupied by an 18th-century farmhouse.

The church contains a wonderful Norman font of about 1150. A masterpiece of the Herefordshire School of Carving (see page 52), it depicts two men, possibly knights, fighting; the details of their clothing are as remarkable as when first carved. There is also a traditional Harrowing of Hell, and a splendid lion, deprived of his (human) lunch, with a comic expression of rage.

In 1233 a licence for fairs and markets was granted to Eardisley, but today only the Stampede, a 'tradition' introduced in the 1970s, remains. On the May Bank Holiday Monday a rodeo hits town – great fun for local 'cowboys'.

Eaton Bishop

Map Ref: 84SO4439

Eaton Bishop is approached from the south over a rough flat area of common land, and modern estate building, particularly on the north of the village, is creating some danger of eventual absorption into Hereford. The old centre of the village is very interesting; including one attractive black-and-white house that used to be the post office; its studded door may have come from the church. Opposite the church is the Rectory, now called Martin's Croft, and the manor house. The rectory is architecturally interesting, dated about 1700 with traces of an earlier building, but the manor house is more attractive; a top storey was removed in the 1950s, restoring its typically Georgian proportions.

The charming, mainly Norman church stands in a raised churchyard. Its famous east window contains 14th-century stained glass which one of the world's leading authorities on medieval church glass has described as 'unsurpassed . . . anywhere'. By comparison with the bright colours of the 15th century, this window in greens, browns and yellows may appear a little sombre, but it is distinguished by its composition and remarkable detail. The Crucifixion panel in the centre is flanked by a Madonna and Child, St Michael weighing souls, and the Archangel Gabriel. The fleurs-de-lys around the borders suggest a French origin, but the window seems utterly appropriate for this rural setting.

A short distance from the village is a hillfort, standing at the junction of the Cage Brook with the Wye. From this vantage point, probably colonised in the 5th century BC, there are fine views of the river meandering through water meadows as it approaches Hereford.

Ewyas Harold

Map Ref: 86SO3828

At the time of Domesday Book, Ewyas Harold was one of only five boroughs in the county, but it never really developed and is now a modern village easily overlooked by those anxious to explore the rest of the Golden Valley. Yet, because of its situation at the junction of the Dore and Monnow rivers, Ewyas Harold has a long and complex history.

The castle was started by Osborn Pentecost, one of the earlier Norman settlers in Herefordshire. Indeed, some experts have suggested that this was the first defensive earthworks to be called a castle – in a reference in the *Anglo Saxon Chronicles* in 1051. It continued to be strategically important until Owen Glendower's death in 1416 brought a lessening of tension in the area. The castle has long since disappeared – when Charles I was here after Naseby it was 'all ruined and gone' – and only the scrub-covered mound remains.

The much restored Early English church is reached by crossing the chattering Dulas Brook, and there is a good view of the castle mound from the churchyard. Ewyas Harold church is well known for a curious effigy of a lady holding a heart-shaped casket in her hands. The modern Catholic church, dedicated to the 17th-century martyr John Kemble, is a reminder of later troubles (see Welsh Newton). Between the village and Abbey Dore is the common, over which villagers still exercise traditional grazing rights.

Fawley Chapel

Map Ref: 85SO5929

There has been a place of worship on the site of Fawley Chapel since the early Christians came here; it was a monastic settlement until the Reformation and the chapel is now run by a trust for the benefit of local parishioners. A tiny place surrounded by farm buildings, the Norman chapel (it has an unusual triple chancel arch and a tub-shaped font) retains a marvellous atmosphere of tranquillity.

In an area containing many beautiful houses, Fawley Court, once the home of John Kyrle (see page 60) is one of the best. Basically Elizabethan in style, the front of the house is red sandstone with elaborately mullioned and transomed windows; by contrast the rear is timber-framed. It stands in the most delightful gardens – open very occasionally – with a group of attractive farm buildings to complete the picture of a perfect small manor house. The road from How Caple to King's Caple passes the front of the house, separating it from parts of the garden, and the charming duckpond.

Fawley Court dates from the 1600s

The Dymock Poets

In the years before World War I the peaceful Gloucestershire village of Dymock was home to a number of young influential poets – Lascelles Abercrombie, Rupert Brooke, John Drinkwater, Wilfred Gibson, Robert Frost and Edward Thomas. Abercrombie was the first to arrive in 1911 and the idyllic surroundings inspired him to compose some of his best works. In the spring his house at Ryton was surrounded by daffodils and he wrote *Ryton Firs*:

From Dymock, Kempeley, Newent, Bromsberrow
Redmarley, all the meadowland Daffodils seem
Running in golden tides to Ryton Firs
. . .

Next came Rupert Brooke and John Drinkwater, followed by Gibson, ' and by 1914 they were joined by the American Robert Frost and by Edward Thomas. Seldom has such a group of poetic genius and influence been gathered together in such a small area. Their work brought fresh vision into the poetry of the time. In February 1914 the first issue of Lascelles' quarterly *New Numbers* appeared, which first published some of the best-loved poems of the Dymock poets, many of which are familiar to readers today. But the outbreak of the Great War scattered them; Frost returned to America, Brooke died of blood poisoning in 1915 on the way to Gallipoli and Thomas was killed at Flanders in 1917. Gibson, Abercrombie and Drinkwater survived the war and often returned to Dymock, and Gibson recalled the golden years before 'August brought the war and scattered us . . .'.

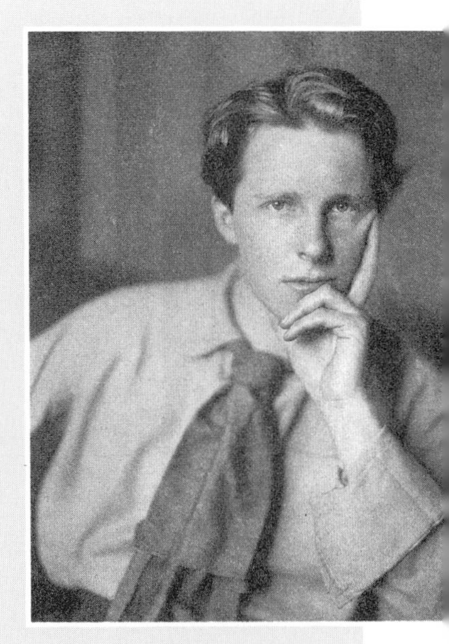

Brooke's idealism and charm made him popular with his contemporaries

The last issue of *New Numbers* appeared in early 1915 and contained Rupert Brooke's best-known poem. He died four months later.

If I should die think only this of me
That there's a corner of a foreign field,
That is forever England. There shall be
In that rich earth a richer dust concealed;
A dust whom England bore, shaped, made aware,
Gave, once her flowers to love, her ways to roam,
A body of England's breathing English air,
Washed by the rivers, blest by the suns of home . . .

Fownhope

Map Ref: 85SO5834

Fownhope lies close to the Wye between the hill-top camps of Cherry Hill and Capler Camp (see Brockhampton), both commanding fine and strategically important views of the river. More recently, the river has been commercially important to the village; barges carried bark downstream to Lydbrook, returning with coal. At the end of the 18th century, when Wye tours became popular, there was a thriving trade in pleasure boats travelling to Ross, Monmouth and Chepstow.

This pleasant, prosperous village with both old and modern housing, retains the old custom of celebrating Oak Apple Day, in memory of Charles II's entry into London at the Restoration. The local version involves the carrying of clubs – probably acknowledging an even older symbolism. Oak Apple Day celebrations end at the Green Man Inn, interesting both architecturally and historically. Changing tastes in architecture are shown in a wall of the inn; once-fashionable brickwork is sandwiched between two timber-framed walls – the latest, added in 1965, reflecting current fashion. The Green Man has been a coaching inn and a courthouse – the judge's room and the cell still exist. Tom Spring, bare knuckle Champion of All England in 1823 and 1824, was landlord here under his real name of Tom Winter.

As a reminder of the coaching days, the village retains a milestone giving very precise distances to Ross, Hereford and Hoarwithy Bridge. Precise, but not entirely consistent, as the distance to Ross by one road is given as 8¼ miles and 165yds; by the other road, 8⅜ miles! Near the milestone, low down beside the churchyard wall, are the remains of the combined stocks and whipping post, easily overlooked and so close to the road that they place the viewer in considerable danger from passing traffic!

The large church, although mostly Transitional, contains examples of many periods of architecture, including a central Norman tower and 14th-century shingle spire. Inside there is a marvellous 14th-century parish chest, carved from a single oak log, but the highlight of the church is the tympanum, now fixed on the west wall of the nave. A fine example of the carvings of the Herefordshire School of Norman Sculpture, it shows the seated figures of the Virgin and Child, hands raised in blessing.

AA recommends:
Hotel: Green Man Inn, 2-star, *tel.* (043277) 243
Guesthouse: Bowens Farmhouse, *tel.* (043277) 430

The suspension bridge linking Foy and Hole-in-the-Wall dates from 1876. Right: the dovecot at Garway

Foy and Hole-in-the-Wall

Map Ref: 87SO5928

A tiny hamlet scattered along the banks of the Wye, Foy was important enough in 1285 to have been granted a three-day annual fair. Nowadays there is no fair, but the laughter of children lasts throughout the summer months as they enjoy holidays at the canoeing centre at Hole-in-the-Wall on the opposite bank of the river. The two hamlets are linked by a suspension bridge – one of several on this section of the river. Explanations for the name Hole-in-the-Wall range from the esoteric to the ridiculous, but it probably came from a post-house operating here in the 19th century. Just above Hole-in-the-Wall, at Perrystone Court, a more important mystery concerns the remains of a massive earthwork which experts think is pre-Offan; possibly a boundary of the Magonsaete people, rulers in the 7th century, which may have been used as part of the Dyke.

The little Church of St Mary at Foy stands among fine, mature trees on a low bluff overlooking the river. Beside it is the 18th-century vicarage now called, rather grandly, Foye Hall. Inside the church the urchin or hedgehog, heraldic sign of the Abrahall family, is much in evidence – their monuments fill the church. The font is claimed to have the largest bowl in the county, there is a Jacobean pulpit and an east window which is an almost exact replica of one at Sellack. The two churches share a priest and, remarkably, between 1816 and 1923 there were only two incumbents!

Garway

Map Ref: 86SO4622

Garway, on the English side of the border formed by the River Monnow, is long and straggly, with attractive houses in its centre, and some modern building towards Garway Common. The Church of St Michael stands on the side of a hill overlooking the river. Important historically and architecturally, it is one of only six in England attributed to the Knights Templar, who were granted the land by Henry II. But the unpopularity of the Order, due to an increasingly feudal attitude of many of its members, led to its dissolution in 1308 and the land at Garway passed to the Knights Hospitaller in 1312.

Architecturally, the largely Norman church is a good example of an early border church, with its square tower set at what appears to be an odd angle to the nave. The tower originally combined a defensive role with that of a prison, and was not linked to the church until the 17th century.

The Knights Hospitaller built the chancel roof of the church and the circular stone columbarium, or

dovecot, which stands among farm buildings to the south. Under its truncated roof they provided nesting boxes for 666 birds with alighting ledges on alternate rows. The lane past the dovecot leads to Skenfrith. Narrow and difficult, it hugs the English bank of the Monnow, but any inconvenience is rewarded by the beauty of the riverside scenery through which it passes.

Gloucester

Map Ref: 82SO8318

Now bypassed by a fast modern ring road system, Gloucester is within easy reach of the Forest of Dean and the Wye Valley. The city's strategic position on the River Severn has ensured it an important place in British history. From it first the Romans and then the Normans launched attacks on Wales. The Saxons considered the town important enough for Edward the Confessor to hold court here – a custom which William the Conqueror was to follow. It was during a meeting of the Witan at Gloucester in 1085 that William conceived the idea of the Domesday survey. The courses of the original four roads of Roman *Glevum* remain, fanning out from the city centre and taking their names from the gates in the wall to which they once led.

Gloucester has also long been strategically important in a commercial sense. It has a port, granted by Queen Elizabeth I, and the Severn flows through the extensive and rejuvenated dockland area of the city to meet the Gloucester and Sharpness Canal. This was constructed for shipping 160 years ago, as the Severn was often difficult to navigate at this point; the canal is still used.

Inevitably Gloucester was a religious centre from its earliest days. From a Saxon monastery the Normans built an abbey church here, and they extended and altered it in the 13th century. In the 14th century further extensive alterations and additions were made, including the graceful cloisters. The tower – so much a feature of the skyline even today – was added in the next century. The cathedral has a superb east window – the largest medieval stained-glass window in Britain, although this is disputed by York! It depicts the Coronation of the Virgin, and was designed to commemorate those who died at Crécy in 1346.

There are many fine old buildings including some good churches – and the Cathedral Close has some beautiful Georgian houses. The City Museum contains relics of the Roman settlement; there is also a Regimental Museum and a Transport Museum.

AA recommends:
Hotels: Bowden Hall, Bond End Ln, Upton St Leonards, 3-star, *tel.* (0452) 614121 (3m SE B4073)
Crest, Crest Way, Barnwood, 3-star, *tel.* (0452) 613311
Gloucester Hotel & Country Club, Robinswood Hill, 3-star, *tel.* (0452) 25653 (2½m SE B4073)
Hatton Court, Upton Hill, Upton St Leonards, 3-star, *tel.* (0452) 617412 (3m SE B4073)
Guesthouses: Alma, 49 Kingsholm Rd, *tel.* (0452) 20940
Claremont, 135 Stroud Rd, *tel.* (0452) 29540
Lulworth, 12 Midland Rd, *tel.* (0452) 21881
Rotherfield House Hotel, 5 Horton Rd, *tel.* (0452) 410500
Campsite: Red Lion Caravan Park, Wainlodes, Norton, 2-pennants, *tel.* (0452) 730251
Garages: Page and Davies, 100 Barton St, *tel.* (0452) 25291
Painswick Rd, Painswick Rd, Matson, *tel.* (0452) 29866
Westgate Motorhouse, Westgate St, *tel.* (0452) 34581

Tall ships feature in a major tourist development in Gloucester Docks

Goodrich

Map Ref: 87SO5719

Sandstone rock becomes sandstone castle without any apparent break at Godric Mappestone's castle, set on a beautiful hill with superb views in all directions. The keep is the oldest remaining section; it was built about 1150 to guard the ancient ford at a time when Stephen's rule barely extended to the Wye. During Edward I's reign the castle was extended by his uncle, William de Valence, to its present massive proportions, and for several centuries it was the home of the Talbots, Earls of Shrewsbury.

Perhaps its sheer size intimidated the Welsh, and everyone else, for it was not until the Civil War that the defences of Goodrich were formally tested. Held for the king by Sir Henry Lingen, its walls were breached in 1640 by the famous 'Roaring Meg' – a cannon alleged to fire balls of 200 pounds, cast at nearby Whitchurch – after a siege lasting four and a half months. Even this did not end the siege; only the loss of the castle's water supply and the knowledge that the king had surrendered ensured that further defence was impossible. Parliament later ordered the 'slighting' of the castle which has ever since remained a ruin, if, as an Ancient Monument, a well-maintained one.

Lying in a hollow in the shadow of the castle is the village. The houses are mostly of sandstone, but the village has a slightly unreal air because of the number of Gothic buildings – including Ye Hostelrie, a turreted folly of 1830. The hotel itself aped an earlier house, Goodrich Court, which was pure Gothic and drew Wordsworth's scorn as 'an impertinent structure'. It was demolished in the 1950s but an indication of the style of the house can be gained from the only remaining gatehouse, beside the A40. Close to Ye Hostelrie is Y Crwys, a hospitum dating, like the castle, from Edward's time. It was probably used as a place of rest by pilgrims on their way to Llanthony Abbey.

AA recommends:

Hotel: Ye Hostelrie, 2-star, *tel.* (0600) 890241

Self Catering: Yew Tree's (cottage), Coppett Hill, *tel.* (0989) 62051

The deep, wide moat of Goodrich Castle is very impressive, with underlying shelves of red rock frequently exposed

Grosmont

Map Ref: 86SO4024

A lovely, well-kept village high in the hills on the Gwent side of the Monnow, Grosmont was probably created a borough by the de Lacys in the 12th century. Certainly the considerable size of the Early English church and the quality of some of the sandstone houses points to a village of importance, as does the possession of a small town hall. On the west of the main street the houses, including the inn, back on to the churchyard, creating a pleasing picture. Modern street lighting has been kept out of Grosmont, and the only lighting in the main street is by old-fashioned lanterns. There is an excellent view of the village from a precarious viewpoint in the castle, and the general views of the rolling, heavily wooded border countryside are magnificent.

The remains of the castle stand on the site of a wooden Norman motte-and-bailey structure, one of the 'Trilateral' castles – Skenfrith and the White Castle are the others – built to guard the area. These medium sized castles were designed as a unit to be held under a single command, usually the Crown, and they remained so throughout the Middle Ages. The bulk of the ruin is 13th-century, built by Hubert de Burgh, Henry III's guardian, but the fine and rare cylindrical chimney is 14th-century. Surrounded by a deep dry moat, Grosmont Castle is an impressive place with a strong sense of history.

On entering the church it is clear that the large nave is not in use, except for miscellaneous storage,

There is a startling contrast between the rich chancel and the 'abandoned' nave in Grosmont church

and the floor consists simply of roughly laid tombstones, put down in 1972. Opinion suggests that, following the plague of 1349, the population of Grosmont was insufficient to justify completing the building and work on the nave was abandoned. The church was considerably restored by Seddon in the 1870s. Much was undoubtedly necessary and was sensibly handled, but the long glass screen dividing the nave and chancel has been the subject of differing opinions; it probably achieves one aim – keeping the congregation warm.

In the nave are two interesting items – the Grosmont 'hutch' and a large, rough and unfinished effigy of a knight in armour. The 'hutch' is one of the many chests carved from 'hollow trunks' surviving from the orders of the Synod of Exeter in 1287 – Fownhope has another. The effigy may be of one of the early lords of the castle, although the legend persists that it is of Jack o' Kent, who sold his soul to the Devil (see page 28).

Below: Hay-on-Wye huddles around its castle on the south bank of the river

Hay-on-Wye

Map Ref: 84SO2342

Over the centuries Hay has had many names and a chequered, often unhappy, history. The names Welsh Hay and English Hay do more than hint at the cause of much of the trouble afflicting this old market town on the boundary between the two countries. It is a town which still seems to arouse strong views – some love Hay, others dislike it.

Set on a hill, the town clusters around a 17th-century mansion called the Castle, which stands on the site of Maud de Valery's early 13th-century stronghold. Burnt first by King John and later by Glendower, only the gateway and tower survive, and are incorporated into the present building. The narrow, winding streets of the town seem to follow no pattern, permitting walkers to become lost in the mixture of old and new.

It was after Richard Booth bought the Castle and established his first secondhand bookshop in it that Hay's modern 'industry' began to develop. Today the town welcomes thousands of visitors each year to its new and secondhand bookshops, and thousands more use it as a base from which to explore the mountains of the Brecon Beacons National Park, the moorlands of Radnor and the soft pasturelands of Herefordshire.

The Parish Church of St Mary stands aloof from the town, as if uncertain of its loyalties. Much restored, it retains some evidence of Early English architecture, and offers good views over the Wye. The Bailey Walk starts near the church, a justifiably popular riverside promenade. Nearer the centre of the town, St John's Chapel, where Wesley preached in 1775, has had a varied career – college, school, prison and fire station – since its foundation over 700 years ago.

Not far away is Cusop, virtually a suburb of Hay, where the church has a Norman chancel and door. To the south is Cusop Dingle, where the Dulas Brook flows through a wooded valley over a number of waterfalls.

Mouse Castle is the site of another motte-and-bailey castle on the B4348 Golden Valley road – decked with trees, it provides splendid views of the Wye, the Brecon Beacons and the Black Mountains. Kilvert, who observed a strange family party on Mouse Castle, gave a lovely description of it which is still apt today.

Some five miles south of Hay, and reached only by footpath – sometimes very damp – are the remains of Craswall Priory. Founded by Walter de Lacy in 1222, it was suppressed during the reign of Edward IV. Over the centuries its stones have been used in local farm buildings. Slowly being engulfed by trees and scrub, soon Craswall will exist only as a placename on maps – an unhappy end for a once fine Cistercian building.

AA recommends:

Hotel: Olde Black Lion, Lion St, 2-star, *tel.* (0497) 820841

Restaurant: Lion's Corner House, Lion St, 1-fork, *tel.* (0497) 820175

Self Catering: Rose Cottage, *tel.* (04973) 324

Guesthouses: York House, Hardwick Rd, Cusop (1m SE in England), *tel.* (0497) 820705

Crossway (farmhouse), Clyro (1¼m N off A438 at Clyro), *tel.* (0497) 820567

Campsite: Hollybush Inn, 1-pennant, *tel.* (04974) 371

Richard Booth's bookshop extends to several buildings in the town, including the former cinema and the old fire station

Hentland

Map Ref: 82SO5426

Beside a bungalow at the end of a narrow lane with pretty cottages lies a small, considerably restored church. Its setting, in a lovely, remote wooded valley grazed by sheep, justifies a visit, but the Church of St Dubricius, Hentland offers more – this is the heart of ancient Archenfield.

Men came to Hentland in the Dark Ages to study and worship at a college established in the early years of the 6th century by St Dubricius, one of the most famous of early Welsh saints. In seven years, before he moved to Moccas, 2,000 priests and scholars joined Dubricius in the college, remains of which have been tentatively identified at Llanfrother Farm in the parish. Later he was to become first bishop of Llandaff, and, according to Monmouth, he was the man who crowned Arthur King of Britain. As late as 1066, Hentland was recognised as one of the major religious establishments in the Border area; five were in Archenfield, showing how strongly the influence of Dubricius and other 'British' saints had endured.

The church, of local sandstone, has some late 13th-century work, including an attractive north arcade, and the scissor-beam roof extends from the nave to the chancel. The churchyard cross is thought to be late 14th-century; a Crucifixion and the figure of a bishop are recognisable in two of the recesses. Attractive National Trust parkland extends from the churchyard boundary south towards the Pengethley Hotel and the A49 road, less than half a mile away.

Hentland is one of three local parishes (Kings Caple and Sellack are the others), where Pax cakes are still distributed on Palm Sunday with the blessing 'Peace and Good Neighbourhood'. The tiny cakes, decorated with the Agnus Dei, are paid for from a 16th-century bequest of the Scudamore family.

Near by on the A49 is Llandinabo, with its pretty church dedicated to the little-known St Dinabo, who may have been related to Dubricius. The church contains a rare and remarkable Renaissance screen with a frieze of angels, dolphins and mermaids. There is an odd little brass to Thomas Tompkins, a local boy drowned in a pool – he is standing in water, a cross around his neck.

Hereford

Map Ref: 85SO5039

Perhaps 'city' is a rather grand word to describe a relatively small market town which, even in the latter half of the 20th century, serves an almost exclusively agricultural community. But once within the walls of Hereford every visitor responds to its rural charm, the beauty of its buildings and, most of all, its sense of history.

The see of Hereford was founded in 676 when Putta, bishop of Rochester, came here to Mercia following a ruinous raid on Rochester – by Mercians! Hereford has always been strategically important in the defence of the Wye, and excavations have confirmed that there was a defensive circuit here during the 8th century – probably installed by King Offa. In the 11th and 13th centuries the walls were extended; several sections still stand, the best preserved near the six-arched Old Wye Bridge, dating from 1490.

Hereford is a city best explored on foot; the geographical centre, High Town, is a pedestrian area, and the city has one of the most confusing one-way street systems in England! High Town is a busy, cheerful place. A popular meeting point here on Saturday mornings is the remarkable Old House. Once part of a row of similar houses, this fine black and white building, typically Jacobean in style, is now a museum filled on all three floors with Elizabethan and Jacobean furniture.

A hundred yards or so to the west in the narrow High Street is the Church of All Saints with its memorable twisted spire. Dating mostly from the 13th and early 14th centuries, it is entered directly from the street. This spacious church contains 14th-century canopied stalls with beautifully carved misericords, a Jacobean pulpit and a chained library of 300 books, exceeded in size only by that in the Cathedral. Running south from All Saints is Broad Street, with several interesting buildings including the Green Dragon and the eye-catching façade of the city library with its animals peering down on the street below.

The Cathedral, at the end of Broad Street, is on a site where there have been places of worship since the early 8th century. Bishop Athelstan began building the present church, but part of his work was destroyed when Gruffyd of Gwynedd sacked the town in 1055. Rebuilding began during the last 20 years of the century, and has continued until this century when the west front was replaced.

Above: this tryptich is among the rich treasures of Hereford Cathedral.
Left: the Wye and the Cathedral from Bishops Meadow

Cider-making

No better cider does the world supply
Than grows along thy borders, gentle Wye
Delicious, strong and exquisitely fine.
With all the friendly properties of wine. (E Davies 1786)

The Wye Valley area has long been renowned for its cider and perry, and the orchards are a glorious sight in spring when the trees are in blossom. Herefordshire once had more orcharding than any other county and Gloucestershire perry was highly prized – some varieties were so strong as to flash in fire. Pear trees 60ft high and 300 years old can be seen, bearing fruit as well as ever.

The origin of cider is lost in the mists of Celtic mythology, when the apple tree was sacred and the fruit was worshipped, but the earliest ciders would have been made from the bitter wild apples growing in the forests. Cider was a very cheap and popular drink in medieval times, and records in Monmouth tell of 60 gallons being sold for two shillings. When Daniel Defoe visited Herefordshire during his 'Tour of the Whole Island of Great Britain 1724–1726', he noted his surprise at the unavailability of ale at the inns of the county, but said with delight that the cider was 'so good, so fine and so cheap that we never found fault with the exchange'.

Cider-making was essentially a craft of cottage and farmhouse, each with its own orchard and cider press – a craft which continues today. Over 2,500 of these mills have been recorded in Herefordshire alone. The apples had romantic and unusual names – Hangdowns, Skyrmes Kerne, Golden Ball, Slack-my-Girdle, Hansome Mauds, Ladies Finger, Cat's Heads, Sheep's Nose and the most famous of them all, developed from the time of Charles I, the Herefordshire Red Streak. Up to 350 different named varieties have been recorded in all.

The season for cider-making begins in autumn when the apples ripen. They are shaken from the trees, gathered and then dispatched to the cider mill. Here the fruit is tipped into silos where streams of water wash and carry it into the mill which extracts the juices from the pulp. The juice is then fermented into cider in oak vats.

Posters recalling the past – from the Museum of Cider in Hereford

Among its treasures are the Norman font; the Mappa Mundi, a map of the world drawn by Richard di Bello in about 1290; the crypt, home to the Diocesan treasures, including an enamel reliquary casket made in Limoges in the 13th century and showing the murder of Thomas à Becket; tapestries by John Piper and, of course, the chained library – the largest in the world, containing more than 1,400 books. It was almost lost to posterity in 1842 when the Dean decided that, unless shifted, the 'rubbish' would be burnt! The 'rubbish' includes an 8th-century Anglo-Saxon book of the four Gospels with illuminated initials similar to those in the Book of Kells; a 9th-century manuscript in Carolingian miniscule; the Herefordshire Breviary – the only known copy with music – and the famous 'Cider' Bible of the 15th century.

In addition to the Old House, there are a number of other museums in Hereford, from the Railway Centre and the Cider Museum, through costume collections and the archaeology and natural history of the county, to the remarkable St John and Coningsby Chapel and Museum, housed in the Coningsby Hospital which incorporates part of the 13th-century chapel and dining hall of the Order. It is claimed that the distinctive red dress of the Hospital pensioners inspired Nell Gwynne with the idea for the uniform of the pensioners of the Royal Hospital, Chelsea.

Mistress Gwynne (her plaque is in Gwynne Street beside the rather plain Bishop's Palace) is just one of a long list of famous people associated with Hereford – historians Giraldus and Geoffrey of Monmouth; poets John Davies of Hereford and Thomas Traherne; actors David Garrick and Roger Kemble, father of Sarah Siddons. John Bull and Samuel Wesley played the organ here and Sir Edward Elgar came to live here in 1904, regularly contributing to and taking part in the oldest of all musical festivals, the Three Choirs Festival.

AA recommends:

Hotels: Green Dragon, Broad St, 3-star, *tel.* (0432) 272506
Hereford Moat House, Belmont Rd, 3-star, *tel.* (0432) 54301
Castle Pool, Castle St, 2-star, *tel.* (0432) 56321
Somerville House, 12 Bodenham Rd, 2-star, *tel.* (0432) 273991

Self Catering: Poolspringe Farm (5 cottages), Much Birch, *tel.* (0981) 540355
Tupsley Court Cottage (house), *tel.* (0432) 55754

Guesthouses: Breinton Court, Lower Breinton, *tel.* (0432) 268156
Ferncroft Hotel, 144 Ledbury Rd, *tel.* (0432) 265538
Munstone House, Munstone, *tel.* (0432) 267122
White Lodge Hotel, 50 Ledbury Rd, *tel.* (0432) 273382

Campsite: Hereford (TRAX) Caravan Club Site, Hereford Racecourse (adjacent to A49 Leominster road and A4103), 2-pennants, *tel.* (0432) 272364

Garages: R F Brown & Son, 77-83 Whitecross Rd, Whitecross, *tel.* (0432) 272589
Victory (A W Marriot Ltd), 101-107 St Owen Street, *tel.* (0432) 276268

Hewelsfield

Map Ref: 87SO5602

Hewelsfield appears to be a remote village yet it is only yards from the St Briavels to Chepstow road. On a grassy island surrounded by a loose grouping of some of the most attractive houses in the whole of the Forest of Dean, stands the Church of St Mary Magdalene. Its history begins as a Saxon church, although there is some tenuous evidence suggesting that an even older place of worship may have stood here. Between 1971 and 1985 the church underwent a loving and faithful restoration involving the whole parish, and today it is full of beauty with a quite delightful sense of welcome. Outside, the roof of the nave sweeps nearly down to the ground, overhung by some magnificent chestnuts and fine old yews.

Hewelsfield stands on the boundaries of the English and Welsh Churches. Within the parish boundary there are two sections of Offa's Dyke, a reminder of the bloody past of this part of the country – yet the history of the parish is remarkably lacking in incident and even changes of ownership to the Manor of 'Hiwoldstone' have been accomplished with relative ease.

The 'Golden Knight' at Holme Lacy

Hoarwithy

Map Ref: 85SO5429

Entering Hoarwithy from the Kings Caple road, the visitor will see how the Church of St Catherine's, high on the side of the valley above the Wye, bears a remarkable resemblance to an Italian church. Around it clusters a group of modern – some very modern – houses, many in an architectural style which heightens the impression of being in Italy.

Perhaps the most surprising moment comes after the climb up the steps, through the cloistered walkway and into the church – it is even more 'Italian' inside than out. Marble, gold mosaics and lapis lazuli are everywhere, richness of ornamentation is the norm, and it invites suspension of critical judgment by its sheer panache.

The church was designed by Seddon in 1885, its sandstone walls enclosing an earlier chapel 'with no pretensions to any style'. The man who dismissed the worth of the old chapel was Prebendary William Poole, vicar of the parish of Hentland, to which Hoarwithy is attached, and the 'onlie begetter' of St Catherine's. Poole inherited property in Ledbury and in the north country and used money from the rents to beautify Hoarwithy chapel. Work on the interior was carried out over a period of almost 20 years by a number of local craftsmen, several from Italy and one from St Paul's in London.

The outstanding impression within the church is of marble – on the floor, the pulpit and in the four graceful pillars supporting the highly decorated domed apse, and the marble altar is inlaid with lapis lazuli. Magnificent carvings of the sanctuary stalls – representing British saints of the district – were carved by Harry Hems of Exeter, using seasoned oak said to be from Poole's estates.

AA recommends:
Guesthouse: Old Mill (farmhouse), *tel.* (043270) 602

Offa's Dyke

The great Saxon King Offa ruled over the Kingdom of Mercia from 757 until his death in 796. By his conquest of Essex, Kent, Surrey and East Anglia, by fair means and foul, he dominated all England south of the Humber. The imprint of his power is visible throughout England, but his most lasting and spectacular monument is Offa's Dyke. This mighty earthwork stretches from Sedbury Cliffs on the River Severn through the Wye Valley and Herefordshire and northwards towards the mouth of the River Dee, a distance of almost 150 miles. The Dyke marked Mercia's western boundary with Wales where the defeated but still warlike Ancient Britons had retreated from their Saxon oppressors. Opinions differ as to the exact purpose of the Dyke. For many years it was thought to have been constructed as a purely symbolic frontier and a show of political power. But recent archaeological discoveries of occasional stone breastwork and of staking on top of the Dyke suggests that it may well have been defensive and patrolled by Mercian soldiers during times of Saxon–Celtic conflict. The Dyke was probably constructed very quickly, maybe within a single year, by numerous groups of workers building in sections. Wooden tools were used to dig a ditch and the excavated earth was thrown to the east to form a mound averaging 6ft above ground level. The total breadth of ditch and mound is almost 60ft. But there are several 'missing' portions. From Sedbury to Tutshill the sheer river cliffs seem to have been considered a sufficient natural boundary and, in parts, the River Wye itself forms the frontier. Some of the best preserved sections of Offa's Dyke are to be found in the hard limestones of the Wye Valley where the ditch has remained well defined and the bank steep and narrow. Offa's Dyke probably only lasted as a meaningful political border for about 40 years. But for well over 1,000 years it has remained as a visible symbol of the cultural divisions between Celt and Anglo-Saxon. Like many relics of the Dark Ages, Offa's Dyke continues to hold many unsolved mysteries.

In 1971 Offa's Dyke Long Distance Footpath was created by the Countryside Commission. It stretches from Sedbury Cliffs near Chepstow to Prestatyn on the North Wales Clwyd coast. The route of the path was chosen partly for its scenic beauty and partly to follow the Dyke. Out of a total of 173 miles only about 60 are on the Dyke itself. The waymarked sign for Offa's Dyke Path is a white acorn and a yellow arrow. One of the best preserved and most beautiful sections of the Dyke is along Shorn Cliff and the Devil's Pulpit, which has magnificent views of the valley, the river and Tintern Abbey.

Offa introduced a coinage based on the silver penny

Mutmaßliches Siegel von König Offa.
Nach einem Abdruck im Brit. Mus. zu London.

Holme Lacy

Map Ref: 85SO5535

This village has some pleasant older buildings, a growing number of small modern estates and the county's Agricultural College, close to the sunken track of the old Ross to Hereford railway. There is a fine view of Haugh Wood on the far bank of the Wye from the Mordiford road as it dips down to the modern suspension bridge at Even Pits.

For centuries 'brinkers' (owners with property adjoining the river) claimed the right to fish the 'free waters' between Holme Lacy and Strangford, near Foy. Following the route of the railway this is a matter of no more than six miles but, as the Wye travels, the distance is considerably longer and the section contains some of the best fishing on the river. It was not until 1911 that the matter was resolved when a bitter legal battle went against the brinkers in favour of the Earl of Chesterfield, the then owner of Holme Lacy House.

A tree-lined avenue leads to the house, the largest in the county and long used as a hospital. The original house on the site was built for the Scudamore family in the reign of Henry III, but in the 17th century the second Lord Scudamore pulled down the old brick house, replacing it with a grand stone building. Some of the internal woodwork is reputedly by Grinling Gibbons; it is now at Kentchurch Court (see page 51), the present home of the family. The original plaster ceilings remain at Holme Lacy House.

Away from the village, beside the often flooded water meadows of the Wye, is the parish church (not always open). It seems light and roomy because of the unusual width of the nave and south aisle, divided by a 14th-century arcade. Very plain 17th-century benches contrast with decorated medieval choir stalls and a gilded lectern. Both inside and outside the church there are tombs and memorials to the Scudamore family – Holme Lacy was their principal seat for centuries.

The Wye at Hoarwithy

View from Hoarwithy church. Inside (left) four Devonshire marble columns support an inner cupola

How Caple

Map Ref: 85SO6030

How Caple Court and its Church of St Andrew and St Mary stand on the last sweeping bend of the Wye between Hereford and Ross. High above the river in densely wooded country, this delightful little grouping is easily missed, but can be found by following the signs to the recently opened nursery. Since 1200 only three families have lived in How Caple Court – the Caples, the Gregorys and the present owners, the Lees. Sir William Gregory was Speaker of the House of Commons in 1679.

The house has some Victorian additions but is largely 17th-century, with fine views from its mullioned windows of the Wye Valley. The garden, opened to the public, is being reclaimed by Mr and Mrs Peter Lee after a lengthy period of neglect – terraces have been uncovered, walls rebuilt and ponds refilled.

The church is small, superbly maintained (as befits what is, effectively, a private chapel), full of interest – and the darkest in all Hereford! Happily there is (once located) effective modern lighting. It has a fine wooden Jacobean screen supporting the arms of William III, which has been taken as a sign of William Gregory's acceptance of the king. There are fragments of 14th-century stained glass in the north window and several fine modern windows in the nave, including memorials to members of the Lee family, five of whom were killed between 1915 and 1921. But the great treasure of How Caple is its 16th-century diptych. Believed to have been painted in southern Germany, it hangs on the north wall of the chancel over the choir stalls. A total of eight paintings – four each on back and front – represent such subjects as the Death of St Francis, the Seven Joys of the Virgin, the Washing of the Feet and the Death of St Clare. Beautifully restored by the Courtauld Institute in 1984, it would alone justify seeking out this lovely, remote part of the Wye Valley.

AA recommends:
Hotel: How Caple Grange, 2-star, *tel.* (098986) 208
Self Catering: Rugden Granary Flat, *tel.* (098986) 224

Kempley

Map Ref: 85SO6729

A few miles from Newent in a quiet part of north-west Gloucestershire are a group of wall paintings which are among the best in the country; they are in the little Church of St Mary, Kempley. The nave and chancel of the church are early Norman and the best, and oldest, of the paintings are the frescoes in the chancel; the paintings in the nave date from the 13th century.

The frescoes (dated about 1130) appear almost as fresh as when first painted – probably due to a combination of Reformation whitewash and Victorian varnish. The whitewash was removed in 1872 but replaced by the varnish; in 1955 the wall paintings were finally restored to their original condition. The scenes in the chancel include Christ sitting on a rainbow blessing the world, while in the nave St Michael weighs souls.

Kempley also has an interesting modern church, St Edward the Confessor. Built of sandstone it contains several good modern sculptures.

Kenchester

Map Ref: 84SO4342

Near the A438 about four miles from Hereford is the 22-acre site of the city's predecessor, the Romano-British town of Magnis (*Magna Castra*). The town was probably occupied for about 400 years – from the 1st to the 4th centuries.

Traces of the walls remain on the north-west side; pottery, coins and jewellery have all been found, and sections of tessellated pavement are now in Hereford museum. The virtual destruction of the town has been a gradual process – when Leland visited it there were clear signs of buildings, but he reported that 'of the decaye of Kenchester Hereford flourished'. Almost certainly many of the remains of Magnis are incorporated into the city which replaced it. The small Norman church here has a beautiful 16th-century roof truss.

Kenchester itself probably replaced the great hillfort of Credenhill, known to have been occupied from about 400BC to AD75. Now the village of Credenhill has been almost obliterated by an RAF base, but the church is interesting, with some 14th-century stained glass which, though not perhaps of the quality of that at Eaton Bishop, (see page 40), is very beautiful. Thomas Traherne was vicar here, writing the meditations which were published shortly after his death. These were lost for over 200 years before their rediscovery and publication in the early years of this century, establishing his reputation as one of the great metaphysical poets.

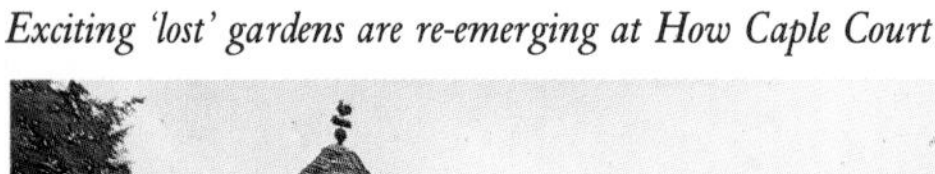
Exciting 'lost' gardens are re-emerging at How Caple Court

The sumptuously carved doorway of Kilpeck church, and (left) comic-strip carvings at its exterior eaves

Kentchurch Court, extending from its mighty medieval tower

Kentchurch

Map Ref: 86SO4125

The 'English' road from Garway to Kentchurch climbs above the valley of the Monnow for much of its length, clinging to the side of Garway Hill, and offering glorious views of the lovely Border country below. The road descends to the floor of the valley and joins the river just before Kentchurch church with the entrance to Kentchurch Court opposite (open only by prior appointment). The present church is 19th-century but has several interesting Scudamore tombs – mainly 17th-century.

Kentchurch Court was a fortified manor house rather than a castle like Grosmont – visible high on the hill on the opposite bank of the Monnow. Set in a deer park, it retains some 14th-century building – the gatehouse, tower and part of the north end – incorporated into Nash's early 19th-century house. The lovely wood carving in the house is attributed to Grinling Gibbons; some was originally at the Scudamore family's main seat, Holme Lacy House.

Sir John Scudamore of Kentchurch married Alice, one of the daughters of Owen Glendower and it is popularly believed that the old chief spent many of the last years of his life in hiding at Kentchurch. The Scudamores have lived here continuously since the 14th century, playing a prominent role in the turbulent history of the area. Members of the family fought and died for the Lancastrians against the future Edward IV at the battle of Mortimer's Cross in 1461.

Kilpeck

Map Ref: 84SO4430

In a county rich with ecclesiastical treasures Kilpeck church ranks high, with its unsurpassed examples of stone carvings. The village, too, is a delight; stone and timbered houses form a small, tight-knit community. There is evidence of an earlier, enclosed village, particularly from the sparse motte-and-bailey remains of the Norman castle which probably replaced an earlier stronghold.

Kilpeck church, built of sandstone, is primarily 12th-century Norman and virtually unchanged since it was built. Around the church is a remarkable profusion of works of the Herefordshire School of Carving, a large Norman font on a modern pillar, a Norman stoup – the bowl clasped in two hands and arms – and an early Jacobean gallery in which to sit and absorb everything this unique place offers.

Less than half a mile from Kilpeck but almost entirely ignored is the little church of St Devereux. It stands along a narrow lane with a farm and a couple of other buildings. Unspectacular but lovingly tended, it makes a pleasing counterpoint to its famous neighbour.

AA recommends:
Guesthouse: Priory (farmhouse), *tel.* (098121) 366

King's Caple

Map Ref: 87SO5628

The beautiful red sandstone Church of St John the Baptist dominates the view of King's Caple from almost every angle. It stands on high ground beside the medieval Castle Tump, site of a motte-and-bailey castle, but used in recent years for festivities. The church is of several periods – the chancel late 12th-century, nave 13th-century, tower and recessed spire 14th-century. The south porch is 15th-century and very attractive with its rib-vaulted roof.

Inside, the box pews are original; there is a good, ornate, Jacobean pulpit and tester. The 14th-century Aramstone Chapel has an excellent vaulted roof, and tombs of the owners of a large house (now demolished) on the edge of the village, from which the chapel takes its name. The benefaction board lists a bequest of five shillings by a member of the Scudamore family, vicar here in the 15th century, for 'cake money so called'. The beneficiaries were Hentland, Kings Caple and Sellack, and Pax cakes are still distributed every Palm Sunday.

The village has been developed in recent years with new housing estates and buildings eroding the paramount position of the church.

Ledbury

Map Ref: 85SO7137

A truly lovely market town, Ledbury has managed to keep its centre almost unspoilt. Nor does its setting, among hop fields and orchards, with the sharp outlines of the Malvern Hills in the background, leave anything to be desired.

The church is basically Norman, but has been added to over the centuries. It has a particularly lovely 14th-century Decorated chapel, which contains an outstanding monument of a priest at prayer. The church has almost an embarrassment of monuments, many medieval; there is good glass, including some modern windows by Kempe.

Outside is the fine detached tower and Georgian spire. Few calendars or books on Britain appear able to resist the genuinely graceful view up Church Lane to the spire – the many well-maintained black and white houses framing the lane, with their hanging flower baskets, add to the charm. A few yards away is the old market house, supported on wooden pillars, an outstanding example of a 17th-century timber-framed house.

In the High Street are the almshouses of St Katherine's Hospital. Founded in 1232, the present hospital was rebuilt in 1822 but a 14th-century chapel and hall remain – the latter has a particularly fine roof of about 1340 and is sometimes open. On the crossroads at the top of High Street is Ledbury Park, one of the largest timber-framed houses in the whole county. Two outstanding inns grace the centre of the town, the late 16th-century Talbot and the Feathers. The top floor of the timber-framed Feathers is about a century later than the rest.

AA recommends:
Hotels: Feathers, High St, 3-star, *tel.* (0531) 5266
Hope End Country House, Hope End, 2-star, country house hotel, 1-rosette, *tel.* (0531) 3613 (2½m NE unclass)
Royal Oak, The Southend, 2-star, *tel.* (0531) 2110
Verzons, Trumpet, 2-star, *tel.* (053183) 381 (3m W A438)
Garage: Parkway (Gittings Bros Mtrs), *tel.* (0531) 2320

Attractive Ledbury Market House stands on huge oak pillars

Littledean

Map Ref: 87SO6713

Littledean is an attractive, well-maintained village cradled in a bend of the A4151. Littledean Hall, a truly remarkable building, is claimed to be the oldest known house in the country.

Recent excavations have indicated that there was a Roman temple on the site. Identified as Springhead Temple, it has proved to be the largest rural temple discovered in Britain. The core of the present house – built for the Dene family in the 11th century – stands on Roman foundations. The cellar was originally a Saxon open hall and, from a later era, there is extensive Jacobean panelling throughout the house. Inevitably, it is said to be haunted and, given its uniquely long occupancy, by not one but several ghosts! The gardens are most attractive with a panoramic walk and fine views over the serpentine twists in the nearby Severn. A little to the north of the hall are the remains of a motte-and-bailey castle said to have been occupied from the 11th to the 12th century.

The Herefordshire School

The Wye Valley and surrounding areas are rich in wonderful church architecture. Almost every village has its own church, and many of them are thought to have been built on ancient Celtic sites. But the most interesting are the unique creation of a group of 11th-century travelling masons who toured the countryside from job to job throughout Herefordshire and the neighbouring counties of Gloucestershire, Worcestershire and Shropshire. Today they are known as the Herefordshire School of Norman Sculpture.

This group of artists came into being in about 1140, at the height of the terrible civil war which erupted after the death of Henry I, when his daughter Matilda disputed the right of Stephen (her cousin and the grandson of William the Conqueror) to the English throne. The war lasted for eight years. Hereford, the centre of some of the fiercest fighting, was severely damaged by fire and siege. It is remarkable that at this time the Herefordshire School emerged.

The masterpiece and best-preserved church of the school is the Church of SS Mary and David at Kilpeck. Located in a remote district eight miles south-west of Hereford, this small Norman church has one of the most amazing collections of Romanesque sculpture to be found in Britain. Without doubt the most lavish is that of the portal over the south doorway which is in excellent order of preservation. This is thanks to a wooden porchway, removed during the last century, which had protected the stonework from weathering for hundreds of years. The carvings depict 'The Creation' and 'The Temptation in the Garden of Eden' represented by intricately twisting serpents, foliage, fruits, dragons and warrior-like human figures in a mass of detail. The style of sculpture was most unconventional for its period and appears to have gathered inspiration from the art of the Anglo-Saxons, Normans and Vikings with some influences from Italy and Spain. Around the church at eaves level are a series of 60 or so extraordinary carvings of grotesque figures, heads and animals. One or two of the more immodest fertility symbols have escaped destruction by prudish Victorians.

The Herefordshire School was responsible for much of the sculpture in at least three other notable churches in the *Wyedean* area: Fownhope and Rowlstone in Herefordshire, and Ruardean in the Forest of Dean. All are in beautiful settings and a day's tour to all four would lead through some of the most delightful countryside in the Wye Valley.

Lydbrook, Upper and Lower

Map Ref: 87SO6015

Both Upper and Lower Lydbrook contain an interesting mixture of architectural styles along a narrow, steep-sided valley which widens and relaxes as it enters Lower Lydbrook. The road through the villages enters the Wye Valley opposite Courtfield (see Welsh Bicknor), and from the small car park at the end of the road there is a typically attractive Wye view upstream.

Nowadays, Lydbrook has several hotels and is developing as a useful centre for exploring both the Wye and the Forest of Dean, yet its traditional connection is with industry – indeed, a book published in 1861 compared it to Sheffield. The first commercially successful blast furnace in the Forest of Dean area was sited here and was working as early as 1608.

Lydbrook was particularly important as a loading place for coal to be taken by barge to Hereford. The flat-bottomed barges were dragged originally by teams of men and later – after the construction of a tow-path in 1811 – by horses. The trade only declined when the canal from Gloucester to Hereford was built in the 1840s. The canal, in fact, was almost at once superseded by the railways; the Severn and Wye line linked with the branch from Ross at Lydbrook.

Lydney

Map Ref: 87SO6303

Lydney is a sprawling town spreading down to the wide Severn Estuary. Its major feature is Lydney Park, which contains a deer park, two museums and an attractive woodland garden, the work of the 2nd Viscount Bledisloe. The 1st Viscount was Governor-General of New Zealand in the 1930s. Within the boundaries of Lydney Park there is a virtual microcosm of the long occupation by man of this part of Britain. Included are an Iron Age promontory fort and the site of a 4th-century temple. Simple designs on pottery pieces found in the fort suggest a connection with similar work produced at Glastonbury. The Romano-Celtic temple is dedicated to Nodens, a benign Celtic god of healing. Close to it are traces of Roman iron mines and there is evidence that the fort was strengthened after the Romans left – probably against the next group of invaders, the Saxons.

Sarah Kemble left this house in Lydbrook to become – as Sarah Siddons – a great tragic actress

A blaze of colour at Lydney Park, a mile from Lydney at Aylesburton

Just north of Lydney are the headquarters of the Dean Forest Railway which runs up to Parkend, deep in a clearing in the Forest, with a long industrial heritage (see Soudley). There are more Roman mine workings at nearby Bream.

South of the town along the A48, in the churchyard at Alvington, are the graves of several Victorian Wintours – a continuing link with the most famous of Lydney's families. Sir William acquired the estate in 1561 and subsequently played a role in the defeat of the Armada (1588). Less than 60 years later his grandson Sir John was involved in a remarkable escape from the Roundheads at the Battle of Lancaut – commemorated at Wintour's Leap on the St Briavels to Chepstow road.

AA recommends:
Garages: Hardacres, Newerne St, *tel.* (0594) 42447
Watts, High St, *tel.* (0594) 42481

Madley

Map Ref: 84SO4138

Madley is a large red-brick village with a fair sprinkling of black and white houses. One of the little streets near the church has the enchanting name of Pennyplock and Rosemary Lane – it is slightly disappointing to find that this medieval name applies to a street of modern houses. Church Farm, on the edge of the village, is a superb half-timbered building rubbing shoulders with several less beautiful examples of modern architecture. The nearby Methodist chapel is one of the most attractive in the county – a black and white cottage.

Structurally very little altered since its building in the 13th and 14th centuries, the church has a lovely, spacious arcaded nave. The enclosed Lulham Pew, in front of the crypt stairs, was probably constructed from the tracery of the 15th-century rood screen. The memorable stained glass in the east windows, some sadly just a jigsaw of pieces, includes 13th-century work comparable with that at Eaton Bishop. There is a Sanctus bell, possibly of the 13th century, but recast in the early 18th century by Henry Williams, a Welsh bellfounder, whose work is rarely found in England. The huge font is said to be the second largest in England, and the 14th-century churchyard cross is one of the best preserved in the county.

One of the heroes of the battle of Rourke's Drift, Robert Jones VC, lived the last years of his life and died at Madley, though he is buried at Peterchurch. Perhaps more important, the Welsh saint Dubricius is traditionally believed to have been born here.

Mitcheldean

Map Ref: 87SO6618

As the A4136 descends Plump Hill into Mitcheldean there is a sudden dramatic glimpse of the Severn Estuary away to the right and the road passes the Forestry Commission land known as the Wilderness, where there is a nature reserve, a field study centre and a forest trail. The centre of Mitcheldean has the appearance and style of a country town, with some good buildings, but it is ringed by modern houses and there is a large industrial estate on its eastern edge.

The mainly 14th-century Parish Church of St Michael and All Saints has a 15th-century Perpendicular north aisle creating a wonderful impression of size, and the church is one of the widest in the country. Almost inevitably there was a great deal of restoration in the 19th century but the greatest treasure was untouched – the magnificent Doom painting, representing the Last Judgement, was executed in oils by an unknown 15th-century artist and fills the tympanum above the chancel arch.

South, on an attractive minor road to Littledean is Abenhall – for a long time a mining centre, but now largely a farming community grouped around a pretty small church on its island site. Links with the past include the 15th-century font bearing the arms of the Guild of Miners and Free Smiths, and a mounting block against the churchyard wall.

Moccas

Map Ref: 84SO3542

Moccas Court was designed by Adam and finished, in 1783, by the relatively little-known architect Anthony Keck. Its superb setting beside the Wye is a graceful deer park with the stamp of Capability Brown on it. The Court is open only one day a week, but it is possible to drive into the park at most times – the great oaks which deeply impressed Francis Kilvert are worth the visit.

Built of red brick, externally the Court is not a notably attractive house – only the semi-circular porch, added in 1792, breaks the severity of line. Inside, however, the ground floor presents a great contrast. The magnificent circular drawing room decorated with French paper panels and a typically cool and elegant Adam hall with curved staircase are particularly fine. The terraces below the house are the work of Humphry Repton.

The Norman church, built of tufa, stands some way from the house and is small, plain and charming. It has a nave, chancel and rounded apse all, as is usual with churches of big houses, in excellent order; there is some good 14th-century glass, large organ and an overbearing monument to a 14th-century knight.

A mile or so away along the flat flood plain is Preston-on-Wye; between the two villages, at Byecross, the Wye comes very close to the road; a small cottage clings to the upper bank, its garden seemingly suspended over the river. Nowadays, Preston is little more than a hamlet, but its church, although several times restored, still contains some attractive examples of various periods of architecture including a Norman south door. Beside the church is Preston Court, a manor house with a delightful garden and some lovely old outbuildings including a long barn. A peaceful pond, usually frequented by ducks, completes a classic and pleasing scene.

The Monnow Bridge Gateway in Monmouth is the only remaining fortified bridge gate in Britain

Monmouth

Map Ref: 87SO5112

The Romans appreciated the strategic importance of a settlement at a point where two rivers, the Monnow and the Wye, effectively the boundaries of England and Wales, meet, and they founded the military camp of *Blestium* here. Monmouth was to develop as a centre for trade – particularly in agricultural produce – and it very clearly remains a market town today.

Any tour of Monmouth should begin at the Monnow Bridge (perhaps not the obvious starting place), with its unique 13th-century fortified gatehouse. One of four gates into the town, it has small arches on either side added in the 19th century. The bridge leads to the suburb of Over Monnow whose Church of St Thomas, beside the bridge, is of special interest for its fine, original chancel arch.

Back across the bridge is Monnow Street, full of interesting buildings, and a useful shopping centre. The cattle market is to the right. At the top of the street is the old town, a close-packed jumble of public and private buildings. A regular street market is still held in Agincourt Square beside the 18th-century Shire Hall, with its rather uninspiring statue to Henry V who was born here in 1387. A second statue is to the memory of Charles Rolls, co-founder of Rolls-Royce.

Henry was born in the castle, but only parts of the tower and hall remain, alongside Great Castle House, an imposing 17th-century structure built by the first Duke of Beaufort using stones from the castle ruins. The castle was built by William Fitz Osbern and was finally destroyed by Parliamentarians after changing hands several times during the Civil War. The house is occupied by the Royal Monmouthshire Royal Engineers, a Territorial Regiment, and is not open to the public.

The New Market Hall, home to two museums, is in Priory Street; one houses a fine collection of Nelsonian relics, the other covers local history. The church is a disappointment, but many of the small, often Georgian, houses around it (few sadly in use as private dwellings) are of high quality. A little remains of the Benedictine Priory, including a room with a window projecting over Priory Street. For no good historical reason it is associated with Geoffrey of Monmouth who may have been born or educated in the town but wrote his classic history in Oxford. There are relics of John Kemble, the Roman Catholic martyr, in the Catholic Church.

Monmouth School, founded as a free school by the merchant William Jones and now administered by the Haberdashers' Company, is large and mostly 19th-century Gothic – neither it nor the bypass can be said to enhance the view of the town from the A466 Chepstow road which leaves Monmouth over the five-arched Wye Bridge, built in 1617.

The parish church at Dixton, to the north of the town, was consecrated in the early years of Norman rule but the site is almost certainly older. A lovely setting beside the Wye brings problems with flooding but external plaster appears to protect it from damp.

There are outstanding views over the town and into Wales from the Round House, a summer house erected by 'the first gentlemen in Monmouth' on the 800ft hill known as the Kymin. The Naval Temple was added in 1800 to commemorate the Battle of the Nile and the deeds of various admirals including Nelson – who visited the Temple for breakfast in 1802. (This, apart from the museum, is the only connection he has with Monmouth.) The road to the top is narrow and winding; for those with stamina the bridle-path is better.

This statue to motoring and aviation pioneer Charles Rolls stands in Monmouth's main square

AA recommends:
Hotels: King's Head, Agincourt Sq, 3-star, *tel.* (0600) 2177
Talocher Farmhouse, Wonastow Rd, 1-star, *tel.* (060083) 236
Guesthouse: Queens Head (inn), St James Street, *tel.* (0600) 2767
Garages: County, Monnow St, *tel.* (0600) 2366
St James (E & B Manns), St James Square, *tel.* (0600) 2773

Monnington-on-Wye

Map Ref: 84SO3743

The tiny settlement of Monnington Court, its church and a few estate buildings on the flat land near the Wye is a sheer delight. Monnington is worth visiting at any time but is possibly best approached in spring through the numerous orchards which surround it, each more riotously blooming than the last.

The approach to the church is enchanting – a wide, well-kept green lane curves around the wall of the court to the timber-framed lych gate of the little church. The battlemented tower of the church is 15th-century and the remainder was built following the Restoration in 1679. Inside it is quite beautifully maintained, its wooden furnishings, all with barley sugar columns, glowing in the light from the plain windows. A large Royal Arms of Charles II hangs on the wall, a further affirmation of support for the monarch.

Across the main road is Staunton-on-Wye. The village is patchy, with new building diluting the old mixture of timber-framed, stone and brick houses, but the narrow little lanes lead to settlements with lovely names – Duck Street and Little London among them – gained as a result of enclosures. The church has a superb position on a knoll overlooking the A438 with an attractive timber-framed farmhouse and other buildings at its foot. The Victorians have left their mark, but it has a Norman lancet window, a plain and pleasing font, and three 700-year-old worn coffin lids.

Mordiford

Map Ref: 85SO5737

The church, red-brick rectory, and bridge make a very pleasing group on the western side of Mordiford where the Lugg loops lazily through water meadows as it nears the end of its journey to join the Wye just below the village. The village is pretty – the slopes of Haugh Wood rise steeply behind its black and white buildings. The powerful, well-proportioned bridge is part 14th- and part 16th-century.

A stone font, dated 1633, stands in the porch of the church (not always open). Also in the porch is a 'Record of Occurrence at Mordiford, 27th May, 1811' which makes interesting, if sad, reading. During a storm the Pentaloe Brook swept away a barn, cider mill and adjoining cottage – four people, including a child, were drowned. Several other houses in the village were damaged by rock falls and £80 was collected and distributed to the householders 'in proportion to their respective losses'.

Nicholas de Hereford, who was the main collaborator with Wycliffe on the first English translation of the Bible, was born at Sufton, a little way above Mordiford. The Herefords have held the estate since the 12th century; the present house is late 18th-century.

A mile along the B4224 is Hampton Bishop, with half-timbered houses dotted about the fields and orchards beside the road – this rural scene is the more remarkable for being little more than a mile from Hereford. The Wye joins the road briefly at the Bunch of Carrots, a modernised 17th-century inn, but the main attraction is the Norman church hidden away, with most of the village, on the opposite side of the road. Hampton has three reredos, two modern, and the remains of a rare medieval stone one.

AA recommends:
Guesthouse: Orchard (farmhouse), *tel.* (043273) 253

The Severn Bore

Foaming, bubbling and crashing its way 21 miles up the River Severn, the Severn Bore has for centuries attracted people along her banks from Awre to Gloucester. If all the conditions are favourable viewers are rewarded first by the approaching distant roar, and then by the sight of one of Britain's most spectacular natural phenomena. The Bore at its most magnificent is amazing and in mid-stream the wave can reach heights of up to 10ft. But the Bore can be fickle, and sometimes the waiting crowds see only a barely discernible ripple – if anything at all. But the uncertainty is part of the attraction, and the anticipation is part of the thrill and the fun.

The Severn Bore actually occurs about 260 times a year – that is, twice a day on about 130 days with the high spring tides. However, to witness the Bore at its best one must take into account the following factors:

1 The biggest Bores occur from one to three days after the new or full moon near the spring equinox in February, March or April or the autumnal equinox in August, September or October. However, there are smaller Bores on the days just before and just after these times.

2 The Bores occur from 7 am until noon and from 7 pm until midnight, and the best ones are likely to be those predicted from 9 am to 11 am or 9 pm to 11 pm.

3 There should be a good west to south-west wind and the atmospheric pressure should be low.

Several factors cause this phenomenon. At the equinoxes, when the gravitational forces of the sun and moon join to pull in the same direction, the difference between high and low water in the tidal Severn Estuary can be about 14ft. At the turn of the tide the sea sends its waters rushing into the wide estuary to meet the Severn head on. It is the resistance of the Severn where the estuary begins to narrow into the river that causes the great wave to form. Here it can be up to 28yds wide. The Bore begins to gather momentum, and by the time it reaches Sharpness, the swell is moving upstream at about five miles per hour until it forces its way into the narrower bed of the river at Fretherne, where the wave gains height and becomes the Severn Bore, moving at an average speed of 10 miles per hour. Behind the first wave will come a second and then a third followed by the full body of the tide, as one 19th-century writer put it, 'foaming and raging like a hideous whirlpool'.

Local newspapers often publish timetables for the Bore, and there are predictions in the annual *Arrowsmith's Tide Tables*, available at local newsagents and bookshops. Also, the Severn Trent Water Authority have produced a leaflet guide to the Bore, available at Tourist Information Centres.

'Borewatchers' are advised to arrive early, particularly during weekends or bank holidays when local traffic congestion can be a problem. The popular viewing points are at Minsterworth, at Stone Bench on the opposite bank, and also at Over Bridge near Gloucester.

Much Marcle

Map Ref: 85SO6532

In an area of fine villages, Much Marcle takes high rank. It stands off the Ross to Ledbury road, almost on the Gloucestershire border, among fields of fruit trees. This is cider-making country – Weston's are still one of the largest local employers, as they were in the 19th century when Henry Weston started his factory here. The village church is of great interest and there are three outstanding houses in the parish.

The church is approached along an almost concealed cobbled footpath, past a group of beautifully maintained small houses including a timber-framed cottage. Some fine trees stand at the entrance and in the churchyard – where the girth of the yew surely confirms its claim to be one of the oldest in the county. Close to the church are the remains of Mortimer's Castle, a motte-and-bailey earthwork.

The first impression inside the church must be the length of the late 13th-century nave; the second, the beauty of some of the tombs. Perhaps the most outstanding is the late 14th-century altar tomb to Blanche Grandison. The figure of a woman of about 30 lies beneath a five-arched canopy, holding a rosary in her left hand. She wears a tight-fitting dress, its folds falling over the end of the tomb. Her eyes closed, her lips parted, she might be sleeping, such is the remarkable quality and realism of the work.

The church has a second tomb of the same period, this one with figures of an unidentified knight and his lady. The identity of the man in civilian dress on the rare wooden effigy in the nave is also in some doubt, but he is believed to be Walter de Helyon, a franklin or gentleman, who owned lands here in 1357.

The interesting octagonal brick dovecot in the gardens of the old manor house, Hellens

In the churchyard at Much Marcle – the huge yew offers shelter, and (left) a finely carved churchyard cross

It is likely that de Helyon lived in Hellens, a fine example of a late 16th-century brick house, based on the framework of an older building, much of it Tudor. It stands a few hundred yards north of the church, across the Dymock road. Closer to the church is the entrance to Homme House, situated about half a mile to the south. A happy mixture of Tudor, Queen Anne and Georgian architecture, it has been in the hands of the Kyrle family for many centuries – their tombs are in the church.

Hall Court, in the hamlet of Rushhall near Putley, is a fine timber-framed house of 1608. Opposite it is a mound, partially excavated in 1974. The countryside around Putley is very attractive – orchard and hop country under the Woolhope-Cockshoot Hills with beautiful views towards the Malvern Hills across the rolling farmland.

Newent

Map Ref: 87SO7225

Still a small, outwardly sleepy market town, Newent is being expanded by the growth of new estates. The black and white timber-framed Market House stands in the centre, close to the junction of Church Street, Broad Street and High Street. Dating from the early 1600s and supported by twelve posts, it contains just one room. The streets all have interesting houses, including some more that are timber-framed; Church Street has good Georgian buildings near the church. On the edge of the town, virtually under the bypass, is Checkley Mill – it is no longer working but is very pretty.

The church was almost certainly a place of worship in Anglo-Saxon times – in the porch is an important cross-shaft of Northumbrian provenance, probably 9th-century (discovered in the churchyard in 1907). Inside the church is another relic with Northumbrian connections. The unique Newent stone tablet has the 'Harrowing of Hell' on one side and a bishop on the other. It bears a distinct resemblance to grave-slabs found in Northumbria, though it was probably used as a portable altar.

Close to Newent is the well-established Falconry Centre which has an outstanding collection of birds of prey, a museum and flying ground. The Butterfly and Waterlife Centre lies to the north of the town.

AA recommends:
Restaurant: Soutters, Culver St, 1-fork, *tel.* (0531) 820896
Garage: Central (W E Bennion & Son), Broad St, *tel.* (0531) 820333

Newland

Map Ref: 87SO5509

Newland is most attractively set high up in a narrow valley, with its many fine houses indicating an affluent and settled past. The beautifully maintained condition of the village suggests a continuing connection with that wealthy history.

All Saints Church has long been called 'the Cathedral of the Forest' because of its remarkable size. Building was begun in the early 13th century by Robert of Wakering, and one of the many effigies is believed to be of him. The famous 'Miner's Brass' in the Gryndour Chapel depicts a medieval miner with hod and pick and a candle in his mouth. At the rear of the church exhibits in display cases include a beautifully designed and executed modern vestal set used at major church festivals.

The church is set in a square churchyard with a road on two sides, and is surrounded by a number of well-preserved houses from various periods – outstanding are the almshouses, for eight men and eight women, founded in 1615 by William Jones. Born in Newland, Jones moved to London where he made a fortune before returning to live in Monmouth. In 1954 the Haberdashers' Company and the governors of the charity set up by Jones carried out a sensitive modernisation of the houses. Among the other buildings is a pub peculiarly named The Ostrich. Rising triumphantly over all is the church tower with its magnificent flying buttresses, pinnacles and battlements in the Decorated style.

Pembridge Castle

Map Ref: 86SO4819

On both the southern and western borders of England and Wales, stone castles – usually built on sites previously fortified by wooden defensive areas – were in use during the mid-13th century. By the middle of the next century a degree of stability had been established during which only Raglan and Pembridge were built.

Pembridge, a model for the fortified manor houses of the succeeding century, is pleasing because it looks very much like a traditional castle, and it retains a splendid 13th-century gatehouse and an attractive great hall of 17th-century design. As an outpost of the Royalists, Pembridge was captured and recaptured during the Civil War, suffering considerable damage. The castle was restored during the early years of this century and is now in use as a farm.

John Kemble (see Welsh Newton) was chaplain here, and it was from Pembridge that he was taken to Hereford for trial and subsequent execution during the mania which afflicted the country following the 'revelations' of a 'Popish plot' by Titus Oates. Looking out over the Archenfield valleys, some of the quietest and most undisturbed in England, it is difficult to realise that turbulence and violence, both civil and religious, were constant factors here over a long period of history.

The goshawk is one of 60 species of birds of prey at the Newent Falconry Centre

Wellbrook Manor, Peterchurch – one of the best surviving examples of a 14th-century hall house

Penallt

Map Ref: 87SO5209

Hidden away in back roads south of Monmouth, Penallt is an interesting mixture of old houses and very new bungalows. One of its best-known places is the Boat Inn, which most patrons reach by walking across the iron bridge over the Wye from Redbrook.

The church stands 600ft above the Wye and contains work of many periods. It suffered from 19th-century restorers, but still has several interesting features, including a line of 15th-century pillars and arches dividing the nave and south aisle. There is a muniment chest carved from a single piece of oak and probably dating from the 12th century, while the stone-slab altar in the south aisle is believed to be the original pre-Reformation altar.

The main house of the parish is Argoed, built in the 1580s by a member of the Probert family who still live in the area. It underwent various rebuildings in the next two centuries before falling into disrepair. In the 1860s it was brought by Richard Potter, chairman of the Great Western Railway, one of whose nine daughters, Beatrice, married Sydney Webb. The early Fabians held many meetings here, Bernard Shaw writing to Ellen Terry that 'the God who made this country was an artist'. It was at Argoed that Shaw met the Irish heiress, Payne Townshend, who was to become his wife.

Peterchurch

Map Ref: 84SO3438

The unofficial capital of the Golden Valley, Peterchurch has a fine parish church. The original spire – erected in 1320 – was removed some years ago and the one that now looks so graceful when viewed from vantage points along the valley is in fact a plastic replacement.

The church is Norman and has a double chancel with three decreasing arches and a Saxon-like apse – a reminder that the original church on this site was built in AD786. The interior appears long and high – it is often described as 'strong'. The altar stone has clearly visible consecration crosses and may be Saxon. A plaque on the wall shows a carp wearing a chain round its neck – allegedly commemorating the catching of a fish in a nearby well.

The churchyard is large, well-kept and pleasant – the River Dore flows past it. Wellbrook Manor to the east of the church is a 14th-century hall-house on which stone has been used to cover the original timber-framing.

AA recommends:
Campsite: Poston Caravan & Camping Park, 2-pennants, *tel.* (09816) 225

Raglan

Map Ref: 86SO4107

The village and its church – notable only for a medieval churchyard cross – lie south of the A40, but immediately obvious are the romantic ruins of the castle. It crouches to the north of the road, a magnificent example of how a castle should look.

Unlike most of the other Welsh Border castles, Raglan was clearly built mainly for comfort and show. It probably began life in the 14th century as more a defensive manor house than a castle, and even its gallant defence during the Civil War was a largely unnecessary gesture. By the time it finally fell it was the last remaining Royalist stronghold, surrounded by a large number of troops released from other sieges, and it held out because of the pride of its defender, the third Marquis of Worcester. The garrison was allowed to leave with honour, but the octogenarian Marquis was taken to London, imprisoned and died within four months. He was buried at Windsor, fulfilling a promise made to him, and his prophecy 'God bless my soul, they will give me a grander castle when dead, than they took from me when living.'

After the surrender, Raglan was slighted, which included the destruction of the library – the finest existing collection of Welsh Bardic manuscripts and the irreplaceable records of Tintern Abbey. In a sense, the slighting of Raglan was a final, symbolic act of retribution by the native population against the Normans. With Chepstow Castle it represented their power on the Welsh borders, and now that power had at last been broken.

AA recommends:
Hotel: Beaufort Arms, 2-star, *tel.* (0291) 690412
Guesthouses: Grange, Old Abergavenny Rd, *tel.* (0291) 690260
Cripple Creek (inn), Bryngwyn, *tel.* (0291) 690256 (2m W off A40)

Raglan Castle's drawbridge is more typical of northern French castles

Redbrook

Map Ref: 87SO5309

Redbrook straggles along a very attractive section of the Wye which is still partly industrialised, though less so now than for much of the last two centuries. Copper and tinplate works operated in Redbrook well into this century – the tinplate works finally closed in December 1961 – and there are the remains of some 18th-century blast furnaces. Cottages here cling for protection to the steep east banks of the Wye, facing almost sheer wooded slopes rising to Penallt on the west bank. The villages are linked by an iron footbridge which was once a railway bridge carrying the Wye Valley Railway over the river.

AA recommends:
Hotel: Redbrook Hunting Lodge, Wrexham Rd, 2-star, *tel.* (094873) 204

An old engraving of the once-industrial town of Redbrook, on the Gwent – Gloucestershire border

Man of Ross

Around the town of Ross-on-Wye the name John Kyrle seems to appear everywhere; it is the name of the local school, a chapel of rest and even a variety of spicy bun!

John Kyrle was born at Dymock in 1637 to a reasonably wealthy and well-known family, and went on to study law for a time at Oxford. However, he did not complete the course and after his father's death he moved to Ross, living off the substantial annual income from a legacy of £500. He spent the rest of his life alone in a house opposite the market hall.

Kyrle became a great benefactor to the town, using his private income to serve only his basic needs and to pay Mrs Bubb, his housekeeper. The rest he used to the benefit of Ross-on-Wye. He organised – and largely financed – the provision of a water supply for the town; this was pumped from the Wye to an ornamental fountain in The Prospect, a garden he designed and created behind his house, and was then piped to public taps. He erected seats and several public buildings, he restored the church spire, and in 1695 he donated a new peal of bells.

Townspeople came to him for loans to improve their property, which he willingly granted provided he could offer advice on how it was done, for he had an eye for good taste. He loved trees and shrubs and planted many throughout the town. On the market hall opposite his house Kyrle, a great royalist, erected a bust of Charles II, and on the south side of the building outside his window he placed a curious logo consisting of C and F intertwined with a heart – representing Kyrle's loyalties. It stood for 'Faithful to Charles in Heart'.

Kyrle died in 1724 and would probably have been forgotten but for the fashionable poet Alexander Pope. Pope was visiting Herefordshire in 1731, seven years after John Kyrle died, and was surprised to find that there was no memorial to him. He was writing his moral essays at the time and, as an example to the wealthy, praised Kyrle's generous virtues in one of his two poems entitled *Of the Uses of Riches*.

. . . All our praises why should Lord engross?
Rise honest muse! and sing the Man of Ross:
Pleas'd Vaga echoes through her winding bounds
And rapid Severn hoarse applause resounds,
Who hung with woods yon mountains sultry brow?
From the Dry rock who bid the waters flow?
Not to the skies in useless column lost,
Or in proud falls magnificently lost,
But clear and artless, pouring through the plain,
Health to the sick, and solace to the swain,
Whose causeway parts the vale in shady rows,
Whose seats the weary traveller repose?
Who taught that Heav'n-directed spire to rise?
'The Man of Ross' each lisping babe replies . . .

Beneficent John Kyrle, from a painting by Van Aken (1709–1749)

Ross-on-Wye

Map Ref: 87SO6024

The best view of Ross, and the best known, is of the town rising in a series of terraces from its mound of sandstone above a loop of the Wye. Motorists bypassing the town on the A40 have a good view, particularly at night when the church is illuminated. The spire of St Mary's is one of the most famous in England, a soaring landmark reflected elegantly in the waters of the Wye.

The market hall stands at the centre of the town, dusty red sandstone on stone pillars. One room is open as a library and around its steps the lively street market meets. Like so many buildings in Ross, the hall was the brainchild of John Kyrle – the 'Man of Ross', as Pope termed him. Perhaps his best memorial is the Prospect, a public garden close to the church which gives outstanding views over the country he so enriched.

The church is of several periods but dates originally from 1284; the spire is 14th-century; there is original glass in the east window and a number of impressive 16th- and 17th-century monuments. One of these, in the sanctuary, is to John Kyrle, but it was not installed until 50 years after his death in 1724. There is a Plague Cross in the churchyard commemorating the 315 victims of the epidemic.

Ross has few buildings of outstanding architectural merit but a great many are pleasing and create a very harmonious impression which is heightened by the virtually exclusive use of sandstone. Almost opposite the Plague Cross, in Church Street, are the Rudhall almshouses, late 16th-century with some restoration. Parallel to Church Street is Copse Cross Street, containing the almshouses of Thomas Webbe and built in 1616. The impressive town walls and tower passed on the approach to Ross from Wilton Bridge were built in a grand Gothic style in 1833 by the company which cut the road, at the suggestion of Thomas Telfer, to replace the old route up Wye Street (a few yards north).

A mile or so south of Ross on the B4228 – the best road for starting to explore the Forest – is Walford. The main interest here is in the houses, in particular Hill Court and Upper Wythall. Hill Court is an early 18th-century red-brick mansion with fine formal gardens. The approach – part of the gardens are opened as a garden centre – is through a pair of very impressive wrought-iron gates and a double avenue of trees. The newly planted walled gardens contain a water garden and provide an exciting view towards Goodrich Castle.

Upper Wythall is a timber-framed house of the early 16th century. On the garden side of the house two windows form an H, believed by some to stand for Henry VII. The church, minus its spire since a lightning strike in 1813, is largely 13th-century; near by is the site of a camp in which three urns containing thousands of 4th-century Roman coins were discovered in the 19th century.

AA recommends:

Hotels: Pengethley Manor, 3-star, *tel.* (098987) 211

Royal, Palace Pound, 3-star, *tel.* (0989) 65105

Chasedale, Walford Rd, 2-star, *tel.* (0989) 63423

King's Head, 8 High St, 2-star, *tel.* (0989) 63174

Guesthouses: Arches Country House, Walford Rd, *tel.* (0989) 63348

Bridge House Hotel, Wilton, *tel.* (0989) 62655

Brookfield House, Ledbury Rd, *tel.* (0989) 62188

Ryefield House, Gloucester Rd, *tel.* (0989) 63030

Sunnymount Hotel, Ryefield Rd, *tel.* (0989) 63880

Self Catering: The Gate House, 5 Church Street, *tel.* (0989) 62302

Great Howle Farm Cottage, Howle Hill, *tel.* (0285) 713295

Hildersley Farm Cottage, *tel.* (0989) 62095

Howle Green Lodge, Howle Hill, *tel.* (0285) 713295

Old Kilns, Howle Hill, *tel.* (0989) 62051

The Vineyard, Howle Hill, *tel.* (0285) 713295

Garage: Gardner Butchers, Brookend St, *tel.* (0989) 62440

The gardens of Hill Court contain a yew hedge walk and beautiful flower borders and shrubberies

Rowlstone church, its chancel arch and detail of the upside-down saint

Rowlstone

Map Ref: 86SO3727

Rowlstone, a little to the south of Ewyas Harold and off the beaten track, contains one of the most important churches of an area rich in treasures. One unique feature of the church is a pair of wrought-iron candle brackets, dating from the 15th or 16th century and decorated with birds and fleurs-de-lys. Arguments have raged over the possible symbolism of the birds, but it seems probable that some at least, in a church devoted to St Peter, are cocks. Cocks certainly appear in the marvellous chancel arch, while on the capitals are figures said to represent the saint crucified upside down. The tympanum is of Christ in Majesty, and it is one of the great glories of the art of the 12th-century stonemasons. To the north-east of the church are the remains of an undocumented motte-and-bailey castle.

Ruardean

Map Ref: 87SO6117

From this exposed village on the northern edge of the Forest of Dean there are fine views over Hereford towards the Black Mountains. Ruardean straggles along under its hill, merging with both Drybrook and Nailbridge, and has little of architectural note except the church. There is, however, a pronounced change in the 'feel' of the landscape as the B4227 climbs out of the Wye Valley and enters the Forest of Dean. That feeling is heightened by the first of many Forestry Commission signs and the presence of sheep feeding freely along the roadside on the approach to Nailbridge.

The church, dedicated to St John the Baptist, has retained some of its original Norman character and possesses a particularly fine Norman tympanum of St George, mounted with his cloak flying, killing the dragon. It is believed to be the work of the Herefordshire School of Carving as are the stone fish discovered in the 1950s and now set in the wall near the font. Outside, the most striking features are the view northwards, and the splendid flying buttresses supporting the 14th-century spire.

Near by, north of the churchyard, are the clearly defined remains of a motte-and-bailey castle with just a hint of a wall. Very little is known about its occupants or history, although it certainly commanded a magnificent strategic position.

St Briavels

Map Ref: 87SO5504

Although now bypassed by the B4228, St Briavels is well worth visiting – the middle of the village is delightfully compact, with a castle, a good church and a pub at its centre. In addition, St Briavels has a fine position, set about 900ft over the Wye and the surrounding countryside.

Much of the castle is in ruins, but the entrance is through two fortress-like gatehouse towers. Most of the surviving part of the castle (now a Youth Hostel) was built in the 13th century, although it was started in the reign of Henry I. Visitors are able to enter several rooms, including the jury and court rooms and the dismal dungeon with its sad graffiti. The surrounding moat is grassed and contains a very well-maintained garden. Perhaps it is this garden which somehow softens the appearance of the castle; it never saw action, possibly because of its superb strategic position, and it has a civilised air more in accord with some of the later fortified manor houses.

Across the road is the large Norman church, its very size indicating that St Briavels was once more important than it is today. It was the administrative capital of the Forest in the Middle Ages, and was also a major supplier of ammunition in the form of quarrels (bolts for cross-bows) – Henry III placed an order for 6,000 in 1223. The church replaced a Celtic chapel but retained the dedication to St Briavel, a Welsh bishop of the 5th century. Under various names he is quite widely commemorated in Wales, Brittany and in Cornwall – but nowhere else in England. The church was considerably enlarged in the 12th and 13th centuries and suffered in the last century by the demolition and rebuilding of the chancel.

Bigsweir Bridge crosses the Wye below the village, carrying the A466 from Chepstow to Monmouth. This attractive 160ft single-span bridge may have been built by Telford or by Charles Hollis, designer of Windsor Bridge. There is a toll house on the Monmouth side, and Bigsweir House lies on the opposite bank in the shadow of Hudnalls Wood.

AA recommends:
Guesthouse: Stowe Court, *tel.* (0594) 530214

Bread and Cheese

Every Whit Sunday, after the evening service, St Briavels holds a unique ceremony during which small pieces of bread and cheese are distributed to the villagers waiting outside the church, accompanied by the chant:

St Briavels water and Whyrl's wheat
Are the best bread and water King John ever eat.

The history of the custom is uncertain, but according to tradition it came about after the villagers' right to gather wood – and certain other privileges – was withdrawn during the 17th century by the High Constable of the Forest, Milo, Earl of Hereford. The story goes, however, that his wife subsequently pleaded with him to change his mind and the Earl agreed to do so, but only within the area described by a circle she rode on horseback. This turned out to be Hudnalls Wood (known now as the Hudnalls) and local people have retained the right to collect wood here ever since. As a gesture of thanks, Milo's wife suggested that the churchwardens should collect a penny a head from each household which would be given to the poor. The ceremony originally took place in the church, but by the 19th century it had become very disorderly and was banished from the church.

At one time miners were said to keep the pieces of bread and cheese as good luck charms (it was believed that, like the bread of Communion, it would not perish) and in World War II villagers even saved their cheese ration in order to preserve the custom.

Bread and cheese are thrown from the Pound Wall outside the church

St Weonards

Map Ref: 87SO4924

The church is dedicated to St Weonard who is generally believed to have been one of the lesser known Welsh saints – possibly a hermit and woodcutter. There was a church here in the 12th century but the earliest part of the present building dates from about 1300. There are some attractive 16th-century oak screens with linenfold panels and a pulpit of the next century, and a few fragments of glass from 1521 are incorporated into the east window. There is also a panel identified as 15th-century and Flemish – it was bought at Hereford market in 1952! St Weonards has a dug-out chest, carved from one tree trunk and possibly early 14th-century, with some original ironwork.

The village stands on a hill, its houses grouped around the church. The prominent tump near the church is said to be a Bronze Age round barrow. Until 1855 a tree stood on it which was used as the village maypole. In that year the tree was cut down and the tump opened up. A local belief was destroyed – St Weonard was not buried in a golden coffin in the tump!

Treago Castle lies at the bottom of an enclosed valley along a narrow lane starting opposite the village. It is a most attractive fortified stone house in a formal garden. The foundations of a house on this site were laid down in the reign of King Stephen but the present house is late 15th- or early 16th-century.

Who Killed the Bears?

'Who Killed the Bears?' may be familiar to some people as having something to do with the Forest of Dean, and some might think of it as vaguely insulting to Foresters, or as good-natured mockery. But beware! The words are best not uttered at all in the Forest, especially in and around the village of Ruardean where they are likely to cause grave offence. The following true story explains why such emotions still run high today, almost a century later.

One morning in 1889 a wandering group of street entertainers – four Frenchmen with two black Russian performing bears – arrived in Ruardean to the delight of the close-knit village mining community who willingly gave their hard-earned coppers for the rare chance of such unusual entertainment.

Later that day the party moved three miles on to repeat the performance around the much larger and busier town of Cinderford. Here they stayed until well into the afternoon when they decided it was time to return to Ruardean before visiting other nearby villages. So the Frenchmen, the bears and a pied-piper following of admiring children made their way to the outskirts of the town.

Unknown to the happy procession, ugly rumours had been spreading through the drinking houses of Cinderford. Believing that the bears had killed a child and mauled a woman, the drinkers poured out into the streets, their outrage fuelled by alcohol. A gang of about 40 men went after the Frenchmen and their bears and caught up with them just beyond the outskirts of the town. The children scattered and ran for home, and the terrified entertainers were surrounded by the angry mob.

Anger turned to frenzy and the Frenchmen who did not speak enough English to reason or argue, tried to run. They were soon set upon, kicked, stoned and beaten to the ground. But the bears, freed from their shackles, lumbered on towards Ruardean desperately trying to escape their bloodthirsty pursuers and the screams of 'Kill the bears . . . kill the bears'. Eventually, within sight of Ruardean, the smaller of the two animals was killed by a blow to its head with its own keeper's pole. The second bear was not so fortunate, and eventually dragged its battered form about a mile to the other side of Ruardean where it was later found dying and was then humanely shot.

The ringleaders responsible for this shameful incident were eventually arrested, brought to justice and heavily fined. But the memory lives on of a day that every Forester would prefer to forget; especially the people of Ruardean whose village was the setting for the crime, but who had no part in it themselves. Today, anyone who hints otherwise is risking trouble.

Sellack

Map Ref: 87SO5627

A small, scattered village with a long history – Leland refers to 'Beysham alias Cellack'. Today the parish priest has in his care How Caple, Kings Caple, Foy, Sollers Hope, Hentland and Hoarwithy.

The church has a rare dedication, to St Tyssilio. Inside there is a Jacobean gallery and pulpit and a number of memorial tablets to the Phelps family. The tall 14th-century spire stands among old yews and soars over the water meadows fringing the nearby Wye. A damp footpath leads to the suspension bridge, built in 1895 to replace the ancient ford in which one of John Kyrle's descendants drowned in 1819. Beyond the bridge is Kings Caple where, as here and at Hentland, Pax cakes are distributed on Palm Sunday.

A path beside the church leads up towards the shell of the 16th- and 17th-century Caradoc Court. Only the stone part of this fine house remains; the wooden sections were destroyed by fire in the mid-1980s. Along the Ross to Hoarwithy road there is a black and white inn; the present owners have reverted to its old name of Lough Pool – a marshy pool beside the inn – in place of the mid-60s' Love Pool.

The church is at the bottom of a steep lane in a narrow valley. Clustered round it are a few houses and back at the top of the lane there is a tiny cemetery. From this most peaceful spot the ground falls steeply to the river and the views, over the shallow waters of the Wye towards Kings Caple and upstream towards Fawley and the woods of How Caple, are a joy at any season of the year.

Skenfrith

Map Ref: 86SO4520

Skenfrith is one of the Trilateral castles built in this area to protect the Border. All three – Grosmont and the White Castle near Abergavenny are the other two – were built by Hubert de Burgh in the 13th century. The simplest of the three, Skenfrith was originally a simple motte and fortified bank. On its summit de Burgh raised a circular central keep and surrounded it with a curtain wall, defended by four circular towers. Around three sides of the wall was a wide moat and the Monnow protected the fourth.

The castle stands on the Welsh bank of the river; beside it is a working watermill. The village is pleasant, with a row of pretty grey stone cottages facing the castle and a large inn on the other side of the road, beside the bridge carrying the B4521 Ross–Abergavenny road.

The church has a massive square tower with a wooden belfry. Inside there is a magnificent medieval cope enclosed in a glass case and a fine Jacobean box pew and altar-tomb, both relics of the last family to be custodians of the castle.

Skenfrith is noted for its fine round tower and well-preserved curtain walls

Fascinating exhibits at the Dean Heritage Museum, pictured below

Soudley Valley

Map Ref: 87SO6510

South of Ruspidge – now effectively part of Cinderford – is the Soudley Valley. The villages of Upper and Lower Soudley contain little of note, but the valley, with its forest and scenic drives and forest walks, is a popular centre for visitors to the Forest of Dean. The Forestry Commission, responsible for the Forest since 1924, produces excellent guides to the walks and has laid out well-landscaped picnic sites and car parks in this, one of its most successfully managed areas.

The Dean Heritage Centre, sited in Camp Mill on the edge of Lower Soudley, gives a fascinating insight into the industrial past of the area in an exhibition, 'The Living Forest'. Anyone interested in the history of Forest industry could do no better than study the history of the Camp Mill site. In the 17th century it almost certainly housed one of the four forges built by James I in the Forest of Dean for making cannon. During much of the 19th century Hewlett's Foundry occupied the site, one of Samuel Hewlett's most successful products was the 'Lightmoor' beam engine – displayed in the museum entrance. In 1876 the present building replaced the foundry. Constructed as a corn grinding mill employing two overshot wheels, it was served by a millpond considerably larger than the present one, but unprofitable milling gave way to the manufacture of leather shoe insoles and then to the mill's final use as a sawmill.

At Blackpool Bridge, south along the scenic drive, is an exposed section of the Roman road which ran from *Ariconium* (near Ross) to Lydney. The stone-arched Blackpool Bridge is also Roman, built to replace a ford crossing of the Blackpool Brook.

Staunton

Map Ref: 87SO5512

A small village perched high over a deep valley, Staunton has a Norman church and is a convenient starting place for visiting the Suck Stone and the Buck Stone.

Both Norman and Early English styles are displayed in the church's nave arches. Looked at from the centre of the nave, the east window is clearly offset – presumably when the wide chancel and the sanctuary were added in the 15th century the builders got their sight-lines wrong! The most interesting feature in the church is a corkscrew staircase leading to the stone pulpit and on to the belfry door – a similar effect to that at Garway. There are two fonts, one is 15th-century, and the other is believed to be a hollowed out Roman altar. Behind the remains of the old cross in the churchyard are the little almshouses given by Benedict Hall in the 17th century.

A short way across the road a path from the White Horse Inn leads to the Buck Stone (see page 27). The wide ranging view from here is one of the finest in the county. The Suck Stone can also be reached from the village, but finding the right path among several tracks crossing Highmeadow Woods may prove difficult. Although estimates of the weight of the Suck Stone range from 100 to 4,000 tons, there is agreement that it is one of the largest rocks in the country.

At Marion's Enclosure, near by along the road towards Gloucester, there is a standing stone of the Bronze Age.

AA recommends:
Guesthouse: Upper Beaulieu (farmhouse), *tel.* (0600) 5025

Stoke Edith

Map Ref: 85SO6040

One of the great pleasures in Herefordshire is the discovery of quiet, unspoilt villages, often less than a mile off a main road. Stoke Edith is perhaps the most remarkable of all for it is almost within shouting distance of the busy A438 road yet is a village largely ignored by time. That situation may change in coming years as Hereford expands but at present tiny Stoke Edith, huddled into its hill, can still be enjoyed as a curio.

The church was rebuilt in 1741 although the tower, minus its top, is 14th-century. Inside, the church is spartan, although it does have a three-decker pulpit and marble font. There are memorials to the Foley family – Paul Foley was speaker of the House of Commons (1695–8) – who built Stoke Edith Park and rebuilt the church. A sadly typical memorial of the waste of war is that to Tom Onslow who gained a scholarship to Magdalene College, Cambridge in 1916 but joined the army and died at Arras in January 1917.

The great house was of brick but is now a sorry wreck, destroyed by fire in 1927. An attempt to rebuild it was abandoned in the 1930s. The copper-domed West Lodge on the main road is a strange and rare building, said to be the combined work of Nash and Repton.

Stretton Sugwas

Map Ref: 84SO4642

The church at Stretton Sugwas was rebuilt in 1880 but it retained two remarkable features of the old church. The tympanum over one of the doors is Norman and contains a magnificent carving of Samson astride a lion – another masterpiece of the Hereford School of Carving. In the body of the church is a 15th-century slab monument to Richard Grenewey and his wife – she wears a realistically windswept butterfly head-dress. The tower is half-timbered. Sugwas Court was rebuilt in 1792 on the site of the manor originally built by Bishop Cantilupe; a Norman arch in the stables and a few stones are the sum total of the remains of the bishop's house.

Symonds Yat

Map Ref: 87SO5516

Symonds Yat, one of the major 'honeypots' in all England now has a new attraction – for several years peregrine falcons have been nesting on the site, bringing hordes of bird watchers to Yat Rock to study these aerial masters.

Symonds Yat justifies its popularity – the views from the Rock are indeed spectacular – and the range of facilities provided, if cramped during the summer months, do ensure an enjoyable time for visitors. Canoeing, walking, and camping are just a few of the opportunities provided and the area is a good base for exploring both the Wye Valley and the Forest of Dean.

But the 500ft high Rock is where every visitor wishes to go. A first glance suggests that there are two rivers in the valley far below but in fact the Wye makes a great loop round Huntsham Hill. The views from the Rock extend for many miles in all directions and there is a topograph to make sense of the landmarks, near and far. Take binoculars.

AA recommends:
Hotels: Paddocks, 2-star, *tel.* (0600) 890246
Royal, 2-star, *tel.* (0600) 890238
Wye Rapids, 2-star, *tel.* (0600) 890366
Guesthouses: Garth Cottage Hotel, *tel.* (0600) 890364
Saracens Head (inn), *tel.* (0600) 890435
Woodlea, *tel.* (0600) 890206
Garage: Bridge (Power Plus Autos), Commercial St, *tel.* (0600) 833209

Symonds Yat Bird Park houses 160 species in a garden setting

Tidenham

Map Ref: 87ST5596

Tidenham is a pleasant village with a long history and a church containing a Norman lead font believed to be 11th-century. The tower of the church was at one time used as a beacon for shipping in the Severn Estuary. Within the parish there are several sections of Offa's Dyke and a Neolithic monolith, the Broad Stone, by the Severn at Wibdon.

A mile or so west of Tidenham is Wintour's Leap, high over the Wye from which the gallant – and, if he did it, foolhardy – Sir John Wintour is alleged to have jumped when escaping from the Parliamentarians in 1642. The spot, not a place for vertigo sufferers, is 200ft above the river on the B4228, just below a turning to Lancaut. There is nowhere to park a car – indeed the place is not signposted – and it is best to park along the Lancaut road and walk back to a small gap in the modern houses clinging to the edge of the cliff along the main road. The view repays the effort of finding it.

Lancaut is just a farming hamlet but along the road are the remains of an old church and a promontory fort. There are also glimpses of views up and down the river which are every bit as spectacular as that from Wintour's leap. Immediately opposite is the great limestone cliff, Wynd Cliff (see Tintern).

Tintern Parva

Map Ref: 87SO5301

In a steep-sided valley beside the Wye, the village of Tintern consists of a long main street. The old railway station has been imaginatively restored by the Countryside Commission, and is being used as an Information Centre.

The great Cistercian abbey in its superlative position beside the Wye is second only to Fountains Abbey in quality and appeal. The abbey was founded in 1131 by Walter de Clare, but the present remains are of much later date. In the early 13th century, plans were made for enlarging the church but the work was not completed until the early years of the 14th century. As a result, the church is a mixture of Early English and Decorated styles. During the 15th century new cloisters were added. Along with other monasteries the abbey was suppressed in 1536. Sadly, we have little knowledge of Tintern's history because its records were destroyed during the slighting of Raglan Castle in the Civil War.

The graceful west window of Tintern Abbey

A little less than three miles south along the A466 towards Chepstow is the Wynd Cliff. A steep limestone cliff, covered in woods, it rises 800ft from the river. The views from the top are breathtaking in their range – seven counties may be seen on clear days. The Wye Valley Walk passes over the top of the cliff, having climbed the 365 steps cut in the limestone in 1828 as a tourist attraction. Since being restored some years ago the number is actually 300. The area is now managed by the Forestry Commission which has set up picnic sites and nature trails.

AA recommends:
Hotels: Beaufort, 2-star, *tel.* (02918) 777
Royal George, 2-star, *tel.* (02918) 205
Guesthouses: Parva Farmhouse (guesthouse), *tel.* (02918) 411
Fountain (inn), Trellech Grange, *tel.* (02918) 303

This former branch line station is now an award-winning visitors' centre

Trellech

Map Ref: 87SO5005

The size of the church suggests that Trellech was once a town of some importance and within the parish boundaries there is a remarkable number of interesting features from many ages. Inside the church a 17th-century stone sundial illustrates three of them – an early form of tourist guide! The church has a fine octagonal spire and, in the churchyard, the base of a very old preaching cross.

In a field 200yds to the south of the church are the first of the features recorded on the sundial. Harold's Stones are massive standing stones, respectively 8, 10 and 14ft high and assumed to be Bronze Age. No one has succeeded in discovering their purpose. Tump Terret Castle mound is close to the stones; it is very large and presumably formed the motte of a Norman castle although suggestions have been made that it is a burial mound. North of the Llandogo road is the Virtuous Well, a natural spring reputed in medieval times to have healing qualities. It is enclosed and has stone seating; the water falls into a basin below a small arch.

The Wye becomes tidal at Llandogo and there is still a flavour of the sea in the names of the inns – the Sloop and the Ship Inn among them. Some of the tombs in the churchyard have anchors on them. The church's chancel has painted texts, angels and flowers; there is a marble and alabaster reredos and a decorated nave roof. Antonio Gallenga lived in Llandogo, at first as an exile and later, when a deputy in the Italian parliament, on his return each summer – there is a memorial to his wife Anna on the south wall of the church.

There is no record that the locals had strong views on the Gallengas but they certainly did on the Amberleys of Cleddon, Bertrand Russell's parents, who held radical opinions on a whole range of subjects and were, as a result, largely ignored by the county hierarchy. Russell was born in the village.

Usk

Map Ref: 86SO3701

The lovely old market town of Usk is a good place from which to explore the Wye Valley and the Forest of Dean, and it certainly has much to offer the visitor. Built on the ruins of the Roman settlement of *Burriam*, it is overlooked by a ruined 12th-century castle, destroyed after supporting the Royalist cause in the Civil War.

The Church of St Mary, once attached to a Benedictine priory of nuns, has a fine screen bearing the oldest known Welsh epitaph and the remarkable organ came here from Llandaff Cathedral in 1899. The nave, extended in 1844, was originally the north aisle, built for the use of the parish 700 years ago. All that survives of the priory (unlike the castle, it can be visited) is the gatehouse. The award winning Gwent Rural Life Museum is at Usk which records the history and development of the area.

The large, beautifully situated Church of St Jerome at Llangwm has a fine, elaborately carved Perpendicular rood screen. The village has a second church – in great contrast, it is small and simple. In even greater contrast, there is a grass-skiing centre in Llangwm!

Wolvesnewton Folk Museum is east of Llangwm off the B4235. Housed in a group of 18th-century farm buildings is a collection of remarkable variety. The Model Farm Museum includes sections on early medical instruments, horse-drawn vehicles, a Victorian cottage bedroom, craft workshops.

Trellech's Virtuous Well was probably an early spa
Below: The Sloop at Llandogo

Vowchurch

Map Ref: 84SO3636

Vowchurch is a very pretty village; the setting of the church by the River Dore is exquisite. There is a half-timbered manor house behind the church and the large churchyard has flowerbeds among the graves.

The church has a small black and white timbered belfry and the interior posts and tie-beams which were renewed in 1613, possibly by John Abel, are a delight.

Poston Camp, about a mile north of the church, is an Iron Age hillfort. Excavations in recent years have shown that it was certainly occupied from the 1st century BC until well into the Roman period.

East of the village is Monnington Court, not to be confused with Monnington-on-Wye. Owen Glendower's daughter was married to the owner and it is generally agreed that it was here that Glendower sought refuge before his death.

AA recommends:
Guesthouse: The Croft (farmhouse), *tel.* (09816) 226
Self Catering: Old Coach House & Mews Cottage (cottages), *tel.* (09816) 226

Welsh Bicknor and English Bicknor

Map Ref: 87SO5817

Welsh Bicknor is both east of English Bicknor and in Herefordshire – the result of the wanderings of the Wye, and of centuries of dispute.

Welsh Bicknor is a difficult place to find – high on a hill over Goodrich it looks down onto Kerne Bridge. The 'no through road' to the village starts beside the entrance to Goodrich Castle. The church houses a fine 14th-century tomb with an effigy of Margaret Montacute – quite possibly Henry V would have seen it during his childhood at Courtfield.

Courtfield is a place with a very long history, although the present house on the site is early 19th-century. It was the seat of the Vaughan family for centuries and still has a connection with them – the college founded by Cardinal Vaughan, builder of Westminster Cathedral, for young men training for missionary work, now occupies the house. Glen Wye, the dower house to Courtfield, has an interesting Italianate garden with lovely views over the Wye; the garden is opened occasionally.

English Bicknor has a small Norman church within the boundaries of a motte-and-bailey castle, probably built in Stephen's reign. The church has a wagon-roofed nave, Early English chancel, two 14th-century effigies and a royal coat of arms of George III.

Top: a Victorian bedroom at the Wolvesnewton Folk Museum. Above: the Golden Valley near Vowchurch

Welsh Newton

Map Ref: 87SO5018

Passing through this village, scattered beside the A466 Monmouth to Hereford road, it is easy to miss the most important part of Welsh Newton – its church and graveyard, lying off the road.

The interior of the mainly 13th-century church contains a rare Decorated stone rood screen with ball-flower design, typical of the period. Very few other stone screens of this age or quality have survived. The screen was presumably installed by the Knights Hospitaller who held the land from after the suppression of the Knights Templar in the early 14th century until the Dissolution of the Monasteries. On the screen would have stood the Great Rood, or crucifix, illuminated by light from the dormer window, another rare 14th-century survival. In the porch, built in the same period, are seats made of gravestones probably removed from the ruins of a chapel to St Wolstan, sited at the farm of that name near by.

The neat graveyard contains an interesting cross with both medieval and modern parts. The grave of the martyr John Kemble (canonised in 1970) lies to the west of the cross. Kemble, whose tomb is simply marked 'JK died the 22 of August Anno Do 1679', was a priest who spent most of his life among the Catholic communities of Herefordshire and Monmouthshire. When the Titus Oates affair was at its height he was arrested at Pembridge Castle (see page 58) where he was chaplain, taken to Hereford, charged with complicity in the plot and executed on Widemarsh Common aged 80!

Westbury-on-Severn

Map Ref: 87SO7114

Westbury Court Garden, on the A48, a few miles south-west of Gloucester, makes a delightful start to a leisurely tour of the Forest of Dean.

Twenty years ago, when the National Trust acquired Westbury Court, the formal gardens laid out at the end of the 17th century were in a ruinous condition. A programme amounting almost to land reclamation was launched and slowly the outlines of this 'Dutch' water garden emerged.

Happily, an engraving by Kip was available to the Trust's advisers, together with the original planting records. With the aid of various grants the Trust was able to restore the only remaining building, the pavilion, dredge the canals, rebuild the walls and replant hedges. The lawns had reverted to hayfields and were ploughed up and resown.

Westbury is, of course, a lovely garden; more significantly, it is of great historical interest as one of the very few examples of early formal planting to survive the onslaught of the 18th-century landscape gardeners.

Weston-under-Penyard

Map Ref: 87SO6323

Weston-under-Penyard lies right across the A40, east of Ross, and for most travellers is memorable probably for the large hotel on the right of the road. Most of the considerable interest in the village lies away from the main road. Hidden away on Penyard Hill are the few stones which are all that remain of the medieval Penyard Castle. On the north of the village, at Bury Hill, excavations have uncovered the foundations of buildings and some fragments of tessellated pavement. The area has been speculatively identified as the lost Roman town of *Ariconium*, but there are no signs of defensive works and it is possible that it was simply an industrial site – large quantities of iron slag have been unearthed on the Bromsash side of the hill.

Weston contains several interesting houses including Lower Weston, a beautiful Jacobean manor, the Rectory and Bollitree Castle, both of which may include some of the stones from Penyard Castle. The late 17th-century Bollitree Castle has a remarkable range of barns which were converted in the 18th century to resemble a Gothic castle.

Westbury Court was influenced by Dutch designs emphasizing intimate spaces and horticultural content. Here, part of the water garden and a statue of Neptune

Whitchurch

Map Ref: 87SO5417

Whitchurch is the gateway to the thriving tourist honeypot of Symonds Yat, where a maze of flyovers and roundabouts has altered the character of the village.

One of the best views of Whitchurch is from the little United Reformed Church crouching on the side of the Doward, interestingly contrasted by the modern triangular-shaped Catholic church in the centre of the village. The heavily restored Parish Church of St Dubricius has an attractive setting. St Dubricius, it is claimed, preached on this site a century before St Augustine arrived in Britain. The finest house in the village is Old Court, a 16th-century stone-built mansion with mullioned and transomed windows. Inside the house (now a hotel) is some very attractive woodwork.

The famous cannon, 'Roaring Meg', used in the siege of Goodrich Castle, was cast at Whitchurch. It is now in the Churchill Gardens Museum, Hereford.

Like Whitchurch, Ganarew has been affected by the route chosen for the A40; the bulk of both villages lies west of the road. Settlement here goes back centuries: near Ganarew church a 16th-century house stands on foundations of one 300 years older; the present church is Victorian, but the site was occupied by a chapel attached to the Priors of Monmouth as early as 1186.

Opposite Ganarew, and looming over it are the Dowards, Great and Little. Part of a limestone outcrop, the whole area is a botanist's paradise. Because of its height and position it attracted early settlers, and in King Arthur's Cave some Palaeolithic remains have been found in this century. Sadly, the site was 'excavated' using dynamite in the 1870s, and, although it yielded bones of mammoth, hyena and woolly rhinoceros (now imaginatively displayed in the museums of Monmouth and Hereford), we have to speculate on what may have been destroyed. The 26-acre hillfort on Little Doward is traditionally said to be the site of the final stand made by Caractacus against Scapula, before his capture and exile to Rome in AD51. Logically, the area on the opposite bank of the Wye known as Slaughter is the more likely spot.

AA recommends:
Restaurant: Gallery, Wayside, 2-fork, *tel.* (0600) 890408
Guesthouses: Portland, *tel.* (0600) 890757
Crown Hotel (inn), *tel.* (0600) 890234

Whitney

Map Ref: 84SO2747

Whitney has suffered more than most villages from the flooding to which the Wye is prone. Three bridges were built and destroyed in quick succession before the present toll bridge was installed in the early 19th century. Both church and rectory disappeared in the great flood of 1735 and the church was rebuilt on a new site. The Norman font remains and there is a good Jacobean reredos given by the long serving rector, Henry Dew.

Wordsworth lunched at the rectory, remarking to Henry Dew, without much originality, that he had never seen a more beautiful scene! Kilvert often visited the Dews, on at least one occasion staying the night. It was after one of his visits that he noted as he passed over the Rhydspence border brook that 'the English inn was still ablaze with light and noisy with the songs of revellers, but the Welsh inn was dark and still'.

Rhydspence is indeed no more than a hamlet astride the border between England and Wales. The Rhydspence Inn, a pleasant timber-framed place, with a jettied porch, is 16th-century. It was once known as the Cattle Inn and served as a meeting point for the Welsh cattle drovers who shod the beasts here in readiness for their journey through England. It was, as Kilvert noticed, the last and first inn in England, and a useful watering hole for more than just cattle.

AA recommends:
Guesthouse: Rhydspence (inn), *tel.* (04973) 262 (2m W A438)
Self Catering: Cwm-yr-Afor (cottage), *tel.* (04973) 324 (2½m W off A438)
Wooden House, *tel.* (04973) 324

The tollbridge at Whitney dates from about 1820. Charges on the board show that a horse-drawn vehicle exacted 4½d

Below: Rhydspence Inn stands by the road west of Whitney

Woolhope

Map Ref: 85SO6135

Not the easiest village to find – the simplest route is probably from Mordiford via Haugh Wood – Woolhope stands on the plateau of the Woolhope Dome, a great ridge of Silurian limestone hills.

On the Haugh Wood approach, at Broadmoor Common, there are some timber-framed houses, said to be 18th-century, but the majority of buildings in Woolhope are of stone. The church has a collection of 13th- and 14th-century coffin lids. East of the village is The Wonder, the site of a landslip in 1575. The main sufferer when some 20 acres slid down the hill was the chapel at Kynaston – its bell was buried for over 200 years and is now in Homme House at Much Marcle.

Part of the fame of Woolhope rests upon the importance of the Woolhope Society of Naturalists and Archaeologists. Like most areas of limestone and shale, this region has a great variety of fossils, flora and fauna and in 1851 local naturalists founded a club which has developed into the county's leading society; the British Mycological Society grew out of studies of fungi carried out by the Woolhope Club. The society still meets in the museum and library in Hereford.

There was once a chapel to St Dubricius in the parish, the only dedication to the saint east of the Wye; it was probably near Buckenhill Farm where a piscina was uncovered in the 1950s. Buckenhill is close to Sollers Hope which today consists almost solely of a church and a half-timbered farm – the whole group set amidst orchards in a totally remote spot. Court Farm is one of several black and white 17th-century farms in the area; most have ornamental brick chimney-stacks – Court Farm's is superb. The farm even has a dovecote. The lovely 14th-century church has a wooden belfry and a restored churchyard cross.

AA recommends:
Guesthouse: Butchers Arms (inn), *tel.* (043277) 281

The village of Woolhope

Below: rubbing from the brass of a Forest Free Miner in Newland church. It is unique for its subject and technique – the figure is shown in relief

Free Miners

The Free Miners of the Forest of Dean are an extraordinarily interesting people, whose ancestry probably goes back well over 2,000 years to the original Celtic discoverers of iron ore in the Forest. Today, there are about 30 full-time Free Miners in the Forest, and there are about 200 to 300 working part-time. The mines are small, mostly occupying two or three men working a coal level (a horizontal tunnel) or a drift (an inclined tunnel) into a hillside.

The Free Miners have special traditional rights and privileges in the working of coal, iron ore and ochre, and stone in the Forest. The origins of their exclusive rights are obscure, and even in the year 1300 they were documented as being in existence since 'tyme out of minde'. It was during the reign of Edward I (1272–1307) that the king formally confirmed the rights, privileges and customs and they were written on a parchment roll known as the Book of Dennis. Legend says that this was done as a reward for the part played by the Forest miners at the siege of Berwick-on-Tweed, when they undermined and blew up the fortifications during the wars with the Scots. But the original document has been lost for centuries and the oldest surviving document, which is supposed to be a transcript of the original, dates from 1610.

The Book of Dennis allowed miners to take coal and iron ore from the Forest 'without withsaying of any man', to build roads to the mines and to take timber for use in the mines from the Forest. In return, the miners had to pay royalties to the Crown on all minerals extracted from the ground. The woods of the Forest within which the Free Miner could dig were: 'First betweene Chepstowe Bridge and Gloucester Bridge, the half deale of Newent, Ross Ash, Monmouth Bridge and so far into the Seasoames as the Blast of a horn or the voice of a man may be heard.'

In the Middle Ages a Free Miner would simply go into the Forest, choose a spot and dig. But it soon became apparent that, in fairness to everyone, stricter controls were necessary, and the Free Miners agreed to set up their own court and laws to administer the tracts of mining land known. A grant to a Free Miner was called a 'gale', and the principal officer of the Forest whose duty it was to grant the gales was the Gaveller. Disputes were heard at St Briavels Castle and witnesses took the oath by touching a branch of holly.

By the 18th century a Free Miner claimed a gale by calling for the deputy Gaveller of the Court to visit the site. If the proposed gale did not encroach or interfere with another gale the deputy Gaveller cut a turf from the ground and two sticks, one straight and one forked, from a nearby tree. On the straight stick he cut two notches, one for the king and one for the miner. He then pinned the notched stick to the earth with the forked stick and covered them with turf and the miner then paid a fee of five shillings and considered himself to be in full possession of the gale. To become a Free Miner a man has to be born and reside within the Hundred of St Briavels of a Free father, and has to have worked for at least a year and a day in an iron or coal mine.

In Newland Church there is a 15th-century brass of a Free Miner carrying his 'mattock' for chipping the ore, his 'nellie' – a stick held between his teeth which held his candle away from his line of sight, and his 'billy' to carry ore. This was the traditional way of mining the ores of the Forest nearly until the closure of the iron mines in the early years of this century.

Directory

ACTIVITIES AND SPORTS

ANGLING

The pure water of the Wye, with its rapid rise and fall, makes an ideal habitat for migratory fish – especially salmon – and it is one of the premier salmon-fishing rivers in the country. Although salmon fishing is somewhat exclusive, there are still a few places where day and weekly permits are available, and the Wye also supports good quantities of freshwater fish – chub, dace, grayling, roach and pike. The best trout fishing in the area is probably in the Monnow and its tributaries.

There is virtually no free fishing in the Wye Valley and the Forest of Dean. Anglers will require a licence from the relevant water authority, as well as a fishing permit from the owner/controller of the water to be fished.

Licences are available from the Welsh Water Authority (WWA) or the Severn Trent Water Authority (STWA), see *Useful Adresses*, page 78. Charges vary depending on the authority, and on what sort of angling is to be done. Detailed information on fishery byelaws is available from the water authorities, as well as full information on angling in their area. Most tackle shops are worth a visit for details of local angling facilities.

Licences are also available from:

Cinderford Roberts Sports, 31 Market Street, *tel.* (0594) 23905. STWA and WWA

Coleford Sport and Leisure, Market Place, *tel.* (0594) 33559. STWA and WWA

Hereford Hatton Tackle, 54 Owen Street, *tel.* (0432) 292317. STWA and WWA

Lydney P J Sports, 24 Newerne Street, *tel.* (0594) 42515. STWA and WWA

Monmouth R Hutton, 32 Wyesham Avenue, *tel.* (0600) 4104. WWA

Ross-on-Wye 10 Broad Street, *tel.* (0989) 63273. WWA

Skenfrith D Hawes, Post Office, *tel.* (060084) 201. WWA

Availability of permits and permit fees are entirely at the discretion of the owner/controller of the water. Most of the salmon fishing is let by the season, or longer, but a few daily and weekly permits are granted. The availability of permits tends to fluctuate; local tackle shops – including the shops offering licences listed above - are a good first stop when trying to get permits for specific waters.

BOATING AND CANOEING

Canoeists enjoy the right of 'free navigation' on the Wye below Hay-on-Wye (though motor vessels are not allowed). But most of the land on the banks of the Wye is private; public access is limited and permission should be sought before canoes are launched or landed. Only experienced canoeists should venture below Tintern, since the tides are considerable and dangerous weirs are exposed at low water. All canoeists travelling to Chepstow should leave Tintern not later than one hour after high water.

CLIMBING AND CAVING

There is limited climbing and caving in the Wye Valley and Forest of Dean, and it is suitable only for the very experienced. For these activities, prior clearance is required from the Forestry Commission (see *Useful Addresses*, page 78).

GOLF

Chepstow St Pierre Park, 3 miles south-west of Chepstow off the A48, is parkland and meadowland with numerous large trees and a picturesque lake. There are two 18-hole courses. *Tel.* (02912) 5261

Coleford Bill's Hotel and Golf Club has an 18-hole course and a swimming pool. *Tel.* (0594) 3262

Hendre On the Rockfield road, 3 miles from Monmouth, these 18 holes are in a beautiful setting. *Tel.* (0600) 5353

Hereford A nine-hole course is at Hereford Racecourse, but is closed on race meeting days. The Leisure Centre, Holmer Road. *Tel.* (0432) 271959

Lydney At Lakeside Avenue, this nine-hole course is on flat parkland and meadowland, with a prevailing wind along the fairways. *Tel.* (0594) 42614

Monmouth At Leasebrook Lane, 1½ miles north-east of Monmouth off the A40, this nine-hole course is set in high undulating land with attractive views. *Tel.* (0600) 2212

Ross Golf Club On the north side of junction 1 of the M50 on the B4221, Two Park has an 18-hole undulating course which has been cut out of the silver birch forest. *Tel.* (098982) 267

HIRE FACILITIES

Bicycles

Little and Hall, Broad Street, Ross-on-Wye have cycles available for hire during spring, summer and autumn. *Tel.* (0989) 62639

Canoes and Boats

The Old Ferry Inn, Symonds Yat West. *Tel.* (0600) 890232

The Paddocks Hotel, Symonds Yat West. *Tel.* (0600) 890246

PGL Adventure Ltd, Station Street, Ross-on-Wye (canoes for groups only). *Tel.* (0989) 64211

River Wye Canoe Hire, Unit 4, Wye Street, Ross-on-Wye. *Tel.* (0989) 81506

Wyedean Canoe Centre, Penny Royal Cottage, Symonds Yat East. *Tel.* (0600) 890129

Fishing for salmon on the Wye near Lower Lydbrook. The Wye has some of the best salmon fishing in the country, with an official catch of between 2,500 and 5,000 a season

RIDING AND PONY TREKKING

Ms Pauline Cook, Tretawdy Farm, Llangrove. Hacking or tuition, one hour to half a day. *Tel.* (098984) 316
Lea Bailey Riding School, Lea Bailey, Ross-on-Wye. *Tel.* (0989) 81360
Littledean Trekking Centre, Wellington Farm, Littledean. Beginners welcome for riding in the Forest of Dean. *Tel.* (0594) 23955
Merryweather Farm, Coleford. Riding or pony trekking. *Tel.* (0594) 33257

WALKS AND TRAILS

The area around the Wye Valley and the Forest of Dean is a wonderland for the walker. From spectacular viewpoints overlooking the Wye, to the serene undulations of the Marches, to the silent trails through the Forest - steeped in history and legend, the walker will find interest and variety here to rival the best in Britain.

There are hundreds of miles of footpaths through the Valley and Forest. The Forestry Commission and the Ramblers Association have laid out a system of paths and trails using coloured arrows and signposts to lead walkers through scenic areas they would be unlikely to find without help. They also produce useful leaflets guiding visitors through forest trails. The leaflets are available from the Forestry Commission Offices in Coleford, 'Log Cabins' at Symonds Yat and at Tourist Information Centres.

Wardens in the Wye Valley Area of Outstanding Natural Beauty lead regular guided walks in the area. A free programme of the walks is published quarterly, and is available from local Tourist Information Centres, libraries, post offices, Goodrich Castle, and at the Old Station, Tintern.

Offa's Dyke Long Distance Footpath
A walk into the past – this ancient earthwork takes its name from the 8th-century Mercian King Offa. Occasionally the path deviates from the Dyke in favour of more outstanding scenery, but a great deal of it can still be seen. In this area, the path goes from Hay-on-Wye, south to Monmouth, and ends at the Severn Estuary at Sedbury Cliffs near Chepstow. Further information is available from the Offa's Dyke Association, see *Useful Addresses,* page 78.

Wye Valley Walk
The Wye Valley Area of Outstanding Natural Beauty covers 127 square miles of superb countryside, and the Wye Valley Walk passes through the heart of it, following the Wye for 52 impressive miles between Hereford and Chepstow. The path is well maintained and clearly marked with yellow arrows. The Wye Valley AONB produces a 'Wye Valley Walk Map Pack', containing weatherproof OS 1:50,000 route cards and descriptions and guides to places along the way. It is available from local shops and Tourist Information Centres.

On longer walks it is important to be properly equipped. Terrain can be rough and weather conditions can change quickly and unexpectedly. Sturdy comfortable shoes are a must, and extra clothing, food and drink, and waterproof outerwear are recommended.

CRAFT WORKSHOPS

Most of the workshops listed will welcome individual visitors without an appointment. However, in some cases where workshops are run by one person, the shop may be open irregularly. Before making a special journey for a favourite craft, do telephone first to ensure that the workshop will be open.

Brockweir
Just north of Tintern Abbey off the A466 is Brockweir and the *Malthouse Pottery.* A wide range of stoneware items is produced, decorated in greens, browns and blues using local river mud. *Tel.* (02918) 291

Chepstow
The *Ned Heywood Ceramics Workshop and Workshop Gallery* are at 13 Lower Church Street. There is a shop with ceramics demonstrations, and a gallery with art and craft exhibitions. *Tel.* (02912) 4836

Stuart Crystal is in Bridge Street, where visitors can see craftsmen applying decoration to handmade crystal. There are tours and an exhibition of crystal – past and present. *Tel.* (02912) 70135

Hay-on-Wye
The Ice House Pottery in Brook Street offers a large selection of pottery and ceramics, as well as a wide range of crafts and exhibitions. There are demonstrations in the pottery workshop. *Tel.* (0497) 820107

Hereford
The *Kemble Gallery,* 29 Church Street, is the retail outlet for work by members of the Society of Craftsmen. A wide range of crafts is represented: ceramics, sculpture, weaving, knitting, book-binding, woodwork, jewellery, painting and screen-printing. *Tel.* (0432) 266049

Lydney
The *Brambles Craft Shop,* 2½ miles north of Lydney, specialises in spinning, weaving and natural-dyeing supplies, as well as the repair of spinning wheels and looms. A wide selection of local crafts is always for sale. *Tel.* (0594) 562780

Much Birch
In Trump Lane, Much Birch (between Ross-on-Wye and Hereford on the A49), *H J and D Hobbs and Co* manufacture leaded-light windows, panels and screens. The glass can be stained, painted, etched or blasted in traditional or modern designs. *Tel.* (0981) 540516

At *Cottage Clocks,* Bryn Garth Cottage, there is an attractive selection of wall clocks in pine and other woods. The faces are hand painted in floral designs to complement interior decor. *Tel.* (0981) 540419

Peterchurch
At the *Craft Inn* in the High Street, dried and pressed flower pictures are made using a variety of frames and flowers, and orders are undertaken using bridal bouquets or other special flowers. *Tel.* (09816) 651

On the Old Forge Industrial Estate, the *Pine Factory* manufactures solid pine furniture. Welsh dressers, wardrobes, chests, tables etc are based on traditional designs in a range of coloured finishes. *Tel.* (09816) 527

Pontrilas
Ornamental and functional hand-forged ironwork is produced at the *Paradise Forge.* There are modern or traditional designs for everything from candlesticks to church gates, and special commissions are undertaken. *Tel.* (0981) 240374

At Rowlstone, 1½ miles west of Pontrilas, the *Rowlstone Pottery* produces domestic stoneware, garden pots and studio pottery in rich natural colours, or decorated with an oak leaf design. Commemorative pieces can be inscribed to order. *Tel.* (0981) 240759

Ross-on-Wye
At *Blades Jewellers,* 54 High Street, all types of jewellery are designed and manufactured in precious metals. Titanium jewellery is a speciality. *Tel.* (0989) 64560

Morel and Partners, in Old Gloucester Road, are cabinet makers specialising in custom-built furniture for kitchens and bedrooms, tables, chairs, display cabinets and fire surrounds. *Tel.* (0989) 67750

At *Multi-Crafts,* 25 High Street, high quality pine furniture is hand-made on the premises, and special items are made to order. *Tel.* (0989) 62438

Just 400yd north of the end of the M50 at Gatsford, *J Arthur Wells - Craftsman in Wood* produces furniture and purpose-made woodwork of all descriptions. A selection of turned items is always in stock. *Tel.* (0989) 62595

One of the smaller border castles, Pembridge has a monumental gatehouse with semicircular towers which have been recently restored

St Briavels
At *St Briavels Pottery* studio potters produce a wide range of stoneware, mostly for domestic use. Records are kept so that pieces can be repeated if required. *Tel.* (0594) 530297

Skenfrith
West of Skenfrith 1½ miles on the B4521 is *Wool Wheels Weaving*. Demonstrations of spinning and weaving can be seen during working hours, and hand-dyed yarns and Hob-Nob knitting kits and knitwear are on sale. There is also a selection of spinning wheels and looms, and comprehensive information on fibre-related crafts. *Tel.* (060084) 607

Soudley
As well as a museum for the Forest of Dean, the *Dean Heritage Museum Trust* is a thriving crafts community, and visitors are welcome to watch the resident craftsmen at work. Traditional forest crafts such as charcoal-burning are regularly demonstrated; other crafts include wrought-iron work, pottery, engraved glass, pokerwork, knitwear and leather goods. A wide choice of souvenirs, paintings and other craft work is available in the gallery. *Tel.* (0594) 22170

Winforton
About 5 miles north-west of Hay-on-Wye on the A438 at Winforton Court, *Gerald and Vera Taylor* operate a complex for the sale and restoration of fine antiques. Clocks, oil paintings and furniture are restored, and gilding and lacquer work are undertaken. *Tel. (05446) 226*

Wolvesnewton
Just off the B4235 at Llangwm, 10 miles north of Chepstow, the *Wolvesnewton Folk Museum and Craft Centre* has a variety of craft workshops, a Victorian collection and changing exhibitions. Crafts include jewellery and resin work. There is a gift shop, licenced restaurant, picnic area and children's play area. *Tel.* (02915) 231

PLACES TO VISIT

This is a sample of the variety of attractions in the Wye Valley and Forest of Dean. The area is rich in history; the borderland between England and Wales has been disputed territory for over a thousand years, so the castles and fortifications are a prominent part of the scene. The gardens and arboreta, however, are also a feature of the area. And what better backdrop to a formal garden could there be than the banks of the Monnow or Wye. Together with the museums, railways and wildlife centres, these guarantee a wealth of attractions for the visitor.

Below are brief details of some of the best-known places to visit. Opening times have been given, but of course these are subject to change.

CASTLES AND HISTORIC SITES

Caerwent Roman Town
About 5 miles west of Chepstow on the A48, this is a complete circuit of a town wall, together with excavated areas of houses, shops and temple. This Ancient Monument is accessible at any time.

Caldicot Castle
Five miles south-west of Chepstow on the B4245, Caldicot is a motte-and-bailey site, rebuilt in stone from the 12th to 14th centuries. It has been extensively restored, and the museum has some fine furniture and costumes. The castle is surrounded by a 50-acre country park, with picnic and barbecue facilities and an adventure playground. Open every day from March to October; Sunday afternoons only.

Chepstow Castle
A memorable Welsh fortress dating from medieval times, Chepstow Castle guards one of the main crossings from England into Wales. In the centre of Old Chepstow, high up on its cliff, the castle follows the curve of the Wye. Open daily.

Goodrich Castle
About 3½ miles south of Ross-on-Wye turn right off the A40 for Goodrich, where Goodrich Castle guards the Wye from its high bluff. The massive Norman keep, rock-cut moat, shaded lawns and breathtaking views over the river make this a Welsh Border castle not to be missed. Open daily.

Grosmont Castle
A castle by Hubert de Burgh, these ruins are on a hill above the church and village at Grosmont, about 9 miles north-west of Monmouth on the B4347. Its huge mound (*gros mont*) gives this fine small border castle its name. Open at all reasonable times.

King Arthur's Cave and Merlin's Cave
These limestone caves on the Great Doward, used by Stone Age hunters for shelter, are reached by a way-marked footpath from Symonds Yat. Excavations in the 1920s revealed they had been inhabited 12,000 years before the Romans came to Britain. Some finds from King Arthur's Cave are displayed in Monmouth Museum.

Monmouth Castle and Great Castle House
The Great Castle House in Monmouth was built on the ruins of Monmouth Castle, and now houses the headquarters of the Royal Monmouthshire Royal Engineers (Militia). The house is not open to the public, but the castle ruins can be seen from the parade ground.

Pembridge Castle
Still a family home, Pembridge Castle is a good example of a small castle farmhouse dating from the 13th century. It is about 5 miles north of Monmouth; turn off the A466 north of Welsh Newton for Broad Oak. For opening times (grounds only) contact Tourist Information Centres.

Raglan Castle
Raglan Castle post dates the years of conflict between the Welsh and English, and belongs to the mid 14th to early 15th centuries. The high bridge over the moat, the shapely towers, the splendour of the castle hall, buttery, pantry, south gate, chapel and state apartments will all stir the imagination. Raglan is on the A40 about 6 miles south-west of Monmouth. Open daily.

St Briavels Castle
This 12th-century castle, in the centre of St Briavels village, sits high on a hill overlooking the Wye. King John was a frequent visitor here when hunting in the Forest of Dean. The castle is now a Youth Hostel and some parts are only open to Youth Hostels Association members, but the exterior may be viewed at all times.

Skenfrith Castle
Built in the early 13th century by Hubert de Burgh, this castle has a beautiful setting beside the River Monnow at Skenfrith. On the B4521 between Ross-on-Wye and Abergavenny, Skenfrith Castle is open at all reasonable times.

Tintern Abbey
Standing serenely beside the banks of the Wye, this old Cistercian Abbey, noted for its majestic arches, fine doorways and elegant windows, is still surprisingly intact. There is a Tourist Information and Visitor Centre on the site, and a picnic area nearby. Open daily.

White Castle
One of the 'trilateral' or 'three castles' in the Monnow Valley (the other two are Grosmont and Skenfrith) which protected the defences of the Welsh Marches here. There are lovely views from the castle tower. Located off the B4233 between Monmouth and Abergavenny near Llantilio Crossenny, White Castle is open daily.

HOUSES, GARDENS AND ARBORETA

Abbey Dore Court
Located 11 miles south-west of Hereford off the A465, the four-acre gardens of Abbey Dore Court include herbacious borders, a circular herb garden and a walled kitchen garden. Gardens only are open daily from mid-March to October.

Bishop's Meadows and Castle Green, Hereford
These open spaces on both sides of the River Wye are near Hereford Cathedral, and there are riverside walks on the Bishop's Meadows.

Brobury House Gardens and Gallery
Located off the A438 between Hay-on-Wye and Hereford, here are eight acres of semi-formal gardens on the banks of the Wye with fine old trees and rhododendrons. The gallery displays thousands of original etchings and engravings. Brobury House is open all year Monday to Saturday; the gardens from June to September only.

Clearwell Castle
North-west of Lydney on the B4231, this is the earliest example of neo-Gothic architecture in England, and is still being restored. Built around 1727, attractions here include gardens, a model train layout and children's adventure playground. Open from Easter to October, Tuesday to Friday and Sundays.

Hellens, Much Marcle
This unique old house has preserved over 700 years of English history in its walls. It has a wonderful collection of art and family heirlooms. Much Marcle is about 7 miles north-west of Ross-on-Wye on the A449. Open Wednesday, Saturday and Sunday afternoons from Easter to October.

Hill Court Gardens
Off the B4228, 2½ miles south-west of Ross, these interesting gardens include a yew hedge walk and an oriental-style water garden and pavilion. Open every day.

Jubilee Maze
At Symonds Yat West, this superbly-presented hedge maze was laid down in 1977 in celebration of the Queen's Silver Jubilee. There is also a 'Royal' garden, a museum of mazes and a viewing platform. Open every day except Friday from Easter to October, and illuminated on certain evenings during July and August.

Littledean Hall
This is probably the oldest inhabited house in Britain, dating from the mid 11th century. A Roman temple is being restored in the grounds, and there are magnificent trees and a water garden, picnic area and children's play area. Located at Littledean, Glos, the hall is open every afternoon from April to October.

Lydney Park
Rhododendrons and azaleas feature in these extensive valley gardens at Ayleburton, Lydney. Open at Easter and on certain days until June. For specific times contact Lydney Park, *tel.* (0594) 42844.

Market House, Ross-on-Wye
Built about 1670 of the local red sandstone, the Market House with its open pillared ground floor now houses the town library. Open standard library hours.

Moccas Court
Ten miles west of Hereford, a mile off the B4352, stands the fine 18th-century Moccas Court. The first floor of the house is open, and seven acres of lovely parkland on the south bank of the Wye were designed by 'Capability' Brown. Open Thursday afternoons from April to September.

The Old House, Hereford
In Hereford's Old Town, the Old House is a fine example of Jacobean architecture, and its three floors are furnished and fitted in the style of the period. Open Tuesday to Friday, and Monday and Saturday mornings only.

Puzzle Wood
At Milkwall, near Coleford, this is a lovely woodland setting for ancient open iron workings going back thousands of years. The paths are arranged in a puzzle, and the walk takes about an hour. There is a tea garden and craft shop. Open every day except Monday from Easter to October.

Speech House
Now a hotel in the Forest of Dean, the Speech House was built in 1680 as a hunting lodge for Charles II. It later housed the courtroom of the Forest Verderers. The Verderers' Court is still held in the timbered dining room, carrying on a tradition of some 900 years. In the Speech House Arboretum nearby, there are over 200 varieties of trees and shrubs. Open daily.

Sutton Court, Mordiford
About 2 miles south-west of Hereford, off the B4224, stands this small Palladian mansion designed by James Wyatt. The park and grounds are by Humphrey Repton. Open irregularly, for details *tel.* (043273) 268.

The Weir
These fine cliff garden walks are owned by the National Trust, and lead through drifts of flowering bulbs in springtime with views of the Wye and the Welsh hills. Open afternoons Wednesday to Sunday

Lindsay Heyes, who, with his brother Edward, built the Jubilee Maze

from March to October; located 5 miles west of Hereford on the A438.

Westbury Court Garden
Laid out between 1696 and 1705, this National Trust property has been restored since 1966 to the now well-ordered formal Dutch water garden with canals and clipped hedges. About 9 miles east of Cinderford on the A48, the garden is open Tuesdays to Sundays from April to October.

MUSEUMS AND GALLERIES

Chepstow Museum
Housed in an elegant late 18th-century town house in Bridge Street, this museum contains a fine collection of illustrations of Chepstow and the Wye Valley, and displays the crafts, trades and industries of this once busy market town. Open daily from March to October, but afternoon only on Sundays.

Churchill Gardens Museum
In Venns Lane, Hereford, the Churchill Gardens Museum contains a costume collection, furniture, glass, porcelain and a corn dolly collection. Open afternoons Tuesday to Saturday, plus Sunday afternoons in summer.

Clearwell Caves
This unique museum near Coleford records the history of iron-mining in the Forest of Dean – the ancient Old Ham iron-mines were worked until 1945. There are eight large caverns open to the public, several vintage stationary engines, plus a shop and picnic area. Open daily from March to October.

Dean Heritage Museum
Surrounded by magnificent woods in a cleft of the hills at Camp Mill, Soudley, this centre reflects the unique heritage of Dean and its ancient laws and customs. Set around an old watermill with its pond, there is also a reconstructed cottage, a coal-mine and archaeological exhibitions, craft workshops, photography and craft exhibitions and special events thoughout the year. Open daily.

Hereford City Museum
In Broad Street, Hereford City Museum reflects the archaeology and natural history of Herefordshire, and displays costumes, toys, embroidery and agriculture. There is also a bee-keeping display with an observation hive. Open Tuesday to Saturday all year.

Herefordshire Rural Heritage Museum
One of the largest collections of historic farm machinery, vintage tractors and rural bygones in the country. About 1⅓ miles from the Doward Hotel on the Biblings road. Open daily.

Museums of Hereford. Left: Roman artefacts from Kentchurch in the City Museum. Above: exhibits from the Museum of Cider

Museum of Cider
See cider-making through the ages – displays here include a French beam press and working cooper, and there are champagne cider cellars and a working cider-brandy distillery. At Pamona Place, Hereford, the Museum of Cider is open every day except Tuesday, April to October.

Nelson Museum and Local History Centre
This centre for local history, in Priory Street, Monmouth, houses a fine collection of Nelson relics – one of the prize exhibits is Nelson's fighting sword. Open daily; Sunday afternoons only.

St John and Coningsby Museum
This early 13th-century hall is arranged with armour and displays of the Order and Chapel of the Knights of St John. Located at 110 Widemarsh Street, Hereford; open from Easter to September, Tuesday to Thursday and Saturday and Sunday.

Wolvesnewton Folk Collection and Craft Centre
This centre houses exhibitions and displays, craft workshops, shop and cafe, and includes a collection of unusual and entertaining everyday items used since the reign of Victoria. The centre is 1½ miles off the B4235 at Llangwm, 10 miles north-west of Chepstow. Open daily April to September and at weekends in October and November.

RAILWAYS AND STEAM

Broomy Hill Engines
At Broomy Hill, near Hereford, this is a complete Victorian pumping station with working exhibits and two steam pumping engines. Open every afternoon from mid July to the end of August, and the first Sunday afternoon in the month from April to September. Broomy Hill Engines are 'in steam' on Bank Holiday Sundays and Mondays.

Bulmer Railway Centre
The 6000 Locomotive Association cares for locomotives and steam engines; industrial locomotives and the Bulmer's Cider Train are on show. Off Whitecross Road, Hereford, the static display is on weekend afternoons from April to September. Contact the secretary, *tel.* (0272) 834430, for details and times of special 'steam' days.

Dean Forest Railways
This line from Lydney Junction to Parkend was part of the Severn and Wye Railway, which itself evolved out of the system of early tram roads built to serve the coal and iron workings of the area. One mile north of Lydney at New Mills on the B4234, the centre has restored locomotives, coaches, wagons and museum displays. There are steam train rides Sundays from June to September, plus Wednesdays in August. The museum and shop are open at weekends all year.

The Old Station, Tintern
Enjoy a picnic on platform one at the Old Station, Tintern. This former branch line station has been charmingly converted into an award winning tourist attraction, with a railway exhibition, refreshments, picnic and barbecue facilities and a children's play area. Half a mile north of Tintern just off the A466.

WILDLIFE CENTRES

Beauford Bird Gardens
At Devauden, near Chepstow, Beauford displays pheasants, tropical birds, peacocks, ducks, geese, rabbits and guinea pigs. Open daily.

Newent Butterfly Centre
Just north of Newent, off the B4216 at Birches Lane this centre contains free-flying tropical butterflies, displays of insects, spiders, giant snails and black scorpions. Open daily from Easter to October.

Newent Falconry Centre
This centre boasts one of the largest collections of birds of prey in the world. There are flying demonstrations, and breeding and baby enclosures. Open from March to October every day except Tuesdays, the centre is 3 miles from Newent on the Clifford's Mesne road.

Symonds Yat Bird Park
Birds on disply here range from matchbox-size nectar feeders to the Indian giant hornbill, with its five-foot wingspan. Located at Symonds Yat West; for opening times *tel.* (0600) 890989.

World of Butterflies
Also at Symonds Yat West, next to the Jubilee Maze, the World of Butterflies houses free-flying exotic butterflies in a landscaped butterfly house. For opening times *tel.* (0600) 890360.

USEFUL ADDRESSES

Forestry Commission
Local headquarters of the Forestry Commission are at Crown Offices, Bank Street, Coleford, *tel.* (0594) 33057. Details of waymarked paths and other work of the Commission are available, and prior permission for climbing and caving must be obtained here.

National Trust
The Severn Regional Office of the National Trust is at 34-36 Church Street, Tewkesbury, Glos, *tel.* (0684) 297747 or 292919. Information is available on National Trust properties, events, concerts and membership.

Offa's Dyke Association
Information on the Offa's Dyke Long Distance Footpath is available from the Offa's Dyke Association, Old Primary School, West Street, Knighton, Powys, *tel.* (0547) 528753.

Ramblers Association
Details of membership and activities are available from the Secretary of the Forest of Dean Group, Ms Fran Parker, 2 Cox's Way, Whitecroft Road, Bream, near Lydney, Glos, *tel.* (0594) 563653.

From the beautiful Beauford Bird Gardens there are commanding views across some of the area's most attractive countryside

Tourist Information Centres

Chepstow
Wales Tourist Board Information Centre, The Gatehouse. Detailed local information is available here. Open Easter and May to September, *tel.* (02912) 3772.

Cinderford
Tourist Information Centre, The Library, Bellevue Road. Open all year for local information only, *tel.* (0594) 22581.

Coleford
Tourist Information Centre, 24 Market Place, *tel.* (0594) 36307. Open all year for local information.

Hay-on-Wye
Tourist Information Centre, The Car Park, *tel.* (0497) 820144. This centre is open daily from Easter to September for local information.

Hereford
Tourist Information Centre, Shire Hall, 1A St Owen Street, *tel.* (0432) 268430. Open all year for general information for the whole country as well as local information.

Monmouth
Wales Tourist Board Information Centre, Church Street, *tel.* (0600) 3899. Open all year for local information only.

Ross-on-Wye
Wyedean Tourist Board and the main Tourist Information Centre for Wyedean, 20 Broad Street, *tel.* (0989) 62768. Open all year for country-wide information as well as comprehensive local information.

Tintern
Wales Tourist Board Information Centre at Tintern Abbey, *tel.* (02918) 431. Open from April to October for local information only.

CALENDAR OF EVENTS

The events below usually occur in the months shown, though actual times and dates may vary from year to year. Also there are other special events through the year, especially in Hereford and the larger towns, and at centres such as the Dean Heritage Museum. Medieval banquets are a feature in the area, and Tourist Information Centres will have details of these. A free magazine, 'What's On - Wye Dean', is distributed annually to Tourist Information Centres, hotels and libraries in the area.

March-April
Pax cakes distributed on Palm Sunday in the parishes of Hentland, Kings Caple and Sellack.

May
Hereford May Fair

Wye Raft Race from Hay-on-Wye to Chepstow, Spring Bank Holiday

Steam Days at the Dean Forest Railway, Spring Bank Holiday Sunday and Monday

Oak Apple Day, Fownhope

Broomy Hill Engines, Hereford 'In Steam', Spring Bank Holiday Sunday and Monday

Rodeo, May Bank Holiday in Eardisley

May/June
Ross-on-Wye Festival of the Arts, biennial celebrations

July
Ross-on-Wye Steam Fair and Rally, at Much Marcle on the last weekend in July

Hereford City Carnival

Madley Music Festival

August
Ross-on-Wye Town Carnival Week

Speech House Antiques Fair, Forest of Dean

Three Choirs Festival – held in Hereford every three years

Steam Days at the Dean Forest Railway, every Sunday

Ross-on-Wye Annual Regatta, August Bank Holiday

Broomy Hill Engines, Hereford 'In Steam', August Bank Holiday Sunday and Monday

September
Ledbury Hop Fair and Ploughing Competition

Hereford Antiques Fair

October
Hereford Antiques Fair

December
Santa Specials on the Dean Forest Railway

FOREST OF DEAN AND WYE VALLEY

Atlas

The following pages contain a legend, key map and atlas of the Forest of Dean and Wye Valley, three motor tours and sixteen walks.

Above: Wye Valley near Fownhope

Legend

TOURIST INFORMATION

Camp Site	Nature reserve
Caravan Site	Other tourist feature
Information Centre	Preserved railway
Parking Facilities	Racecourse
Viewpoint	Wildlife park
Picnic site	Museum
Golf course or links	Nature or forest trail
Castle	Ancient monument
Cave	Telephones : public or motoring organisations
Country park	PC Public Convenience
Garden	Youth Hostel
Historic house	

Waymarked Path / Long Distance Path / Recreational Path

ORIENTATION

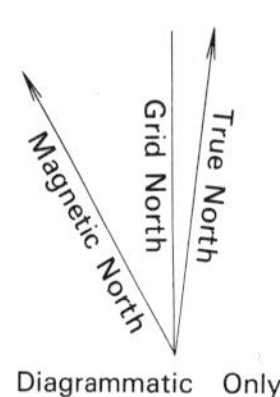

Diagrammatic Only

True North
At the centre of the area is 0°15'E of Grid North

Magnetic North
At the centre of this area is about 5° W of Grid North in 1988 decreasing by about ½° in three years.

GRID REFERENCE SYSTEM

The map references used in this book are based on the Ordnance Survey National Grid, correct to within 1000 Metres They comprise two letters and four figures, and are preceded by the atlas page number.

Thus the reference for Ross-on-Wye appears 87 SO 6024

87 is the atlas page number

SO identifies the major (100km) grid square concerned (see diag)

SN SO 84/85 86/87 SS ST

6024 locates the lower left-hand corner of the kilometre grid square in which Ross-on-Wye appears

Take the first figure of the reference 6, this refers to the numbered grid running along the bottom of the page. Having found this line, the second figure 0 tells you the distance to move in tenths to the right of this line. A vertical line through this point is the first half of the reference.

The third figure 2, refers to the numbered grid lines on the right hand side of the page, finally the fourth figure 4 indicates the distance to move in tenths above this line. A horizontal line drawn through this point to intersect with the first line gives the precise location of the places in question.

Ross-on-Wye 3 4 2 1 5 0 6 7

KEY-MAP 1:625,000 or 10 MILES to 1"

ROAD INFORMATION

M4 S 24 — Motorway with service area, service area (limited access) and junction with junction number

M4 L 29 — Motorway junction with limited interchange

Mid 1988 — Motorway, service area and junction under construction with proposed opening date

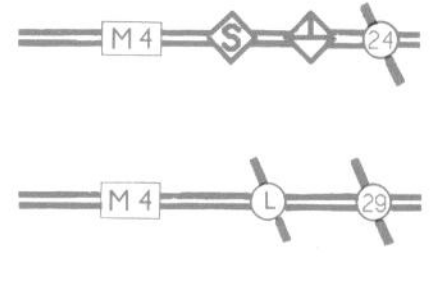

Primary routes / Main Road — Single and dual carriageway with service area

Main Road under construction

Narrow Road with passing places

B 4521 — Other roads: B roads (majority numbered), Unclassified (selected)

TOLL — Gradient: 14% (1 in 7) and steeper, and toll

24 15 — Primary routes and main roads
24 15 — Motorways

Mileages are shown on the map between large markers and between small markers in large and small type

1 mile = 1·61 kilometres

Primary Routes

These form a national network of recommended through routes which complement the motorway system. Selected places of major traffic importance are known as Primary Route Destinations and are shown on these maps thus HEREFORD. This relates to the directions on road signs which on Primary Routes have a green background. To travel on a Primary Route, follow the direction to the next Primary Destination shown on the green backed road signs. On these maps Primary Route road numbers and mileages are shown in green.

Motorways

A similar situation occurs with motorway routes where numbers and mileages, shown in blue on these maps correspond to the blue background of motorway road signs.

GENERAL FEATURES

Passenger railways (selected in conurbations)

AA :A RAC :R PO :T — Telephone call box

National Boundary

County or Region Boundary

Large Town — Town / Village

Airport

427 — Height (metres)

WATER FEATURES

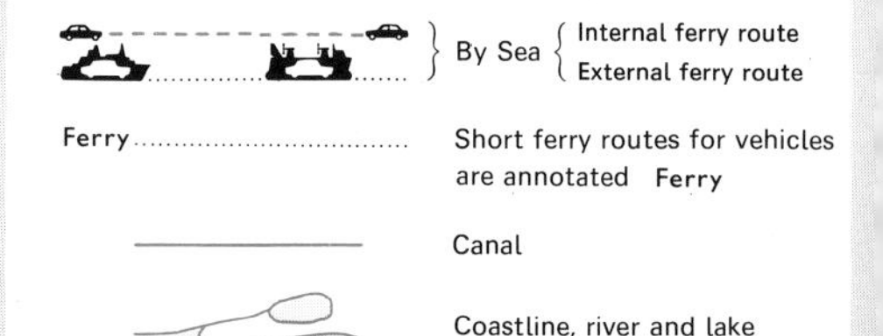

By Sea: Internal ferry route / External ferry route

Ferry — Short ferry routes for vehicles are annotated Ferry

Canal

Coastline, river and lake

ATLAS 1:200,000 or 3 MILES to 1"

TOURS 1:250,000 or 4 MILES to 1"

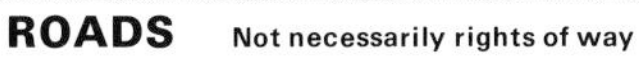

ROADS Not necessarily rights of way

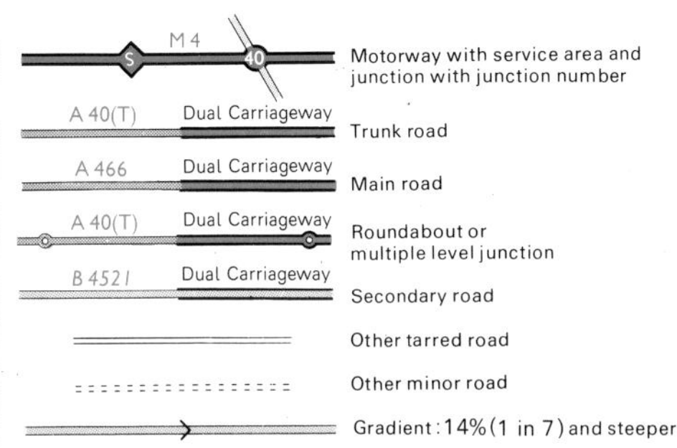

Motorway with service area and junction with junction number

Trunk road

Main road

Roundabout or multiple level junction

Secondary road

Other tarred road

Other minor road

Gradient: 14% (1 in 7) and steeper

RAILWAYS

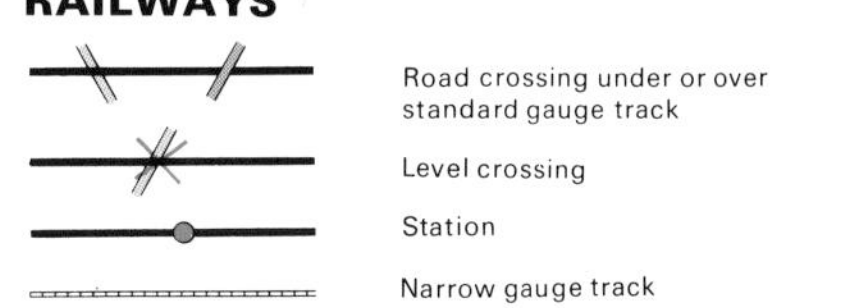

Road crossing under or over standard gauge track

Level crossing

Station

Narrow gauge track

WATER FEATURES

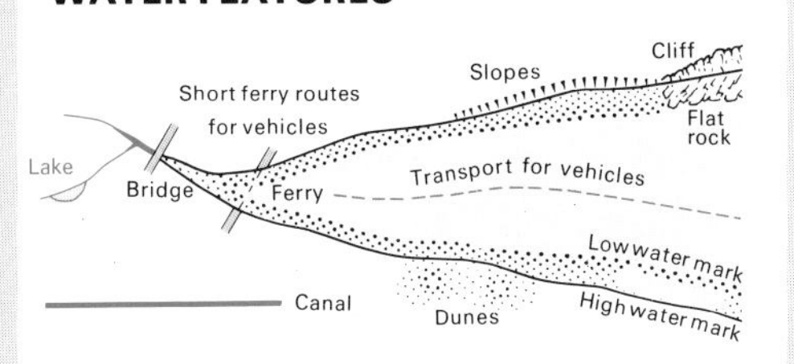

ANTIQUITIES

Native fortress

Roman road (course of)

Castle · Other antiquities

CANOVIVM · Roman antiquity

GENERAL FEATURES

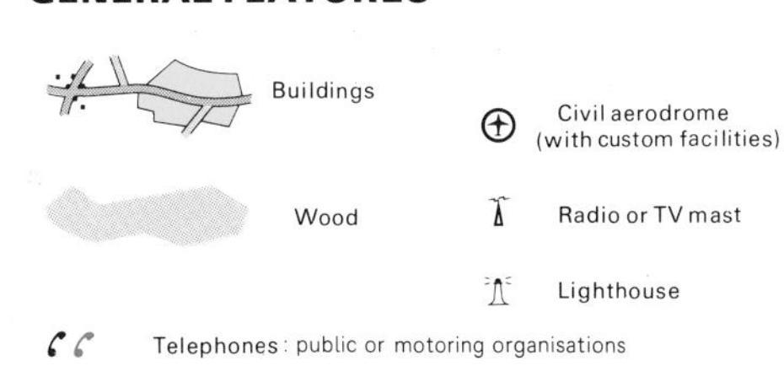

Buildings

Civil aerodrome (with custom facilities)

Wood

Radio or TV mast

Lighthouse

Telephones: public or motoring organisations

RELIEF

Feet	Metres	
		.274 Heights in feet above mean sea level
3000	914	
2000	610	
1400	427	
1000	305	Contours at 200 ft intervals
600	183	
200	61	
0	0	To convert feet to metres multiply by 0.3048

WALKS 1:25,000 or 2½" to 1 MILE

ROADS AND PATHS Not necessarily rights of way

M 4	M 4	Motorway
A 40(T)	A 40(T)	Trunk road
A 466	A 466	Main road
B 4521	B 4521	Secondary road
A 40(T)	A 40(T)	Dual carriageway
		Road generally over 4m wide
		Road generally under 4m wide
		Other road, drive or track

Path

Narrow roads with passing places are annotated

RAILWAYS

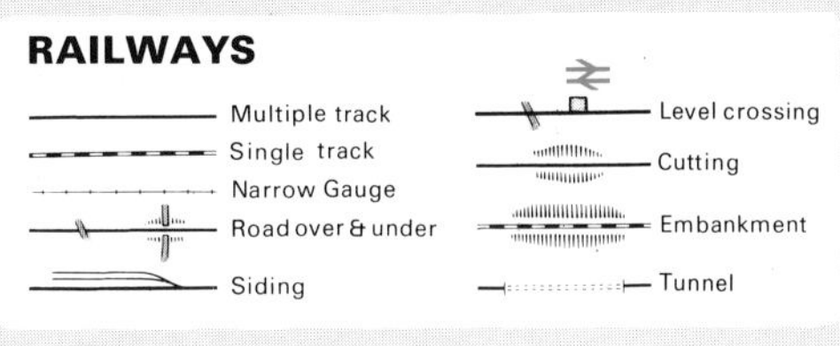

Multiple track

Single track

Narrow Gauge

Road over & under

Siding

Level crossing

Cutting

Embankment

Tunnel

GENERAL FEATURES

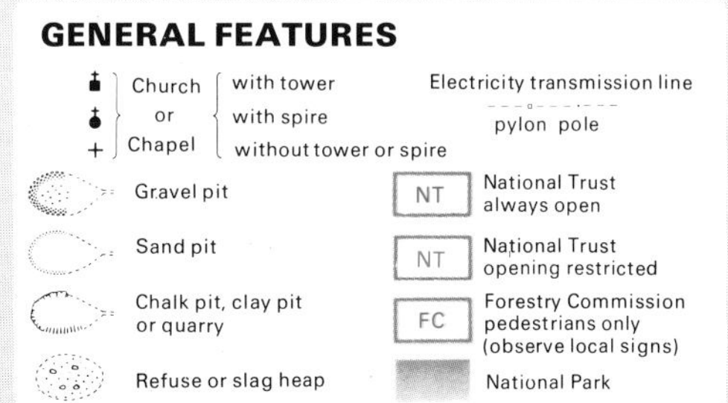

Church or Chapel { with tower / with spire / without tower or spire

Electricity transmission line

pylon pole

Gravel pit

Sand pit

Chalk pit, clay pit or quarry

Refuse or slag heap

NT National Trust always open

NT National Trust opening restricted

FC Forestry Commission pedestrians only (observe local signs)

National Park

HEIGHTS AND ROCK FEATURES

Contours are at various metres / feet vertical intervals

50 } Determined { ground survey
285 · } by { air survey

Surface heights are to the nearest metre / foot above mean sea level. Heights shown close to a triangulation pillar refer to the station height at ground level and not necessarily to the summit.

Vertical Face

75
60
50

Loose rock Boulders Outcrop Scree

PUBLIC RIGHTS OF WAY

Public rights of way shown in this guide may not be evident on the ground

Public Paths { Footpath / Bridleway

By-way open to all traffic

Road used as a public path

Public rights of way indicated by these symbols have been derived from Definitive Maps as amended by later enactments or instruments held by Ordnance Survey between ***1st Aug 1976*** *and* ***1st May 1986*** *and are shown subject to the limitations imposed by the scale of mapping (Note: some walk maps do not show rights of way symbols)*
Later information may be obtained from the appropriate County Council.

The representation on these maps of any other road, track or path is no evidence of the existence of a right of way.

WALKS AND TOURS (All Scales)

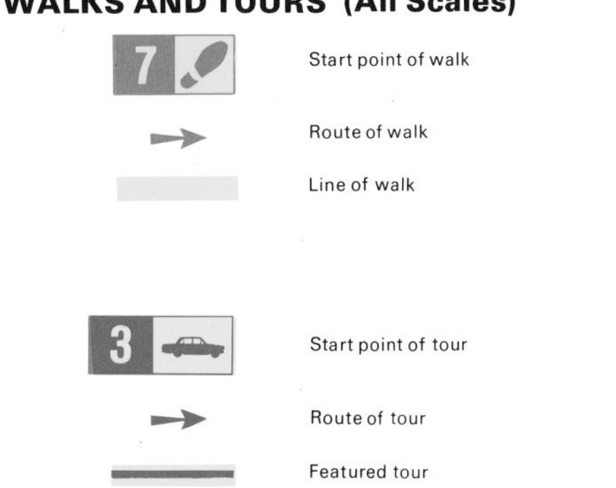

Start point of walk

Route of walk

Line of walk

Start point of tour

Route of tour

Featured tour

82
Key to Atlas pages
Distances in miles to ROSS-ON-WYE
Map Ref: 87 S0 6024
Aberystwyth 94
Birmingham 58
Bristol 44
Cardiff 48
Leeds 188
London 121
Manchester 140
Nottingham 118
Oxford 66
Swansea 75
WYE VALLEY & FOREST OF DEAN
Kilometres 10 20 30
Miles 10 20
BRISTOL CHANNEL

Welshampton
Ightfield
Ashley
Barlaston
STONE
Kirk Langley
Longford
DERBY
Doveridge
Etwall
Hordley
Northwood
Prees
MARKET DRAYTON
Standon
Hilderstone
UTTOXETER
Cockshutt
Hodnet
Cheswardine
Eccleshall
Sandon
Draycott in the Clay
Tutbury
Burlton
WEM
Child's Ercall
Clive
Myddle
Shawbury
Woodseaves
Gnosall
STAFFORD
Abbots Bromley
BURTON UPON TRENT
Nesscliffe
Hadnall
Edgmond
Haughton
Yoxall
Walton-on-Trent
Albrighton
High Ercall
Crudgington
NEWPORT
Church Eaton
RUGELEY
Armitage
King's Bromley
Overseal
Rodington
Donnington
Wheaton Aston
Penkridge
Alrewas
SHREWSBURY
WELLINGTON
TELFORD
Sheriffhales
Gailey
CANNOCK
LICHFIELD
OAKENGATES
Brewood
Whittington
DAWLEY
Shifnal
Minsterley
Cressage
Iron-Bridge
Albrighton
Codsall
BROWNHILLS
ALDRIDGE
TAMWORTH
Broseley
Fazeley
Polesworth
MUCH WENLOCK
WOLVERHAMPTON
WALSALL
ATHERSTONE
Leebotwood
Cardington
WEDNESBURY
SUTTON COLDFIELD
Kingsbury
CHURCH STRETTON
Morville
SEDGLEY
Hope Bowdler
BRIDGNORTH
Claverley
Wombourne
DUDLEY
Ditton Priors
Coleshill
Filton
Wistanstow
Clee St Margaret
Billingsley
Amblecote
STOURBRIDGE
BIRMINGHAM
Craven Arms
Highley
Kinver
HALESOWEN
Meriden
Culmington
Hagley
Clungunford
Bromfield
Bitterley
KIDDERMINSTER
Belbroughton
SOLIHULL
COVENTRY
Leintwardine
LUDLOW
Cleobury Mortimer
Clows Top
BEWDLEY
Chaddesley Corbett
Knowle
Walford
STOURPORT-ON-SEVERN
Alvechurch
KENILWORTH
Hockley Heath
Wigmore
Woofferton
Tenbury Wells
BROMSGROVE
Stoke Prior
REDDITCH
Henley-in-Arden
WARWICK
Orleton
Great Witley
Ombersley
Clifton upon Teme
Holt Heath
DROITWICH
Astwood Bank
Studley
Claverdon
Kingsland
Feckenham
Wootton Wawen
Hatfield
Martley
Bearley
Barford
LEOMINSTER
Whitbourne
WORCESTER
Inkberrow
Alcester
Alveston
Monkland
Crowle
Wellesbourne
BROMYARD
Leigh
Spetchley
Broom
STRATFORD-UPON-AVON
Hope under Dinmore
Powick
Bidford-on-Avon
Weobley
Bishampton
Ettington
Wellington
Malvern Link
Kempsey
Harvington
Long Marston
GREAT MALVERN
Pershore
South Littleton
Halford
Staunton on Wye
Credenhill
Withington
Bosbury
Defford
EVESHAM
Mickleton
SHIPSTON-ON-STOUR
Upton upon Severn
VALE OF EVESHAM
Ilmington
Welland
Chipping Campden
HEREFORD
LEDBURY
Willersey
Madley
Mordiford
Eastnor
Longdon
Bredon
Broadway
Burmington
Kingstone
Blockley
Wolford
Fownhope
Much Marcle
Stanway
Moreton-in-Marsh
Long Compton
Dymock
TEWKESBURY
Little Compton
CHIPPING NORTON
Pontrilas
Staunton
Bishop's Cleeve
Winchcombe
Peterstow
ROSS-ON-WYE
Newent
Hartpury
Guiting Power
Stow-on-the-Wold
St Weonards
Lea
Norton
Staverton
CHELTENHAM
Bourton-on-the-Water
Bledington
Tibberton
Huntley
Churchdown
Whitchurch
Goodrich
Mitcheldean
GLOUCESTER
Great Rissington
MONMOUTH
Staunton
Cinderford
Longney
Birdlip
Withington
Northleach
Burford
Coleford
Newnham
Frampton on Severn
Painswick
Aldsworth
Raglan
Parkend
Blakeney
Stonehouse
Winstone
N Cerney
Carterton
Brize Norton
Trelleck
Bream
St Briavels
Lydney
Eastington
Bisley
Daglingworth
Bibury
Barnsley
Hatherop
Broughton Poggs
STROUD
Minchinhampton
CIRENCESTER
Fairford
Sharpness
NAILSWORTH
Poulton
Lechlade
Kelmscot
Berkeley
Dursley
Uley
Horsley
Avening
Kemble
Ashton Keynes
S Cerney
Faringdon
St Arvans
N Nibley
Hill
Stone
Wotton-under-Edge
TETBURY
COTSWOLD HILLS
CRICKLADE
Shirenewton
CHEPSTOW
TOLL
Falfield
Leighterton
Minety
HIGHWORTH
Caerwent
Magor
CALDICOT
Thornbury
Wickwar
Charlton
MALMESBURY
Purton
Shrivenham
Aust
Alveston
Brinkworth
Redwick
Redwick
Almondsbury
Iron Acton
Chipping Sodbury
Badminton
Wootton Bassett
SWINDON
Wanborough
Ashbury
Easter Compton
Great Somerford
Yate
Hullavington
Wroughton
Avonmouth
Filton
Westerleigh
Tormarton
Chiseldon
Lyneham
Baydon
PORTISHEAD
Mangotsfield
Pucklechurch
Broad Hinton
Aldbourne
Hilmarton
BRISTOL
TOLL
KINGSWOOD
Wick
Marshfield
Cold Ashton
Biddestone
CHIPPENHAM
CALNE
Ramsbury
Oldland
Cherhill
Avebury
MARLBOROUGH
Nailsea
Kenn
KEYNSHAM
Whitchurch
Corsham
Box
Lacock
W Overton
Saltford
Froxfield
Yatton
BRISTOL
Congresbury
Pensford
BATH
Atworth
Bromham
MELKSHAM
Bishops Cannings
Alton Priors
Gt Bedwyn
Chew Magna
Marksbury
BRADFORD-ON-AVON
Seend
DEVIZES
Wrington
Burbage
Blagdon
Pewsey
Winscombe
Clutton
Wellow
TROWBRIDGE
Collingbourne

Black Mountain
1584
Beacon
Pool Hill
1690
Lanllwyst
Dutlas
Llanfair Waterdine
Offa's Dyke
Purlogue
Black Hill
Hobarris
New Invention
Caer Caradoc
Chapel Lawn
Twitchen
Hopton Castle
1300
Hopton Titterhill
Clungunford
Shelderton
1004
Bedstone
Bucknell
B 4367
B 4385
Leintwardine
A 488
Knucklas
Crûg
848
Llanbister Road Station
Bailey Hill
Llangunllo
1373
KNIGHTON
River Teme
Stowe
541
572
Milebrooke
Fort
Buckton
Brampton Bryan
Walford
389
Downton on the Rock
Burrington
Adforton
Elton
A 488
B 4356
1367
7
Offa's Dyke
B 4355
1079
Llan-wen Hill
8
1092
A 4110
ROMAN ROAD
Letton
Leinthall Starkes
Wigmore
Glog Hill
16
Bleddfa
Pilleth
B 4357
Birtley
Ongar Street
1108
Fforest fach
Lower Lye
0 Kilometres 5 10
0 Miles 5
Cascob
Lingen
10
Yatton
Llanfihangel Rhydithon
Stapleton
Castle
Aymestrey
Discoed
934
B 4356
PRESTEIGNE
492
R Lugg
Kinsham
Byton
Radnor Forest
2166
Bache Hill
1218
Slough
B 4362
Rodd
Combe
Combe Moor
Mortimer Cross
Lucton
319
Kinnerton
Evenjobb
Nash
Fort
Shobdon
Ledicot
Esgairnantau
New Radnor
B 4372
B 4357
Burfa Camp
Stansbatch
609
B 4362
Knill
Titley
Staunton on Arrow
Offa's Dyke
Rowe Ditch
A 4110
Shirl Heath
Old Radnor
Walton
B 4355
A 44
Yardro
Burlingjobb
A 44
R Arrow
Eardisland
1284
Llanfihangel-nant-Melan
Dolyhir
KINGTON
3
705
Marston
Pembridge
10
Bryn-y-maen
B 4594
Hergest Ridge
1397
Barewood
A 4457
Sollers Dilwyn
Stretford Court
Lyonshall
Luntley
1745
Gladestry
Moorcot
Haven
245
Rhulen Hill
1777
Hergest
Holme Marsh
Broxwood
Dilwyn
ROMAN ROAD
Huntington
Kingswood
6
Birley
Hengoed
1718
1225
A 480
Glascwm Hill
Michaelchurch-on-Arrow
6
A 4111
Upcott
Almeley
Weobley
Weobley Marsh
King's Pyon
Sarnesfield
Newchurch
Bryn-wyn
16
5
Red Hill
1671
1171
Brilley
Lower Welson
Eardisley
4
Kinnersley
Ledgemoor
Dol-y-cannau
B 4230
Canon Pyon
A 4112
Calver Hill
Rhos-goch
1276
Rhybspence
Whitney-on-Wye
Toll
Ailey
Norton Canon
Wormsley
Yarsop
A 438
Letton Lake
Painscastle
Clyro Hill
Clifford
Winforton
Willersley
River Wye
Moorhampton
Yazor
Mansell Lacy
Letton
380
Staunton on Wye
ROMAN ROAD
Mansell Gamage
334
Priory Wood
Merbach
208
Begwns
363
Bredwardine
Brinsop
Fort
A 438
Clyro
418
B 4348
Brobury
Monnington on Wye
B 4230
ROMAN ROAD
Bishopstone
Hardwicke
HAY-ON-WYE
The Bage
B 4348
B 4352
Byford
Kenchester
Preston on Wye
14
Bridge Sollers
Sugwas
16
Llowes
Cusop
Moccas
Lulham
Wye (Afon Gwy)
Dorstone
Ciltwrch
Blakemere
Ploughfield
R Wye
Canon Bridge
B 4350
Llanigon
Snodhill
4
Tyberton
Glasbury
Madley
Eaton Bishop
Peterchurch
B 4350
1593
1419
Shenmore
Tregoyd
Three Cocks
Urishay Common
Golden Valley
ROMAN ROAD
B 4349
A 4079
2220
Vowchurch
A 4078
Velindre
Hay Bluff
B 4348
Turnastone
B 4347
Kingstone
2263
Craswall
Michaelchurch Escley
Upper Maes-coed
Llanelieu
2306
Thruxton
Twmpa
St Margarets
Talgarth
Kerry's Gate
2338
Middle Maes-coed
Cockyard
Rhos Dirion
Newton
Pen y Manllwyn
Bacton
Didley
Capel-y-ffin
Llanveynoe
Grwyne Fawr Resr
Wormbridge
1
Lower Maes-coed
Castell Dinas
Waun Fach
Abbey Dore
3
2660
THE BLACK
1983
86
Howton
1997
Mynydd Troed
Longtown
Ewyas Harold
Mynydd Llysiau
Priory
Mynydd Merddin
1060
3
2173
MOUNTAINS
Llanthony
Clodock
Bagwyllydiart
Mynydd Llangorse
Grwyne Fechan
230
Pontrilas
13
Afon Honddu
Rowlestone
Hatterrall Hill
Kentchurch Court
1667
Llangua
Kentchurch
Pen Allt-mawr
Walterstone
1743
Grosmont Castle
1202
A 479 (T)
Pen Gwyllt Meirch
25
2360
Oldcastle
River Monnow
White Rocks
Cwmdu
2
Hoaldalbert
4
Pen Cerrig-calch
Cwmyoy
B 4347
3
2300
1805
Pandy
896
Bwlch
2
Gaer
Crug Mawr
Tretower
Stanton
1389
Tretower Court
Crug Hywel
Llanbedr
Forest Coal Pit
Llangattock
Skenfrith

Cangeford
Cleeton St Mary
Catherton
Titterstone Clee Hill
Trimpley Resr
Trimpley
Middleton
Bitterley
1750
Neen Savage
B 4363
B 4194
Buttonoak
Habberley
Henley
Hopton Wafers
Wyre Forest
Farden
1109
Doddington
Cleobury Mortimer
BEWDLEY
Snitton
Knowbury
Cleehill
Knowle
Hints
Far Forest
Caynham Camp
Hope Bagot
Coreley
River Rea
Pound Bank
Callow Hill
Ribbesford
Milson
Bayton
Bliss Gate
Caynham
Whitton
Neen Sollars
Clows Top
760
Rock
STOURPORT-ON-SEVERN
Ashford Carbonell
Nash
Mamble
Areley Kings
Greete
Middleton
Boraston
Frith Common
B 4202
Wooofferton
Little Hereford
Lindridge
Pensax
The Village
Dunley
A 456
Newnham
A 443
Abberley
Brimfield
Burford
Rochford
Eardiston
Stockton on Teme
Astley
Tenbury Wells
Abberley Hill
B 4204
Orleton
R. Teme
Hanley William
Stanford Bridge
Callows Grave
Stanford on Teme
Great Witley
St Michaels
Hanley Child
B 4214
Middleton on the Hill
904
Broad Heath
Woodbury Hill
137
Ashton
707
Leysters
Kyre Park
Stoke Bliss
Upper Sapey
Sapey Common
Little Witley
Shrawley
The Hundred
A 4112
Shelsley Walsh
Shelsley Beauchamp
Garmsley Camp
Bank Street
B 4203
Clifton upon Teme
Kimbolton
Wolferlow
Stockton
Whyle
Grafton
High Lane
Harpley
B 4197
Bach Camp
Wall Hills
Collington
Wichenford
Hatfield
LEOMINSTER
Pudleston
Thornbury
Tedstone Wafre
Martley
Edvin Loach
602
Tedstone Delamere
Horsham
Steen's Bridge
Docklow
818
Edwyn Ralph
Berrow Green
B 4204
Stoke Prior
Humber Court
A 44
Grendon Green
Whitbourne
Broad Green
Bredenbury
739
Bromyard Downs
Knightwick
Lulsley
Fort
Risbury
Marston Stannett
River Lodon
Broadwas
A 44
Newton
Bromyard
Leigh
Hegdon Hill
Linley Green
215
A 417
Pencombe
Stanford Bishop
Suckley Hills
Alfrick
Bowley
Bransford
Bodenham
A 465
B 4214
Munderfield Row
Suckley
Leigh Sinton
Maund Bryan
Little Cowarne
638
Acton Beauchamp
B 4220
Longley Green
R Lugg
Ullingswick
Munderfield Stocks
Acton Green
Urdimarsh
The Vauld
Stoke Lacy
Stifford's Bridge
Storridge
672
Walker's Green
Felton
Moreton Jeffries
Bishop's Frome
Evesbatch
Marden
Burley Gate
Much Cowarne
Ridgeway Cross
Cradley
Sutton Walls
Preston Wynne
Castle Frome
Fromes Hill
West Malvern
Sutton St Nicholas
A 465
Ocle Pychard
Mathon
1394
Newtown
Westhide
A 4103
R. Frome
B 4220
Wyche
Pipe and Lyde
Stretton Grandison
566
Withington
Bosbury
Colwall Stone
Shelwick
Shucknall
Canon Frome
Coddington
Yarkhill
Ashperton
Colwall Green
Malvern Wells
Hagley
B 4214
B 4218
Lugwardine
Weston Beggard
Munsley
Little Malvern
Bartestree
Tarrington
Wellington Heath
Tupsley
Stoke Edith
1114
Dormington
A 438
ROMAN ROAD
Trumpet
A 449
Fort
HEREFORD
865
LEDBURY
Hampton Bishop
Aylton
937
Lower Bullingham
B 4224
Eastnor
Dinedor
Mordiford
Putley
Little Marcle
A 438
Hollybush
Birts Street
167
A 4172
Holme Lacy
Twyford Common
Woolhope
B 4216
A 417
Fownhope
Rushall
Preston
Capler Camp
Sollers Hope
Donnington
904
Aconbury
Bolstone
Much Marcle
M 50
Pendock
Brockhampton
Ryton
Little Birch
Little Dewchurch
B 4024
Dymock
Redmarley D' Abitot
Much Birch
Ballingham
Carey
A 449
Fawley Chapel
How Caple
Poolhill
Hoarwithy
87
Kempley
Staunton
R Leadon
Kings Caple
Foy
Hole in the Wall
Llandinabo
R Wye
Brampton Abbotts
Upton Bishop
Sellack
Crow Hill
Upleadon
Pencoyd
Hentland
344
St Owen's Cross
M 50
B 4221
Gorsley
Bridstow
Rudhall
Linton
Kilcot
Newent
B 4215
Hartpury
Peterstow
ROSS-ON-WYE
Bromsash
Aston Ingham
Kent's Green
A 4137
A 40
Aston Crews
B 4222
Tretire
B 4216
Clifford's Mesne
Highleadon
Weston under Penyard
B 4224
Glewstone
Hom Green
Coughton
Pontshill
Lea
May Hill
Taynton
Tibberton

Three Cocks
Velindre
Talgarth
Hay Bluff
2220
2263
Twmpa
2306
Craswall
Urishay Common
Michaelchurch Escley
Golden Valley
Vowchurch
Turnastone
B 4348
Upper Maes-coed
Middle Maes-coed
St Margarets
Kerry's Gate
Newton
Bacton
Kingstone
Thruxton
Cockyard
Didley
Wormbridge
Kilpeck
2338
Rhos Dirion
Pen y Manllwyn
Capel-y-ffin
Grwyne Fawr Resr
Llanveynoe
Lower Maes-coed
Abbey Dore
Ewyas Harold
Howton
Castell Dinas
Waun Fâch
2660
THE BLACK MOUNTAINS
1983
84
Longtown
Mynydd Llysiau
2173
Priory
Llanthony
Clodock
Mynydd Merddin
1060
Rowlestone
230
Pontrilas
Bagwyllydiart
1997
Mynydd Troed
Mynydd Llangorse
1667
Grwyne Fechan
Hatterrall Hill
1743
Afon Honddu
Walterstone
Llangua
Kentchurch Court
Kentchurch
1202
Grosmont Castle
White Rocks
Pen Allt-mawr
2360
Pen Gwyllt Meirch
Oldcastle
Cwmyoy
River Monnow
Hoaldalbert
Cwmdu
Pen Cerrig-calch
2300
1805
Crug Mawr
Pandy
896
Bwlch
Gaer
Tretower
Stanton
Forest Coal Pit
Llanvihangel Crucorney
Llangattock Lingoed
1389
Skenfrith
Tretower Court & Castle
Crug Hywel
Llanbedr
Mynydd Pen-y-fâl
Bont
B 4521
Cross Ash
Llangynidr
Ffawyddog
B 4558
Crickhowell
1955
Sugar Loaf
Bettws
1595
Llangattock
Llangenny
Allt
Ysgyryd Fawr
Newcastle
Cwrt-y-gollen
Mynydd Llanwenarth
Llanvetherine
White Castle
Glangrwyney
Mardy
Llantilio Pertholey
Llangattock-Vibon-Avel
Mynydd Llangatwg
1735
Llanelly
River Usk
A 40 (T)
ABERGAVENNY
B 4233
Llantilio Crossenny
Gilwern
Govilon
Llanvihangel-Ystern-Llewern
Clydach
Blackrock
Llanfoist
Llanddewi Rhydderch
Llanvapley
BRYNMAWR
A 465 (T)
Llanelly Hill
Blorenge
1833
B 4269
Wernrheolydd
Penrhos
Beaufort
B 4248
Llanellen
Llanarth
Tregare
Sirhowy
NANTYGLO
Garn-yr-erw
The Bryn
EBBW VALE
BLAENAVON
Llanvihangel Gobion
107
216
Castle
1804
Forge Side
BLAINA
Llanover
Raglan
1905
Coity Mountain
Gwastad
A 4043
Llanfair Kilgeddin
Twyn-y-Sheriff
1648
Cefn yr Arail
Varteg
Cwmavon
Mynydd Garnclochdy
1470
290
Nant-y-derry
Bettws Newydd
Kingcoed
Cwm
Cwmtillery
639
ABERTILLERY
Penperlleni
Kemeys Commander
Gwehelog
Manmoel
ABERSYCHAN
Little Mill
Llancayo
72
284
Llandenny
Llansoy
Hollybush
Aberbeeg
Trevethin
A 472
Monkswood
St Illtyd
Brynithel
569
Glascoed
Gwernesney
Markham
Llanhilleth
PONTYPOOL
USK
Llangwm
Glandwr
Trinant
Llandegfedd Resr
Aberbargoed
480
New Inn
Griffithstown
Swffryd
Crumlin
Coed-y-paen
Llanllowell
Gaer-fawr
Oakdale
Penmaen
Sebastapol
BLACKWOOD
1550
608
Llantrisant
NEWBRIDGE
Mynydd Maen
Gaerllwyd
Croesyceiliog
Llangybi
PONTLLANFRAITH
Pen-y-cae-mawr
Earlswood
Llandegveth
Cefn Rhyswg
CWMBRAN
Tredunnock
Newbridge-on-Usk
ABERCARN
1013
Maesycwmmer
B 4591
Henllys
Wentwood
Ynysddu
Cwmcarn
Llanfrechfa
Ponthir
Llanhennock
Llanvair Discoed
Pontywaun
1264
Castell-y-Bwch
Cwmfelinfach
Crosskeys
Croes-y-mwyalch
Parc Seymour
Llanvaches
Sirhowy Valley
Ebbw Vale
1167
Wattsville
RISCA
298
Fort
394
CAERLEON
Llanbradach
Pontymister
Malpas
ISCA
Cat's Ash
Llanbeder
Penhow
ROMAN ROAD
Ynysddu
MACHEN
Bettws
73
Llanmartin
BEDWAS
A 468
Canal
Ebbw River
26
25
24
Lower Machen
Rogerstone
Llanfihangel Rogiet
Rhymney River
M 4
Underwood
CAERPHILLY
27
Llanwern
Bishton
Fort
Magor
23
Draethen
Rhiwderin
Undy
Rudry
Ruperra Castle
Bassaleg
28
Maes glas
NEWPORT
Works
Llandevenny
Duffryn
Caldicot Level
Thornhill
Michaelstone-y-Fedw
Tredegar Park
Pye Corner
Summerleaze
29
Coedkernew
River Usk
Whitson
Redwick
Lisvane
Castleton
Power Sta
Nash
Portland Grounds
Marshfield
Goldcliff
Welsh Grounds
Llanishen
Pentwyn
St Brides Wentlooge
B 4239
Denny Island
St Mellons
Rhymney R
Peterstone Wentlooge
Heath
Rumney

Bullingham
Dinedor
Mordiford
Putley
Little Marcle
Eastnor
Hollybush
Birts Street
Twyford Common
Holme Lacy
Woolhope
Rushall
Preston
Fownhope
Much Marcle
Donnington
Capler Camp
Sollers Hope
Aconbury
Bolstone
Brockhampton
Pendock
Ryton
Little Birch
Little Dewchurch
Ballingham
Dymock
Redmarley D' Abitot
Much Birch
Carey
Fawley Chapel
How Caple
Kempley
Poolhill
Hoarwithy
Kings Caple
Foy
Hole in the Wall
Staunton
Llandinabo
R. Wye
R. Leadon
Sellack
Brampton Abbotts
Crow Hill
Upton Bishop
Pencoyd
Upleadon
St Owen's Cross
Bridstow
Rudhall
Linton
Gorsley
Kilcot
Newent
Hartpury
Tretire
Peterstow
ROSS-ON-WYE
Bromsash
Aston Ingham
Kent's Green
Aston Crews
Highleadon
Glewstone
Hom Green
Weston under Penyard
Clifford's Mesne
Coughton
Pontshill
Lea
May Hill
Taynton
Tibberton
Llangarron
Pencraig
Walford
Glasshouse Hill
Maisemore
Marstow
Castle
Goodrich
Kerne Bridge
Hope Mansell
Mitcheldean
Longhope
Huntley
Bulley
Highnam
Llangrove
Welsh Bicknor
Birdwood
Churcham
Whitchurch
Ruardean
Drybrook
Blaisdon
Oakle Street
Minsterworth
Garnarew
Symonds Yat
Ruardean Woodside
Northwood Green
Hempsted
Fort
Brierley
Lydbrook
English Bicknor
Elmore Back
Elmore
Brierley
Flaxley
Westbury-on-Severn
Farleys End
Dixton
Edge End
Cinderford
Elton
Quedgeley
Christchurch
Berry Hill
Littledean
Boxbush
Longney
Staunton
Mile End
Newnham
Rodley
Broadwell
Ruspidge
Arlingham
Coleford
Coalway
FOREST OF DEAN
Upper Soudley
Upper Framilode
Redbrook
Newland
Fretherne
Saul
Moreton Valence
Whitminster
Penallt
Milkwall
Awre
Parkend
New Mills
Clearwell
Ellwood
The Noose
Frampton on Severn
Whitecroft
Yorkley
Whitebrook
Offa's Dyke
Trow Green
Blakeney
Stonehouse
Trelleck
Bream
Gloucester & Sharpness Canal
ROMAN ROAD
St Briavels
Purton
New Grounds
Eastington
Llandogo
Lydney
Purton
Cambridge
Leonard Stanley
Tintern Parva
Hewelsfield
Sharpness
Halmore
Slimbridge
Frocester
Chapel Hill
Fort
Aylburton
Breadstone
Coaley
Lower Cam
Brockweir
Tintern Abbey
Alvington
Wanswell
Hetty Pegler's Tump
Netherend
Berkeley
The Quarry
Cam
Woolaston
Lydney Sand
Castle
Ham
Stinchcombe
Uley
Tidenham Chase
Newport
Dursley
Wynd Cliff
Boughspring
Stroat
Bevington
St Arvans
Wibdon
VALE OF BERKELEY
Tidenham
Woodcroft
RIVER SEVERN
North Nibley
Tutshill
Tidal Reservoir
Shepperdine
Hill
Stone
CHEPSTOW
Castle
Sedbury
Mounton
Rockhampton
Falfield
Tortworth
Wotton-under-Edge
Mathern
Oldbury Sands
Oldbury-on-Severn
Whitfield
Charfield
Kingswood
Tresham
Beachley
Morton
Milbury Heath
Alderley
Littleton-on-Severn
Cromhall
Severn Road Bridge
Toll
THORNBURY
Cromhall Common
Hillesley
Portskewett
Aust
Elberton
Alveston
Wickwar
Sudbrook
Severn Tunnel
Ingst
Olveston
Rudgeway
Tytherington
Hawkesbury
Northwick
Itchington
Hawkesbury Upton
English Stones
Redwick
Tockington
Rangeworthy
Severn Beach
Awkley
Horton
Pilning
Almondsbury
Latteridge
Iron Acton
Engine Common
Horton Court
Works
Easter Compton
Over
Frampton Cotterell
Nibley
CHIPPING SODBURY
Badminton
Patchway
Coalpit Heath
Yate
Old Sodbury
Hallen
Catbrain
Stoke Gifford
Winterbourne
Westerleigh
Wapley
Dodington
Acton Turville
Filton
Tormarton
M 50
M 5
M 4
A 40 (T)
A 48 (T)
A 38
A 449
A 4136
A 466
A 403
A 432
A 46
B 4224
B 4215
B 4221
B 4222
B 4227
B 4228
B 4226
B 4234
B 4431
B 4066
B 4509
B 4058
B 4060
B 4061
B 4461
B 4427
B 4057
B 4055
B 4040
B 4024
B 4071
85

TOUR 1 77 MILES

The Middle Wye and Golden Valley

This drive goes west from the historic city of Hereford through the Wye Valley to Hay-on-Wye, then turns south east through the Golden Valley at the foot of the Black Mountains and proceeds on down to Skenfrith. Then unclassified roads lead towards Ross-on-Wye, from where the tour returns to Hereford through attractive Herefordshire villages and countryside.

From Hereford *follow signs Brecon to leave by the A438. After some 10 miles there are occasional views of the Wye before reaching Letton. In 1¾ miles turn left into Willersley, then continue through Winforton and Whitney on Wye. In ½ mile turn left onto the B4350, signed Hay and cross Toll Bridge, to reach Clifford where there are the remains of an 11th-century castle. In 2 miles enter Wales and Hay-on-Wye, a market town situated beneath the Black Mountains.* This busy market town set beneath the Black Mountains is known today as a centre for second-hand books, and even over a hundred years ago Francis Kilvert walked here from Clyro to attend the annual Book Club sale at the Rose and Crown.

On reaching the Blue Boar Inn, turn left onto the Peterchurch road, B4348. Re-enter England then in 2½ miles turn right, signed Ross. The drive then enters the attractive Golden Valley to Dorstone and bears left at the church. In just over ¼ mile turn right and continue to Peterchurch. Peterchurch is the main village in the valley and has a large, well-preserved Norman church and a 14th-century hall-house, Wellbrook Manor.

Two miles farther turn right onto the B4347, signed Pontrilas, to reach Abbey Dore. The large parish church is virtually all that remains of the 12th-century Cistercian abbey – very little is left of the monastic quarters and the abbey church has lost its nave. Nonetheless it is most impressive. In the 17th century a magnificent wooden roof was made using Herefordshire oak and there is some fine stained glass.

Continue to Ewyas Harold. The remains of Ewyas Harold Castle, built in the 11th century and one of the most important castles along the Welsh border, can be seen to the west of the church.

Bear left over river bridge. In ¾ mile cross the main road and then the River Dore, then turn right signed Monmouth.

In 1½ miles bear right, cross the River Monnow into Wales and ascend to Grosmont, picturesquely situated high above the River Monnow. In the village are the ruins of the Norman castle, one of the trilateral castles originally built to guard against Welsh raids from the west.

Continue through pleasant hilly countryside and in 4¼ miles at T-junction turn left onto the B4521 signed Ross to reach Skenfrith, another attractive village containing another of the trilateral castles.

Cross the River Monnow then ascend, and in 1¾ miles at the crossroads turn right on to an unclassified road signed Welsh Newton. After 1½ miles to the left lies the 13th- to 17th-century Pembridge Castle.

On reaching the main road turn right onto the A466 into Welsh Newton. Here turn left onto an unclassified road signed Llangarren to reach the village of Llangarren. At the church bear right, signed Ross, and in 1½ miles cross main road for Glewstone. In 1 mile turn left joining the A40 to reach the Wilton roundabout, where the drive takes the third exit, B4260, to enter Ross (see page 61).

Leave by following signs Gloucester, A40. In just over ½ mile at the roundabout turn left onto the A40, signed Monmouth. Almost a mile farther at another roundabout take the third exit, A449, signed Worcester. At the next roundabout take the first exit, then in 1¾ miles branch left to join the B4224 signed Hereford. A quarter of a mile farther turn left, following a pleasant road with distant views to the left, to reach Fownhope. This prosperous village, with its position close to the Wye, was once a centre for commercial trade and for the pleasure boats of the Wye Tours. In the churchyard wall of the Norman church are preserved the village stocks and whipping post. Within the church is a 12th-century tympanum, widely held to be one of the most splendid in England.

The Wye is touched again before Mordiford where it is joined by the River Lugg. Mordiford is associated in legend with a dragon (see page 28).

At the Moon Inn bear left and cross the Lugg to Hampton Bishop. This pleasant village has a good Norman church noted for its three reredoses.

Continue back to Hereford.

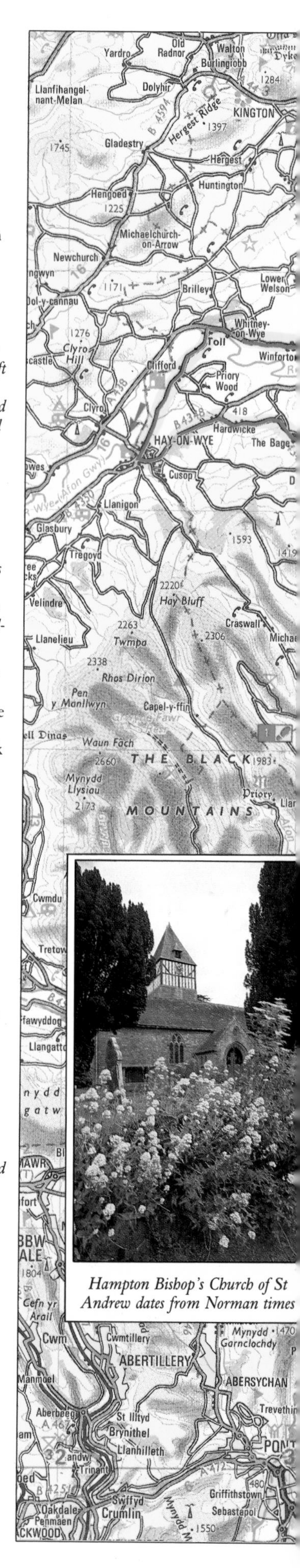

Hampton Bishop's Church of St Andrew dates from Norman times

The ruins of Grosmont Castle stand on an impressive ditched earthwork overlooking the church and village

TOUR 2 50 MILES

The Lower Wye Valley

This tour includes some of the best-known places in the area: busy Ross-on-Wye, historic Chepstow, the ancient mining centre of Clearwell and the spectacular viewpoint at Yat Rock.

The drive starts at Ross-on-Wye, an ideal tourist centre for the Wye Valley and Forest of Dean. The town is attractively situated above a bend of the Wye and from the Prospect, near the churchyard, there is a splendid view of the river and surrounding countryside.

From Ross follow signs Monmouth, A40, to leave by the B4260. Descend and cross the River Wye, then at the roundabout turn left onto the A40. There are occasional views of the river before this scenic dual carriageway main road crosses higher ground and continues past the turning to Whitchurch. From here a short detour to the left along the Symonds Yat West road, B4164, leads to the Jubilee Maze and Museum of Mazes (see page 76).

Remain on the A40 for 2½ miles and enter Wales, then rejoin the River Wye and proceed towards Monmouth. This interesting former county town contains several Tudor and Georgian buildings within a network of old streets. There are scant remains of the 12th-century castle, but the unique 13th-century fortified Monnow Bridge is still in use today. The Monmouth Museum has a collection of Nelson mementoes as well as items of local history.

Approaching the town go forward at the roundabout (for the town centre turn right). At the next traffic signals turn left on to the A466, signed Chepstow. Cross the river and bear right to enter the lower reaches of the picturesque Wye Valley. Pass through Redbrook then in 3½ miles cross Telford's Bigsweir Bridge to reach Llandogo. Continue down the valley and later pass, on the left, a picnic site and interpretation centre situated in an old railway station before entering Tintern. Beyond the village are the beautiful ruins of the 13th-century Cistercian abbey which are in a splendid setting beside the river.

An ascent is then made through pleasant woodland, and 3 miles farther a turning to the right may be taken to visit the fine viewpoint at Wyndcliff (footpath on the final approach).

Beyond St Arvans pass Chepstow Racecourse, then at the roundabout take the first exit (B4293) to enter the historic fortress town of Chepstow. The grand Norman castle, built on a spur of rock overlooking the river, has a 13th-century chapel and looks down on Chepstow's steep, medieval streets. The 16th-century town gate still survives and there are extensive remains of the town walls. Also interesting are the very fine Norman church and the local museum in Bridge Street, portraying the history of agricultural, commercial and industrial development in the area.

Turn left through the archway, then descend through the town and in the square keep left. Shortly cross the River Wye to re-enter England. Ascend and in ½ mile turn left with the B4228, signed St Briavels. Continue through undulating countryside for 7 miles to St Briavels, then branch left on an unclassified road to enter the village and pass (on the left) the restored medieval castle, now a youth hostel. Nearby the Norman church has an unusual Whit Sunday custom of giving out bread and cheese after the service (see page 63).

At the end of the village turn left at the crossroads to rejoin the B4228, signed Coleford. Two miles farther turn left onto the B4231, signed Clearwell, then in ¾ mile pass Clearwell Castle on the left, reputed to be the oldest mock castle in Britain (not open).

In Clearwell turn right at the Wyndham Arms on to an unclassified road and shortly pass the Clearwell Caves Ancient Iron Mines, which include exhibits of local mining and geology from the Forest of Dean.

In ¼ mile turn left on to the B4228 and continue to the small former mining town of Coleford. At the roundabout take the second exit, signed Ross, then in ¼ mile turn right. In just over another ½ mile cross the main road for Christchurch. Here turn left onto the Symonds Yat road, B4432. Almost 2 miles farther is the car park for Yat Rock. The AA Viewpoint on Yat Rock offers fine Wye Valley scenery where attractive woodland forms a backdrop for this great bend in the river.

Continue forward on an unclassified road (narrow in places) and descend steeply (1 in 5). Later cross the River Wye by Huntsham Bridge, then at the T-junction turn right on to the B4229 for the outskirts of Goodrich. Here bear right with the B4229. Alternatively branch left on an unclassified road to visit the 12th- to 14th-century Goodrich Castle – the ruins are on a high bluff overlooking the Wye.

After about ½ mile the main drive crosses Kerne Bridge over the River Wye for the last time. At the next T-junction turn left with the Ross road, B4228. Proceed through Walford before returning to Ross-on-Wye.

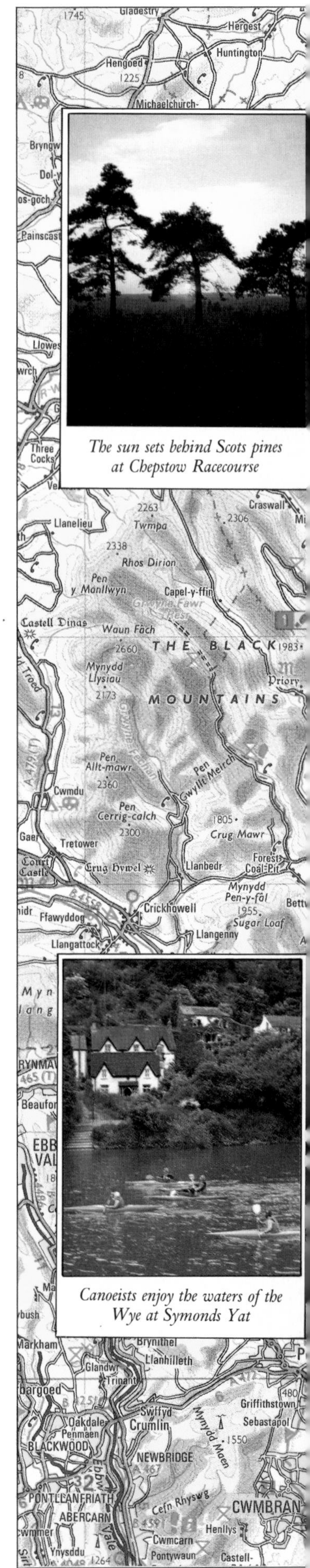

The sun sets behind Scots pines at Chepstow Racecourse

Canoeists enjoy the waters of the Wye at Symonds Yat

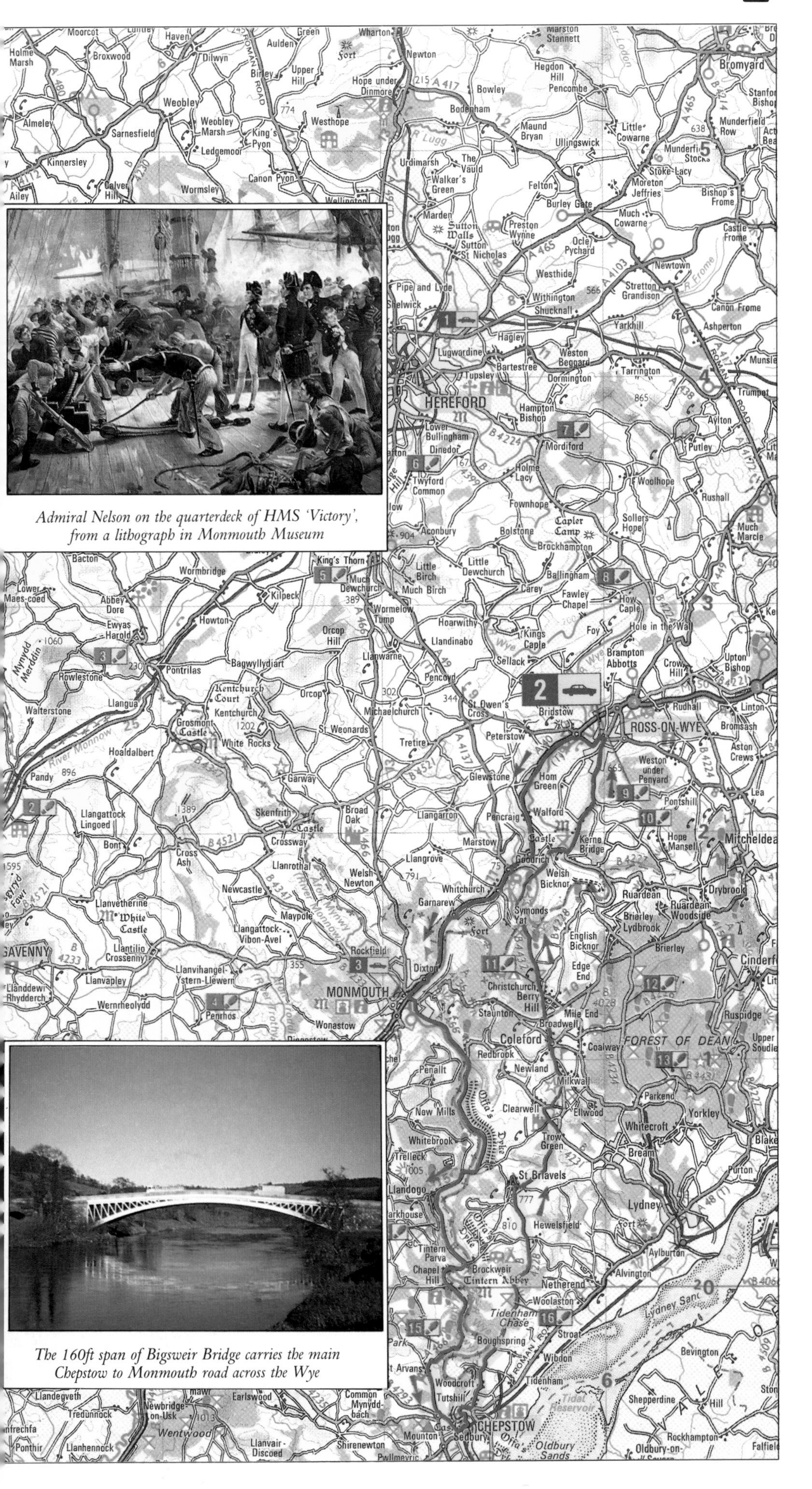

Admiral Nelson on the quarterdeck of HMS 'Victory', from a lithograph in Monmouth Museum

The 160ft span of Bigsweir Bridge carries the main Chepstow to Monmouth road across the Wye

TOUR 3 40 MILES

In the Heart of the Forest

This interesting drive into the Forest of Dean offers an insight into the forest of the past – the ancient mines at Clearwell, the Speech House with its Verderers' Court, the fascinating Dean Heritage Museum near Soudley and the historic Littledean Hall and Flaxley Abbey. The forest scenery of the tour is varied and contrasted by river views of the Wye and Severn.

The drive starts at Monmouth. *Follow Chepstow signs to leave by the A466, cross the River Wye, then bear right and follow the river to Redbrook. At the Bush Inn turn left on to the B4231, signed Lydney. Beyond the village enter England and continue through hilly countryside to Newland.* This attractive village on the edge of the Forest of Dean is noted for its fine 13th- to 14th-century church – known as the 'Cathedral of the Forest' – but it can also delight in its Stuart and Georgian houses, its 17th-century almhouses and the original Bell's Grammar School.

Remain on the B4231 to Clearwell where, at the Wyndham Arms, go forward on to an unclassified road. Shortly to the right are the Clearwell Caves Ancient Iron Mines which include exhibits of local mining and geology from the Forest of Dean area. During the summer months, visitors may enter the mines and go underground to a depth of 100ft.

In almost ½ mile cross the main road then in ¼ mile turn right, signed Ellwood. Take the next turning right and ½ mile farther at the crossroads turn left, signed Parkend. In almost another ½ mile join the B4431 and proceed through woodland to Parkend. To the right along the Lydney road, B4234, is the northern terminus of the Dean Forest Railway.

Continue along the Blakeney road, B4431. Then in 1¼ miles turn left on to an unclassified road, signed Speech House. A fine run is then made through more forest scenery, passing several picnic sites, before reaching the Speech House Hotel. This 17th-century building still preserves the court room of the Forest Verderers.

Turn right with the Cinderford road B4226, passing an arboretum, and continue through the forest. Two miles farther the drive reaches the outskirts of Cinderford. From here a diversion to the right along the B4227 Blakeney road leads through Ruspidge to Lower Soudley. Nearby is the interesting Dean Heritage Museum and Craft Centre.

The main drive continues forward and ascends to skirt the town of Cinderford. Later turn right on to the A4151 (signed Gloucester) then descend to Littledean. At the T-junction turn right with the unclassified Newnham road and shortly pass Littledean Hall. This historic manor house depicts the evolution of a manorial hall from the early Norman period. Other points of interest in Littledean include the gaol, a motte-and-bailey, some lovely houses, a good church and the former pin, nail and glove-making industries. In late summer the Forest 'ship badgers' gather here for the annual sheep sales.

There follows a long descent with views across the River Severn to the distant Cotswold Hills. At Newnham on Severn turn left on to the Gloucester road, A48. The River Severn is then followed for a short distance to Broadoak. One mile farther turn left on an unclassified road, signed Mitcheldean, and proceed along a pleasant by-road to Flaxley. Behind the church is Flaxley Abbey, founded in the 12th century by Cistercian monks who both farmed in the valley and smelted and forged iron. Additions were made to the abbey in Georgian times.

In a mile bear right and continue to the outskirts of Mitcheldean. Here turn left on to the Monmouth road, A4136, and ascend. This undulating main road is followed for the next 9 miles to reach Staunton. Although it generally passes through attractive scenery along the northern extremity of the Forest of Dean, there is occasional evidence of old mine workings and quarries in places. The village of Staunton is pleasantly situated beneath Highmeadow Woods and the fine church dates from Norman times.

A long descent is then made through beautiful wooded countryside, and after 3 miles a worthwhile detour to the left can be taken along a side road to Kymin Hill. From this 800ft National Trust property there are good views over the Wye and Monnow valleys. Near the summit there is a 'naval temple' built in 1800 to commemorate British naval heroes.

Continue the descent, and at the foot turn right on to the A466 for the return to Monmouth.

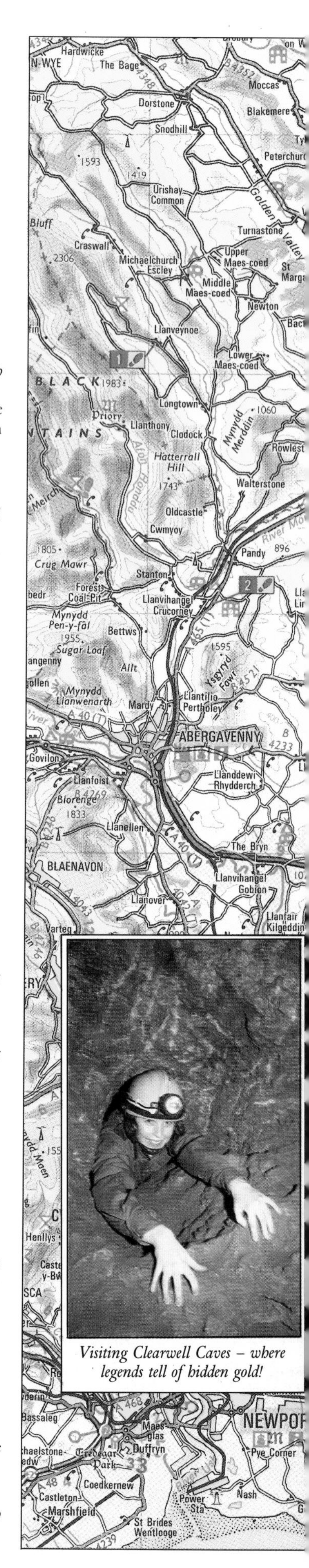

Visiting Clearwell Caves – where legends tell of hidden gold!

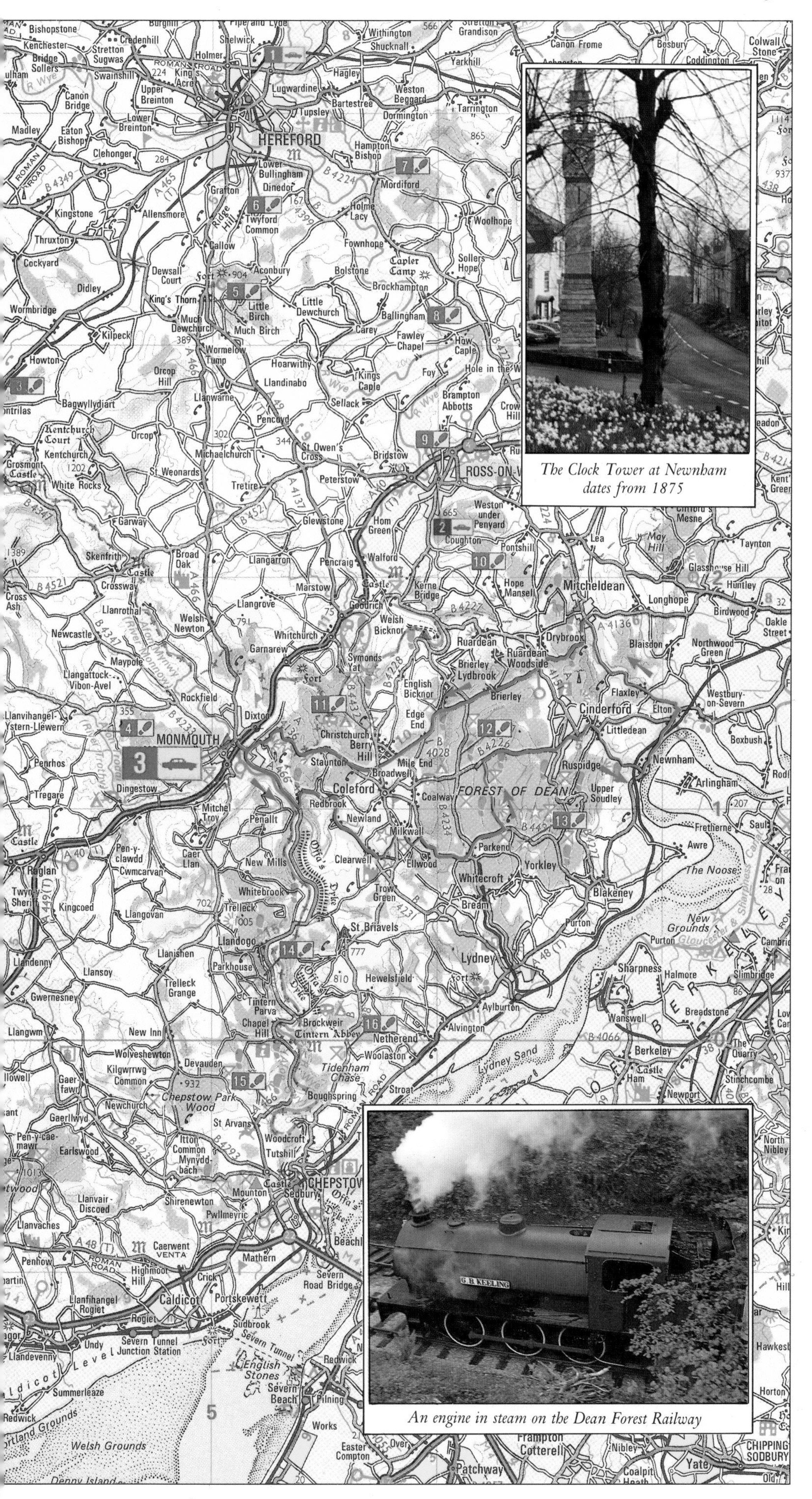

The Clock Tower at Newnham dates from 1875

An engine in steam on the Dean Forest Railway

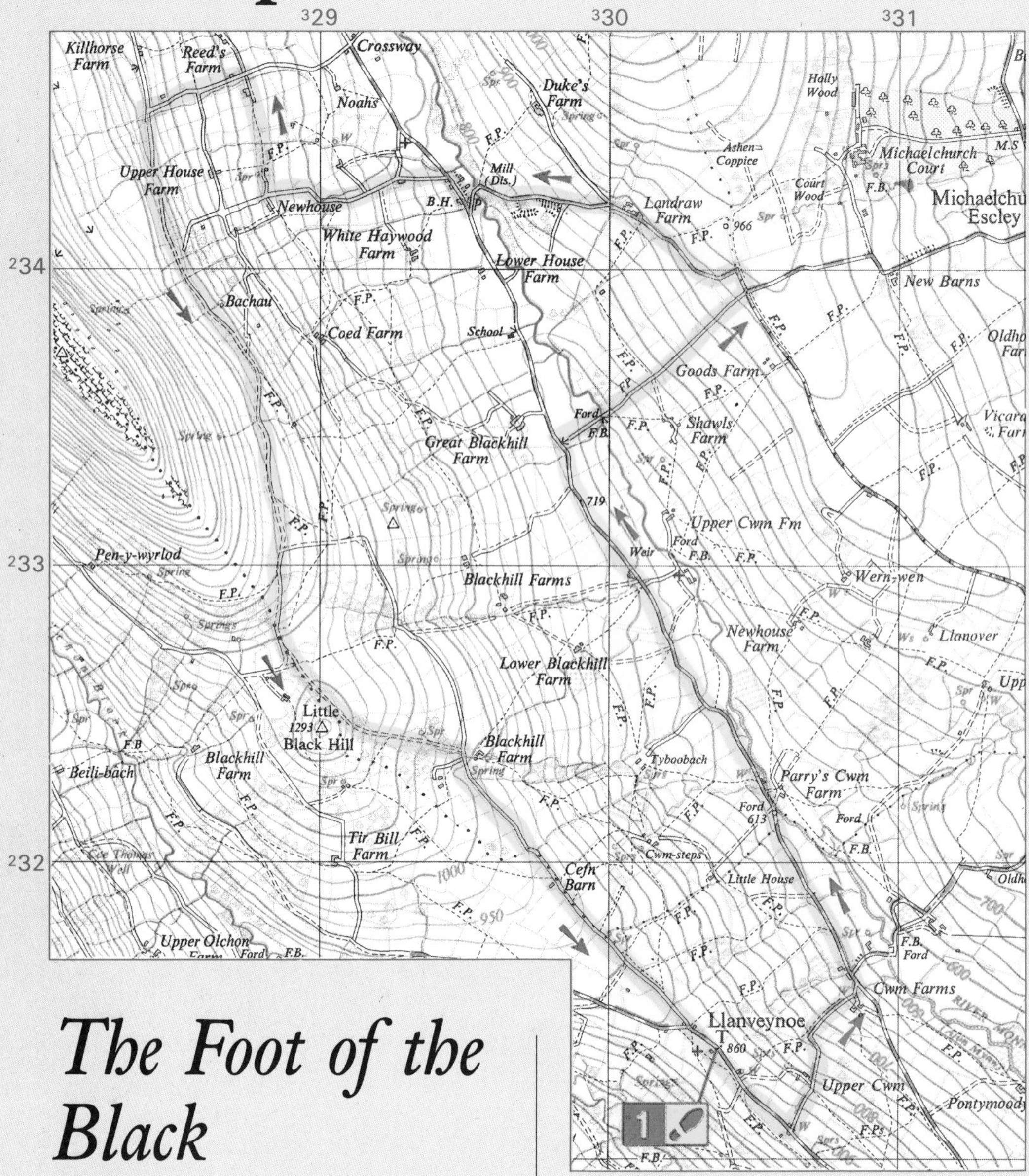

The Foot of the Black Mountains

Allow 3½ hours

This is a delightful but demanding walk suitable for more experienced ramblers. The route crosses the panoramic foothills of the Black Mountains, where trickling streams run through sheltered fertile valleys. From the hamlet of Llanveynoe quiet lanes and tracks lead to the slopes of Black Hill, offering stunning views.

Park beside a telephone box opposite the small stone church at Llanveynoe (SO304314). From here walk southwards and at a recently restored cottage turn left. This lane winds steeply down to join the Crasswall road. Follow this to the left for about a mile alongside the River Monnow. In 500yd, after passing the sign to Blackhill Farm, leave the road and follow a green lane on the right leading to a picturesque footbridge crossing the Monnow. This pretty stream forms the upper reaches of the Monnow, which rises at Crasswall.

After crossing the footbridge, continue ahead to a T-junction. Here turn left to Crasswall. Cross the stone bridge and at the junction turn right. Within 100yd, beyond Rose Cottage, turn left following an unsigned but well-defined bridleway. This becomes rocky underfoot as it climbs uphill.

By a derelict barn at New House turn right through a gate keeping left of stone farm buildings. The right of way continues ahead through open fields crossing two tricky stone slab stiles, keeping right of the hill farm before meeting a metalled lane which is followed to the left. A short climb leads to a T-junction where a well-used bridleway is followed to the left. After passing through a gate the open mountainside is reached, and the route continues for at least a mile along this scenic stretch. Black Hill, known locally as the 'Cat's Back' stands at over 2,000ft. It forms part of the Black Mountains range along the Welsh borders.

From a small picnic site a rocky route follows the ridge to join Offa's Dyke Path at Hay Bluff. At the picnic site follow the tarmac lane, but before it bears right turn left to follow the right of way straight across unfenced rough pastures. Cross the right-hand gate and walk diagonally right across a patch of waste land covered with fallen trees. Reaching an open field, follow the fence on the right to a gap where an irregular track leads downhill through rough wooded pastures. It crosses a brook to reach a gate leading onto a rocky path. Turn right and immediately go through another gate leading onto an unclassified road which descends to the church at Llanveynoe.

Heart of the Borders

Allow 3 hours

From this busy Welsh borderland village an invigorating walk leads high above Crucorney along a section of Offa's Dyke Path, with commanding views of the Black Mountains. Narrow lanes and hilly paths then lead beside the pretty Honddu River, where there is a splendid variety of flowers in spring.

Park in the side road beside the letter box (SO327207) at the northern end of Llanfihangel Crucorney. From here cross the busy A465 and climb over the stile ahead, where the right of way goes diagonally left across the orchard towards a whitewashed cottage. Left of the cottage cross two footbridges before reaching a tarmac lane. Turn right here and ascend past Llanteens Cottage and farm buildings at Whitehouse. After 600yd turn left to follow the clearly waymarked Offa's Dyke Path descending sloping pastures, with remarkable views of Skirrid Fawr and Hatterrall Hill. The Skirrid is easily recognised by its unusual outline caused by a massive landslide at the time of the Crucifixion, hence its other name of Holy Mountain.

Continue following the Dyke Path across the A465, over the River Honddu and the railway track. Beyond Treedw Farm bear right across a hilly field to rejoin a lane beside a stone barn. Here proceed right, past the entrance to Little Llwygy. At the next crossroads turn left. Pass barns and buildings on the right, and within 200yd follow an unsigned footpath on the left through a gate. Keep to the right side of the fields crossing old stone and timber stiles. On reaching a gate in the right corner turn sharp left heading for the bridge at Pont Rhys Powell. During the early months of the year, primroses, bluebells, stitchwort, violets, vetches and forget-me-nots line the wayside banks. Beside the water courses, eye-catching marsh marigolds glow above abundant beds of watercress.

Do not cross the stile on to the lane, but turn left along the banks of the Honddu to a stile and footbridge over a brook. Keep ahead across the next field to a coppice, where another footbridge followed by a stile leads back to the riverside. Follow the banks of the river until reaching a footbridge, here bear left to the cottage and join a woodland path. On reaching fields the footpath keeps to the right hedge until reaching a gate. Here bear slightly left across a field towards the farm at Llwygy. Turn right through the yard towards the house.

Before reaching the farmhouse turn right through a gate on the right. The undefined path descends through fields and over stiles to the railway track. Turn right over a stile then across the railway lines on the left. The path continues along the right hand side of the next meadow to the road. Turn right, cross a stone bridge, then turn left, and left again to return to the car.

The sweet violet, with its white or blue flower, is seen in woodland and hedges

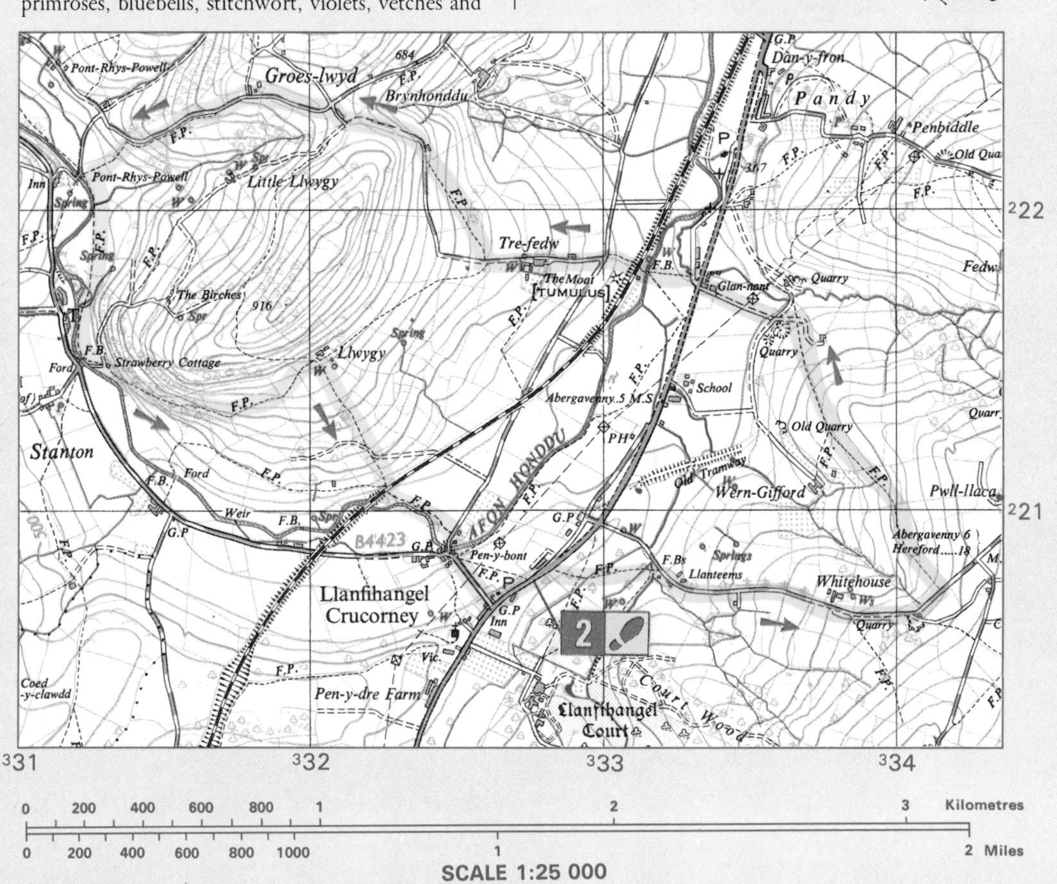

WALK 3

Beside Dulas Brook

Allow 2 hours

A short bracing walk in the peaceful Golden Valley, with ample time to view the lively village of Ewyas Harold and browse around its ancient church. A steep climb to the common is rewarded with fine views of the Dulas and Dore Valleys with the towering Black Mountains in the distance. After a pleasant amble across the common a field path leads to the road where a glimpse of the castle remains may be savoured.

The walk starts from Ewyas Harold church (SO388288). After parking in the village head towards the Church of St Michael. Ewyas Harold church is set prettily beside the banks of the Dulas Brook. Its massive 13th-century tower was formerly detached – a feature of Welsh Border churches.

Walk across the churchyard, through an iron swing gate, then turn right along a tarmac lane. Turn left at the junction where this lane passes Downs House and steeply ascends to Ewyas Harold Common. The bracken and grass-covered common rises to over 500ft.

Immediately after crossing a cattle grid turn right up a steep track, and at a cottage bear left towards a brick-built house called New Holme. From here continue ahead keeping left of the corrugated barn to join a muddy path enclosed by hedges leading onto open commonland, before passing The Barn, a cottage on the right. Here fork left along a concrete track leading to a small modern farm building. Turn sharp left, gently climbing a grassy path. At the top turn left to follow a wide grass-covered path, keeping left of a clump of young trees, each protected by a high fence. Within 100yd turn right, heading west along a pleasant downhill path. Cross a main track and keep right of an old barn before a steeper descent leads to a stile ahead, beside the entrance to a cottage called Weaver's Place.

Cross the stile and follow an undefined field path across the meadow towards a gate, where the path crosses the Dulas Brook over a footbridge. Continue straight across the next field to a stile leading onto the road. Turn left heading back to the village. On the way do not miss a rickety stile on the right where a public footpath leads to the site of Ewyas Harold's castle. This tree-covered mound is the only remaining evidence of a pre-Conquest castle, rebuilt by William Osbern before Domesday. It was one of the most important castles along the Welsh Borders.

Return to the road, which soon re-enters Ewyas Harold.

Britain's most common bird of prey, the buzzard soars in wide circles over forest woodland

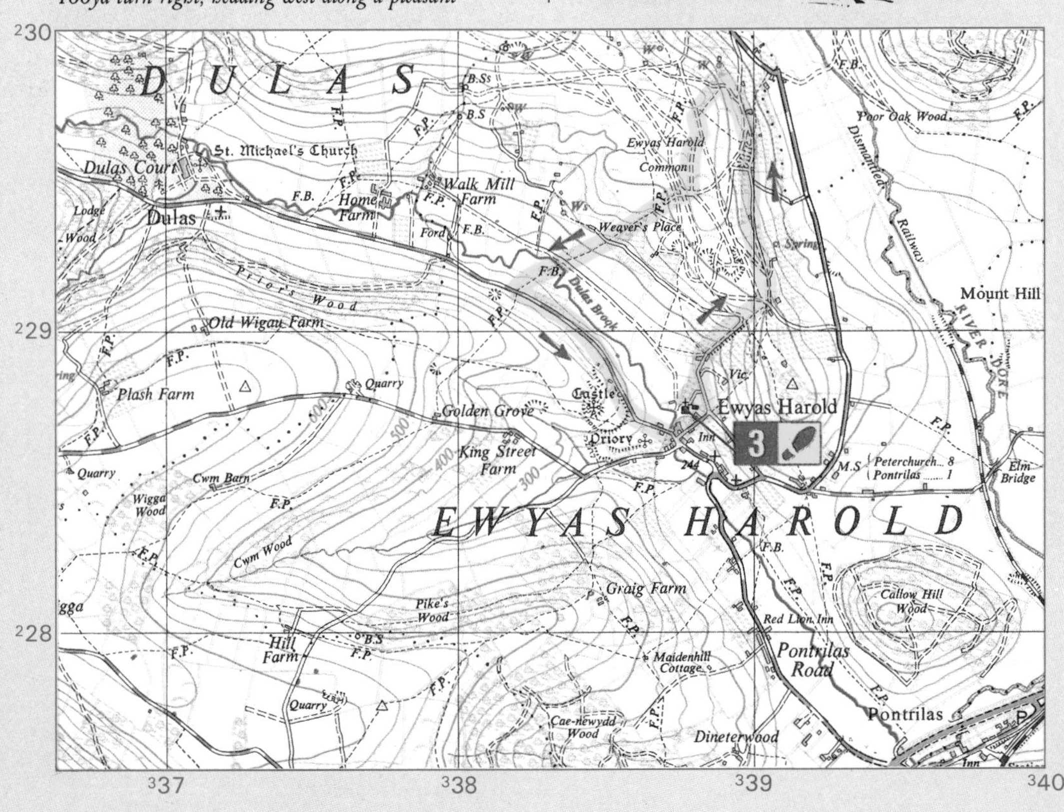

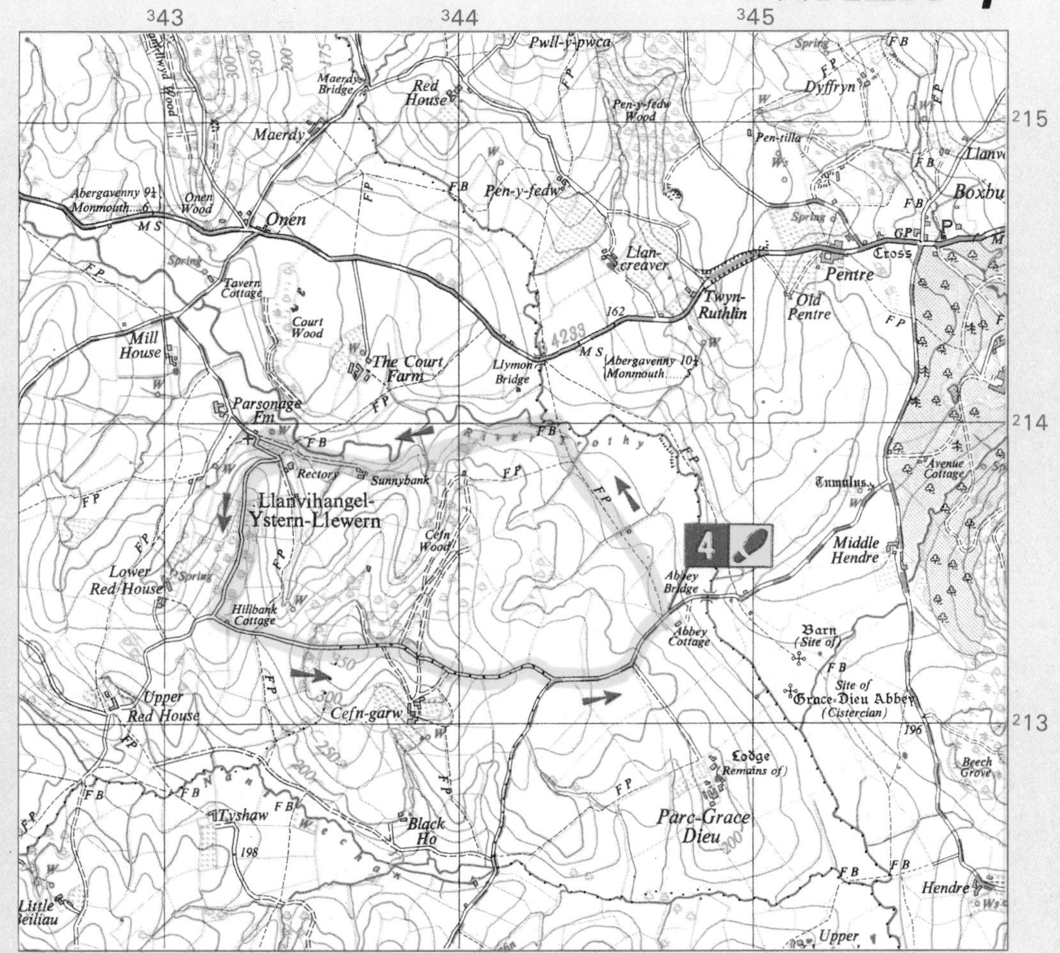

Along Offa's Dyke

Allow 1½ hours

This attractive short walk follows Offa's Dyke Path along the banks of the River Trothy to the pretty, remote parish church at Llanvihangel-Ystern-Llewern. The return route is via hilly lanes surrounded by the rolling country of the Welsh Borders.

The walk starts near Abbey Bridge, about 5 miles west of Monmouth. There is limited verge-side parking beside an Offa's Dyke Path finger post (SO447134). Opposite Abbey Cottage the waymarked Dyke Path leads across fields to the left of a corrugated barn and proceeds through a meadow to a footbridge over a small tributary of the Trothy. Here turn right over a stile, then bear left to walk alongside the delightful alder-lined River Trothy. The Trothy drains the lovely countryside between Monmouth and Abergavenny and enters the Wye a mile below the bridge at Monmouth. A few of its numerous bridges date from the end of the 18th century, which probably includes the neat stone structure at Abbey Bridge, named after the nearby site of Grace Dieu Abbey founded by the Cistercians in the 12th century.

The path continues through riverside meadows which provide ideal sheltered pastures for sheep. After passing the whitewashed farm called Sunnybank, the waymarked route follows the track to a tarmac lane, which proceeds straight ahead. Soon another Offa's Dyke Path finger post directs the way right around the isolated church at Llanvihangel-Ystern-Llewern. Here leave the path by bearing left through the churchyard. This medieval stone-built church with its tiny turret and timbered porch stands on rising ground amid rows of lichen-covered tombstones. The church is reputed to have been founded by Ynyr, a king of Gwent, at a place on firm ground after he had been wandering about in the misty marshes.

Leave the graveyard by the other gate, and turn right to follow a quiet lane steeply climbing around a hairpin bend. The views improve while climbing; isolated farmsteads dot undulating Welsh countryside surrounded by tree-topped hills.

A pleasant oak- and beech-covered ridge leads to a crossways. Turn left here towards Hendre, following a switchback lane for ¾ mile. At a T-junction keep left where a downhill slope leads back to Abbey Bridge.

Sheep vary according to terrain – small, active breeds are found on hilly land with poor pasture

0 200 400 600 800 1 2 3 Kilometres

0 200 400 600 800 1000 1 2 Miles

SCALE 1:25 000

WALK 5

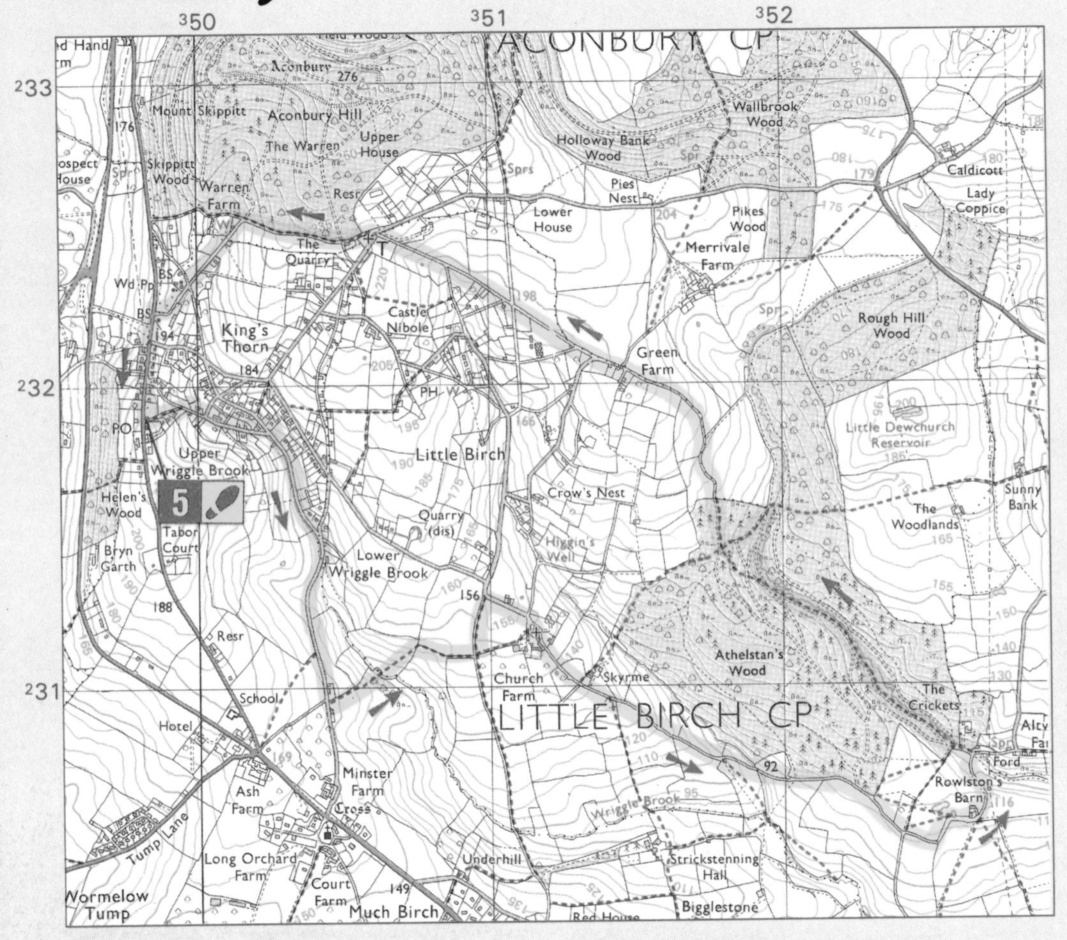

Hills and Woods of Little Birch

Allow 3 hours

Six miles south of Hereford lies the scattered parish of Little Birch, where a maze of lanes and paths lead from the wooded slopes of Aconbury to the thick plantations of Athelstan's Wood. This pleasant ramble from the quiet village of King's Thorne, now bypassed by the main road, includes varied, undulating countryside and shady streams.

The starting point is the post office at King's Thorne (SO498319) – there is car parking by the roadside. North of the post office and General Stores turn right along Aconbury Close where a signed footpath leads down steps to join a rough track to the right. This leads onto a tarmac lane and a right turn is made at a T-junction. The lane is followed for a further 500yd from Wriggle Brook Cottage.

Beyond the next stone-built cottage turn left, go through a gate and follow the signed path across a meadow to a wooden bridge over the Wriggle Brook. Continue ahead where the right of way climbs steeply to the top of the field. Turn right through the gate and continue ahead to another gate leading onto an enclosed track. This turns left at the crossways to meet a tarmac lane, which is followed to the right past Little Birch church. Dedicated to St Mary, this church was rebuilt in 1869 at a cost of £3,500, paid by a long-serving rector of the parish. Built in the Geometric style, with a bellcote and polygonal apse, it contains a tall wrought-iron screen of about 1870. Near the church is a large area of mixed woodland, Athelstan's Wood, managed by the Economic Forestry Commission.

After passing the church and the Old Rectory, the lane becomes a rough track which proceeds between woods and open farmland for about a mile. Beyond the woods turn left at a T-junction onto a partly metalled lane which winds past Rowlston's Barn before descending to another brook. Do not cross the bridge, but bear left passing an isolated cottage called the Crickets, and follow the path alongside the left bank of the stream through Athelstan's Wood.

Within a mile, at the outskirts of the woods, the route turns sharp left climbing gently to a larch plantation. Turn right along a narrower path and out of the woods. Cross an iron hurdle and follow a green lane which passes Green Farm before continuing through Little Birch to join the road at the Methodist Chapel. This was founded in 1834 and rebuilt in 1858 and displays the typically arched windows of the early 19th century. Aconbury Hill, standing at 904ft, is the site of an Iron Age hillfort. The single rampart of Aconbury Camp encloses an area of 17½ acres, and excavations have revealed Iron Age and Romano-British pottery.

Cross the road and alongside the chapel follow a well-defined path on the left below the wooded slopes of Aconbury Hill. Take the next track left past Warren Farm and descend to the road. Turn left along the road and return to the post office.

Atop Dinedor Hill

Allow 2½ hours

From the outskirts of Hereford city this attractive walk follows lanes and field paths to the Victorian church at Bullinghope. The highest point is the wooded hillfort of Dinedor, approached by a sharp climb before returning by a gentle downhill path which joins a tarmac road leading back to the car.

This walk starts from a lay-by on the south side of a railway bridge (SO517378) spanning Lower Bullingham Lane. Walk south along the narrow lane which shortly joins the Hoarwithy road at Green Crize. Cross this road and follow the signed footpath ahead which crosses fields and Norton Brook before reaching the farmyard at Bullinghope Court. Continue through the farmyard on to a lane at Bullinghope which is followed to the left. The ancient parish of Bullinghope is a pretty place. St Peter's, designed by F R Kempson, was built in the Early English style in 1880 at a cost of £2,000, replacing a ruined Norman church. The remains of this earlier building can be seen in a nearby garden belonging to The Cedars.

About 100yd before reaching the church, turn left over a solid stile to the left of a black and white cottage. A well-used and clearly-defined footpath leads through fields, and re-crosses the Norton Brook to join a tarmac lane beside some houses. Turn left along the lane to a road which is then crossed. A signed right of way is followed over a stile, through a small paddock and across the Red Brook. In the next field the path steeply ascends the slopes of Dinedor Hill. From the next stile the walk offers scenic views.

Cross an unmade track where a worn but unsigned narrow right of way bears slightly left uphill through woodland. At a tarmac lane turn left, then right within 50yd to reach the summit of the hill. Dinedor Hill, formerly known as Oyster Hill, is the site of an Iron Age camp occupied between 300BC and AD100. The ramparts enclosing an area of 12 acres and rising to nearly 600ft are now covered by fine, mature beech trees. The city of Hereford, Aconbury Hill, the Black Mountains and the Malverns can all be seen from this attractive elevated site.

Retrace the way back from the hill camp and continue along the lane which soon becomes an unmade track passing several isolated cottages. After the sign 'Unsuitable for Motorists' it gradually descends through woods. At a modern house follow a tarmac lane to the left leaving the slopes of Dinedor Hill. After ½ mile or so the walk comes to the railway bridge then Lower Bullingham Lane. Turn left back to the lay-by.

Hereford Cathedral stands prominent in this old engraving of the city and its environs

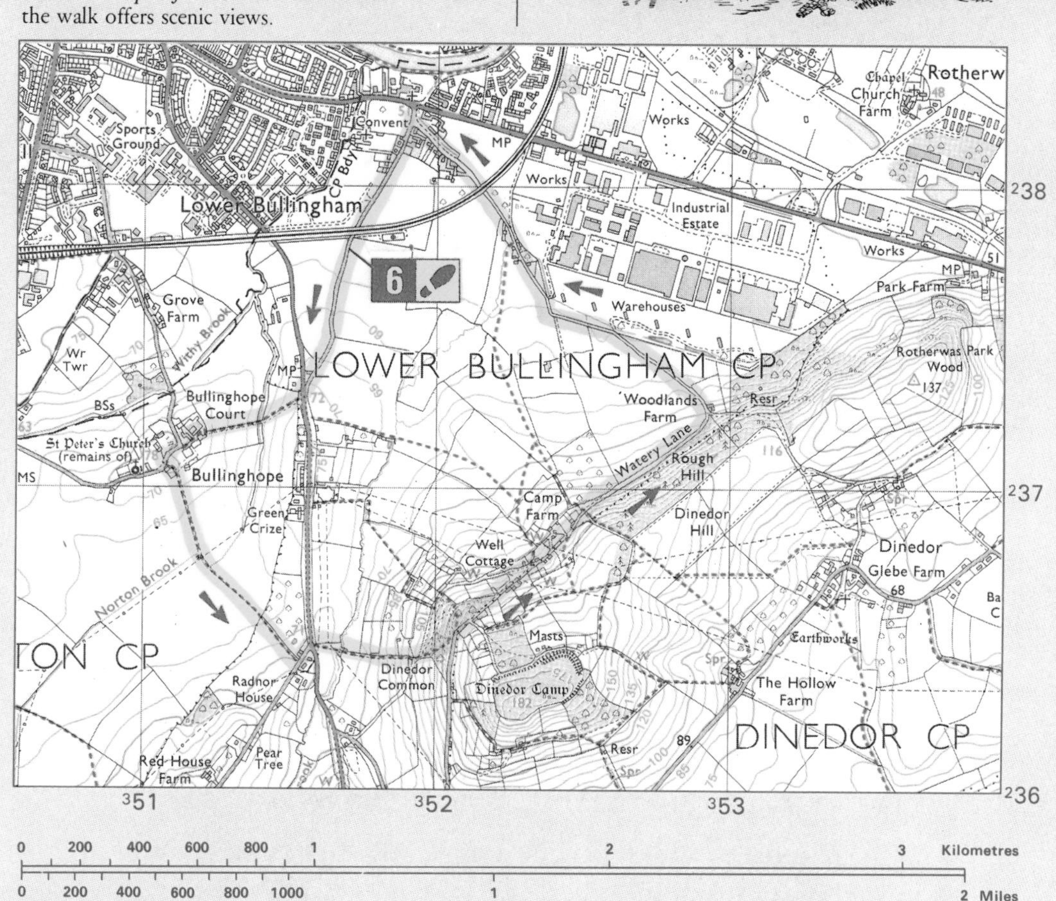

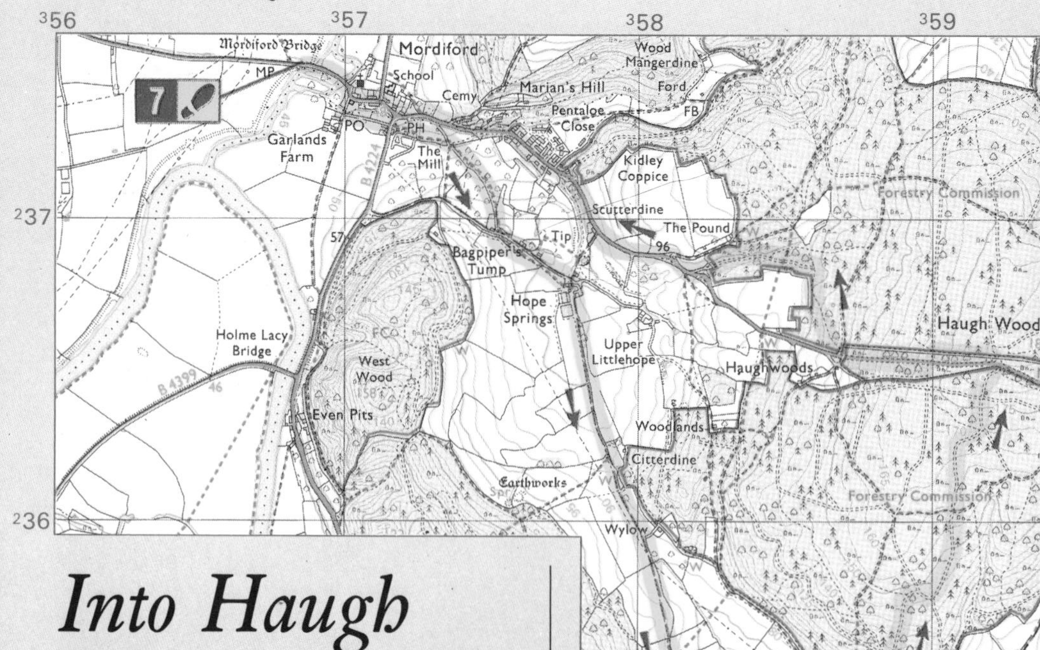

Into Haugh Wood

Allow 3 hours

From the attractive Herefordshire village of Mordiford, lying on the banks of the River Lugg, this ramble follows an easy section of the Wye Valley Walk before climbing the wooded slopes of Haugh Wood. Enjoy views of the surrounding hills before returning through the village via the church path.

Parking is available at the western end of Mordiford Bridge (SO569375). Follow the yellow arrows of the Wye Valley Walk across the ancient bridge leading to Mordiford. Turn immediately right along a track which bears left to cross the road, then leads through the yard of an old mill and continues through pleasant orchards to Bagpiper's Tump. Mordiford's stone bridge, dating back to the 14th century, was built to carry the Hereford to Gloucester road over the swiftly flowing Lugg.

From Bagpiper's Tump a lane is followed before bearing right and passing the farm at Hope Springs. The Wye Valley Walk continues along a well defined bridleway through fields to join the road near Nupend Farm. Turn left along the quiet road, leaving the route of the Wye Valley Walk. At Rudge End investigate the Tom Spring Memorial, indicated by a sign on the right. Tom Spring was born at Rudge End in 1795, and apart from serving as the landlord at a local Fownhope inn, he fought as a bare fist prize fighter, becoming Champion of England in 1823. After his death in 1851, his fellow 'countrymen of the land of cider' erected this apt memorial.

Return to the road and beyond Hill View Cottage turn left to follow a track, steeply ascending Haugh Wood. Take the left fork, then bear right to enter the woods by a barrier where the stony track climbs to a junction beside thick spruce plantations. Here turn right following a wide winding track which reaches a road opposite the Haugh Wood car park and picnic site. The name Haugh is pronounced 'Hoff', and is derived from a Saxon name. This mixed woodland is now managed by the Forestry Commission. A small herd of fallow deer live in these woods together with squirrels, voles, mice and a wide variety of bird and plant life.

Cross the road to the picnic site, but turn immediately left along a narrow woodland path running parallel to the road. At a forest track turn left to join the road which is followed to the right. At the next entrance into Haugh Wood on the right follow a path leading diagonally left through the deep conifer forest. At the outskirts of the wood keep left where the path follows the banks of a brook to a gate leading onto the road. Here turn right. There is delightful scenery as one drops into Mordiford with its inn, school and 13th-century church.

In the village turn right then left to return to the bridge via the churchyard.

Fallow deer, which can be seen in Haugh Wood, are thought to have been introduced into Britain by the Romans

Bow-hauliers, with their flat-bottomed trow, on the Wye near Monmouth in about 1790

The Rural Wye

Allow 2 hours

A lovely walk through beautiful unspoiled countryside between Ross-on-Wye and Hereford. There is ample opportunity to admire far-reaching views from the slopes of Capler Camp before visiting one of the prettiest churches in Herefordshire at Brockhampton. After crossing a delightful valley, the familiar arrows of the Wye Valley Walk lead back along well-defined tracks above the Wye.

Start the walk from a small scenic parking site (SO591324) opposite Capler Lodge on a minor road at Brockhampton, a mile south of Fownhope. Stop and admire this tremendous view of the meandering River Wye, cross the road and follow an unsigned footpath starting from the field gate to the right of Capler Lodge. Capler Camp, which can be seen on the left, is an Iron Age hillfort standing at just under 600ft. At this oval site of 10¼ acres, enclosed by double ramparts, Roman coins and traces of medieval buildings were discovered during the 1920s. From its slopes the panoramic views of the surrounding hills can be enjoyed.

Keep straight ahead close to the right hand hedge. Cross a dividing fence, then a makeshift stile, and turn almost immediately sharp right to cross a rickety stile beside a gate. From here the right of way continues diagonally right over a stile in the hedge and across the next field to a hurdle beside a house and barn at Brand Oak. Follow the track to the road and turn right to inspect the pretty thatched church at Brockhampton. All Saints was built in 1902 in a mixture of architectural styles, and replaces an earlier medieval church whose ruins can be seen in the grounds of Brockhampton Court. Inside, the theme is wild flowers; they are carved on the choir stalls as well as embroidered on altar cloths and hymn book covers.

Opposite All Saints follow another unsigned path through a wooden gate and straight across a delightful valley of sloping pastures. The ruins of the old church can be seen in a clump of evergreens beside Brockhampton Court.

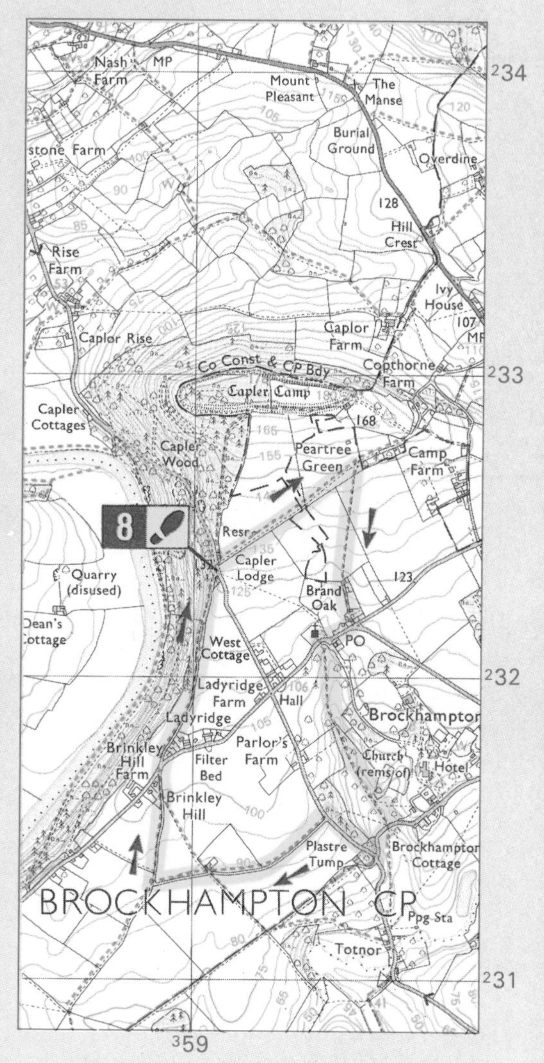

At a tarmac lane turn right then right again at the junction. A short road section of the Wye Valley Walk has now been joined; follow it for 200yd before turning left along a pleasant track which eventually bears right through a field and along another track leading to houses at Brinkley Hill. Cross the road and follow the well-defined track passing the old school and several cottages. A gap in the trees reveals a superb view of fertile farmland and the River Wye far below.

A short climb leads back to the parking site.

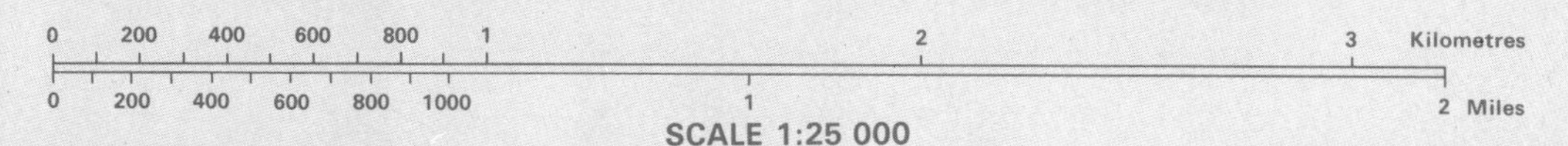

SCALE 1:25 000

WALK 9
Around Ross

Allow 3½ hours

From the historic market town of Ross-on-Wye the walk follows the banks of the Rudhall Brook to Rudhall where country lanes lead through Kingstone and on to Weston-under-Penyard. From here a steep climb up the wooded slopes of Penyard Hill offers splendid views of Ross and the surrounding hills.

Start from the public car park at Mill Pond Street (SO601244) in Ross-on-Wye. Turn left out of the car park and left again on to the footpath. Continue alongside a dismantled railway track and the narrow Small Brook. Cross the footbridge and turn left along a lane passing a short stretch of industrial Ross. Keep straight ahead where the right of way crosses a stile through low-lying fields until reaching steps up and over a new relief road. (This new road is not shown on the map.)

Proceed immediately over a step stile and alongside the Rudhall Brook, lined with alders and willows, and watch mallards enjoy this quiet backwater. Cross the solid bridge over the brook where the path keeps to the right of a drainage ditch, soon crossed by a bridge on the left. Walk diagonally right across the field to join a farm track leading to the road at Rudhall. Rudhall House lies in a hollow partly hidden by trees and a high stone wall. It dates from the 14th century, with more recent additions producing a pleasing mixture of architectural styles.

From Rudhall turn right along the road, which continues for 1½ miles following road signs to Weston-under-Penyard. The road leads past interesting buildings, including a mock 18th-century castle at Bollitree.

Beside the inn at Weston-under-Penyard cross the main Ross to Gloucester road and follow the lane ahead towards St Lawrence's Church. The lane becomes an unmade track winding its way up Penyard Hill between thick conifer plantations before reaching Lawns Farm. Continue past the farm, through a meadow to a stile in the right-hand hedge. Before crossing, glance back to admire the superb views and catch a glimpse of the scanty remains of Penyard Castle. This 14th-century castle was probably built as a hunting lodge, but by the 1600s it was in ruins and a house was built on the site.

Follow the narrow footpath skirting the woods of Penyard Park. At a forest track turn right till a stile is reached on the left. Cross a field to a solitary oak where the route of the Wye Valley Walk is met. Follow the yellow arrows right through more woods and down across a sloping meadow to a kissing gate. Go on to the outskirts of Ross and Alton Court. The lane leads to Alton Road. Turn right to a turning on the left called Waterside which leads to Gloucester Road. Cross and continue ahead along Smallbrook Road to a mini roundabout. From here retrace the route back to the car park along the signed footpath.

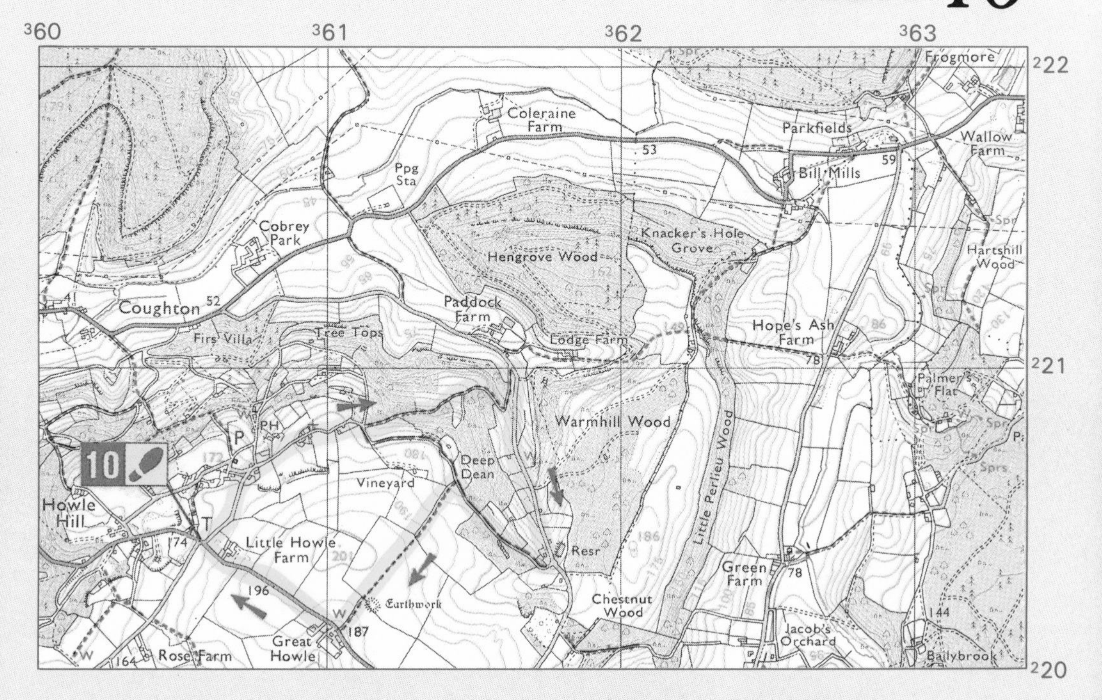

Across the Hills of Dean

Allow 2 hours

This short hilly ramble explores the delightful countryside south of Ross-on-Wye. From the elevated hamlet at Howle Hill quiet lanes, footpaths and bridleways lead across wooded hills offering sweeping views as well as sites to interest the local historian.

The walk starts from the telephone box at Howle Hill (SO606204) where there is limited parking. From the crossroads follow the tarmac lane to Howle church, passing several dwellings, including the Crown Inn, before reaching a small stone-built church. St John's was built as a 'chapel of ease' just over 100 years ago, and was paid for by a lady living in this parish of Walford. The Crown Inn dates back to 1857 when it was called Kiln Cottage, suggesting its connection with either lime-burning or brick making. Remains of these local industries can be clearly identified on this hill, where a network of deep sunken lanes connect lime-kilns, pits and quarries.

Just past the entrance to a house called Wooleys, the lane bears right. Continue ahead here to the road at Deep Dean. During the 18th century this was known as Dib Dean, where a turnpike road from Ross terminated. The original route across Chase and Penyard Hills became so difficult and inconvenient for wheeled traffic that it was abandoned in 1791 and replaced by an easier route through the Coughton Valley.

Turn right along the road where a few scattered cottages add to the charm of this pretty wooded valley. Shortly after passing Deep Dean Cottage, opposite a small reservoir, turn sharp right to follow a signed bridleway leading steeply up an attractive lane. As it levels off there are far-reaching views of Deep Dean and the surrounding hills.

Before reaching the next building be careful not to miss a stile on the left. Here the footpath leads straight across fields and over stiles to the right of a wooded earthwork at Great Howle. The Iron Age camp is a rectangular enclosure with ramparts covering quite a small area for a hillfort. It stands in a commanding position at over 600ft.

From here follow the right of way which continues ahead alongside the right-hand hedge. The road is met at a gate opposite Great Howle Farm. Here turn right to the crossroads at Howle Hill.

Increased industrialisation in the 17th century necessitated a better road system for transportation

0 200 400 600 800 1 2 3 Kilometres

0 200 400 600 800 1000 1 2 Miles

SCALE 1:25 000

WALK 11

Ready Penny

Allow 3 hours

This is an energetic walk through the beautiful Forest of Dean, combining woodland and riverside paths which wind through the scenic Wye gorge and up to the famous viewpoint at Symonds Yat Rock. The route is easily followed on waymarked forest trails and a section of the Wye Valley Walk, but there are a number of steep climbs and descents. Marvellous views and a rich variety of wildlife make this a very worthwhile and enjoyable walk.

Start at the small picnic site at Ready Penny (SO568132), near the village of Christchurch in the Forest of Dean. Follow the track on the right leading to a 'no through road'. Observe the first of the yellow arrows indicating a route through Highmeadow Woods. A narrow path shortly leads down to a wider track where the path follows a stone sign to Buckstone along a majestic avenue of trees. Highmeadow Woods, owned by the Forestry Commission, covers 3,500 acres between Symonds Yat, Monmouth and Coleford. At least 20 different types of tree can be identified, and this encourages a variety of wildlife. Fallow deer are common and can be seen at dawn or dusk.

Before reaching the road at Bracelands turn sharp right and follow a white-arrowed path which gradually descends between conifer and oak plantations. It becomes steeper and rockier before reaching a swift-flowing brook, the banks of which are now followed down to the River Wye at a superb site called the Biblins. The Biblins, situated below steep cliffs called the Slaughter, is an outcrop of conglomerate rock known as pudding stone. A suspension bridge here spans the Wye linking a network of footpaths and forest trails.

At the riverside turn right and follow the shorter yellow arrows of the Wye Valley Walk, which continue through this steep-sided gorge for about a mile. Pass impressive rapids and proceed to the Royal Hotel at Symonds Yat. Here leave the Wye Valley Walk and follow the longer yellow arrows of the forest trail, which bears right beside the left-hand wall of the hotel. A steep zigzag path climbs to the 504ft Yat Rock. Wooden seats and steps ease the steep ascent.

At Symonds Yat picnic site bear left to walk across the road bridge to enjoy the view from the famous rock. Yat Rock is a popular tourist site overlooking the beautiful horseshoe bend of the River Wye. There is a rustic log cabin selling refreshments, and a toposcope erected by the Automobile Association.

Retrace the path back across the bridge to rejoin the waymarked path which leaves the car park to the right of its exit. A pleasant 1¾-mile walk can now be followed through mixed woods called Mailscot. At a cottage called Mailscot Lodge the waymarked trail bears left then continues ahead leading back to the stone sign at Ready Penny. Here turn left and proceed back to Ready Penny picnic site.

Forest Sculpture

Allow 3 hours

Disused railway tracks and old industrial tramroads now provide ideal paths in the peaceful Forest of Dean. This walk follows a stretch of the Severn and Wye Valley Railway line and a waymarked forest trail then leads to the heart of the forest at the Speech House. An interesting feature here is the open-air Sculpture Trail, where rustic works of art are permanently on display.

Start from a small lay-by (SO609125) opposite Vallets Wood depot. Follow the Lydbrook road for 500yd, passing a deep pool fed by the Cannop Brook. Turn right along a forest trail waymarked with yellow arrows over Cannop Brook via stepping stones towards a railway bridge. Scramble up the embankment and follow the track to the left through woodland. The route briefly joins the Sculpture Trail which includes a collection of seven works commissioned by the Arnolfini Gallery in collaboration with the Forestry Commission. With financial support from the Henry Moore Foundation artists were encouraged to interpret the Forest of Dean in creative new works.

Continue ahead along the railway track, passing under a brick and stone bridge, then through the wooded slopes of Serridge Inclosure. The waymarked route of the forest trail goes right over a stile parallel to the railway line then bears right through woodland. At a main track turn left and left again leaving the waymarked path. On reaching a metalled road turn right and continue to Crabtree Hill. At the top of the hill the path veers right alongside a patch of cleared woodland with delightful views. Well to the right of Woorgreens Lake the path joins a wide forest track, descending past Kensley Lodge and continuing over a step stile to the picnic site at Speech House. The Speech House (now a hotel) stands in the centre of the Forest and was built during the reign of Charles II to house the Verderers' Court. The courtroom is now the hotel dining room, and can still be viewed by visitors.

The Speech House, built of local stone, stands at an important crossroads in the Forest

Keep to the right of the picnic site and follow the way as directed by yellow arrows, going sharply right opposite the hotel. After the thick yew trees, planted in 1902, the path opens up offering scenic views and a close-up of a massive oak sculpture, The Giant Chair.

After a gentle, descent do not miss a left fork along a rocky track which becomes soft and muddy and descends to the railway embankment. Continue up and over this to return to the car park.

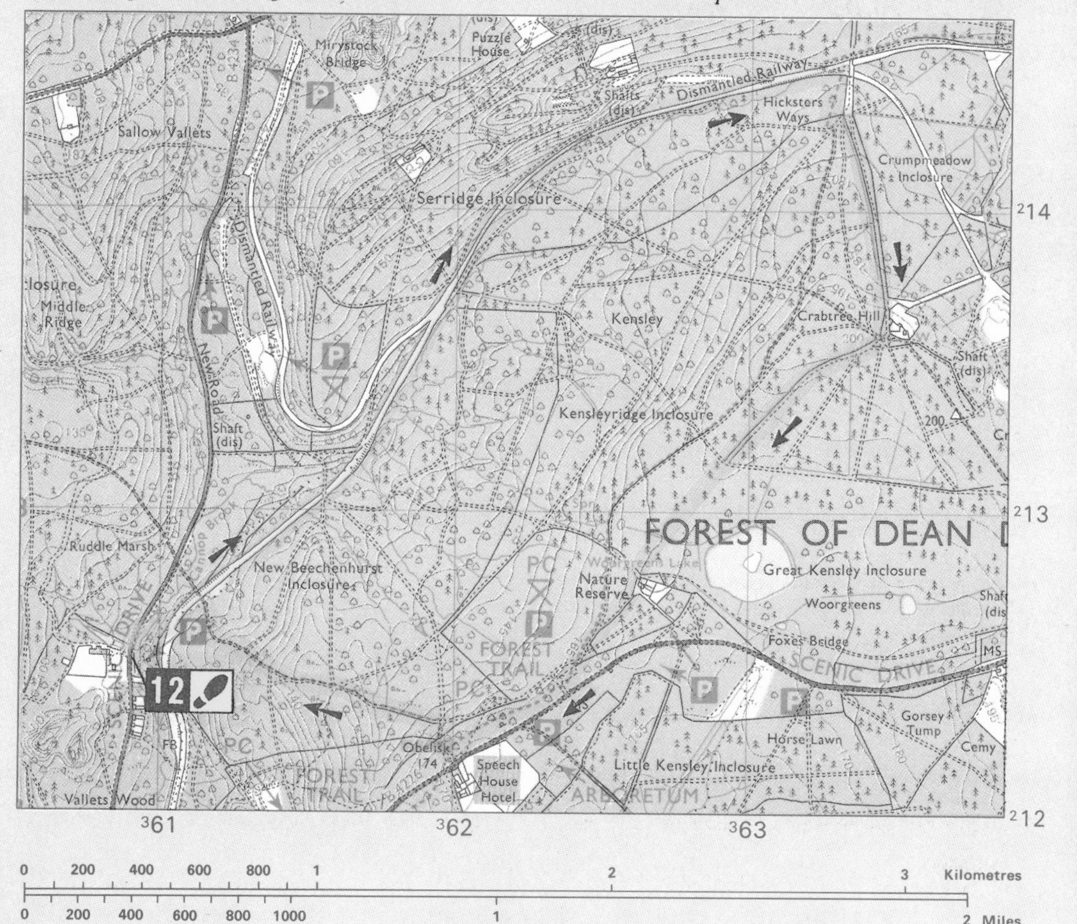

WALK 13

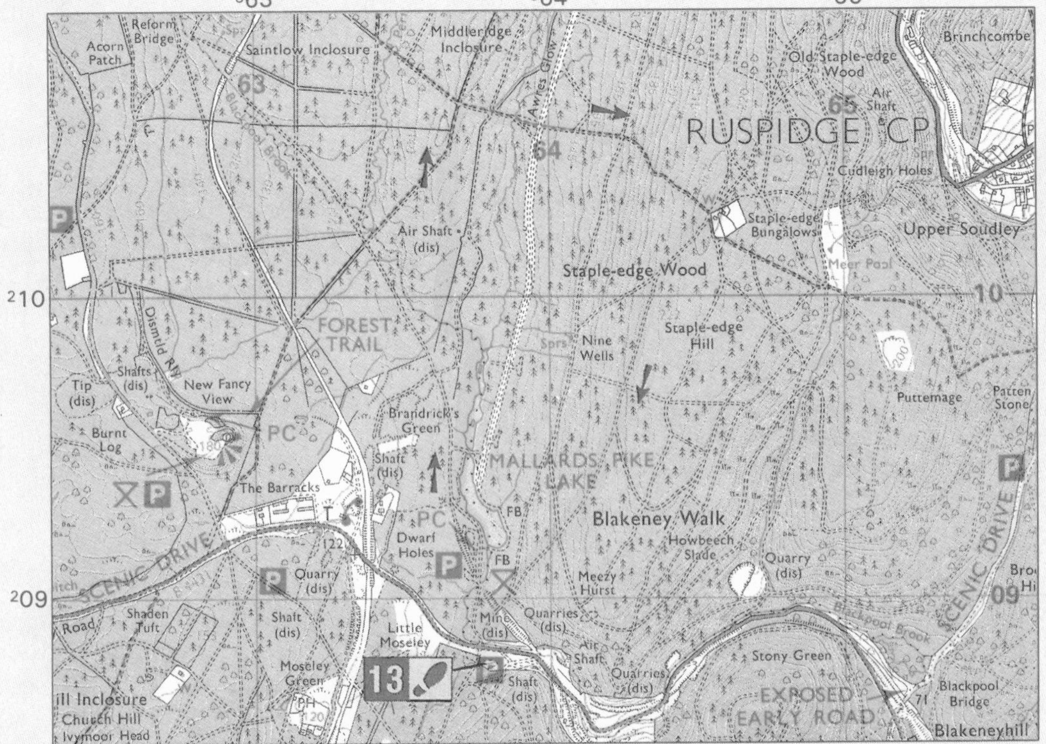

Alongside Mallards Pike

Allow 2 hours

A ramble in the scenic Forest of Dean leads alongside a picturesque lake at Mallards Pike, then along a waymarked forest trail with a strenuous climb to Staple Edge. Here far-reaching views may be enjoyed before returning down an attractive woodland path.

Park at the Forestry Commission car park (SO638088) opposite the entrance to Mallards Pike Lake picnic site. Cross the road and enter the site by following the tarmac lane up to the picnic site and lake. Since Roman times coal has been taken from the Forest of Dean. In the 19th century up to a million tons of coal a year were mined and transported on a network of tramroads and railways. Along this first stretch traces of this old industrialisation are still evident. Mallards Pike is a purpose-built recreational lake constructed by the Forestry Commission in 1982. Swimming is not allowed, but sailing and canoeing are permitted in this delightful pool, surrounded by Scots pine.

Keep to the left of the lake, following a path which becomes narrow and uneven as it winds its way under conifers along the water's edge. On reaching the Blackpool Brook, which feeds this lake, turn left beside the wooden bridge and follow the yellow arrows of the forest trail. This 'yellow arrow route' through the Forest of Dean was created by the Forest of Dean Group of the Ramblers' Association. It is a 10-mile circular walk through East Dean, which can be split into three shorter rambles offering a variety of views and a selection of pools and acres of woodland to be enjoyed along the way.

The rapidly-growing Scots pine will reach a height of 40 to 50ft in just 20 years

Our route now follows this waymarked route to Staple Edge. From the bridge go left then right along a forest track to cross the brook. Turn immediately left through a spruce plantation where the path bears right and continues through woodland before joining a broad path. Follow this to the right, and at the next crossways turn right descending to a main forest track. Be careful to continue ahead along a narrower path which then bears left, becoming broader as it gently climbs between spruce plantations to a clearing at Staple Edge.

At the junction of numerous paths and tracks, turn right and right again to follow the waymarked path along a grass path. Where the waymarked trail bears right, continue ahead. Along this delightful path lined with holly, larch, spruce, gorse and bracken, forest sheep forage.

Ignore all turnings as the path gently descends towards Mallards Pike. Cross over a main track where the narrowing path offers glimpses of the tree-shaded lake below. Once back at the picnic site proceed ahead, cross a stone railway bridge and return to the car park.

Waterfalls and Valley Views

Allow 2 hours

This short walk provides plenty of interest, especially for children. Leafy paths lead through delightful woods in the lower Wye, offering fantastic views. A spectacular feature is the Cleddon Falls, a high and rocky waterfall which, when in full spate, leaps and bounds over boulders and down a misty gorge through which the route steeply descends to the riverside village of Llandogo.

Start from the Forestry Commission's picnic site at Whitestones (SO525029), situated on a minor road 2 miles north of Tintern. From here follow a recently altered part of the Wye Valley Walk northwards through Bargain Wood. Whitestones was created by the Forestry Commission, whose policy is to make the forests accessible and attractive to the public, as well as producing a cash crop from timber. The site has ample parking, picnic tables, superb views of the River Wye and forest trails for the disabled.

After passing the last viewpoint leave these woods by the barrier, then turn right still following the yellow-arrowed route of the Wye Valley Walk. This bridleway leads straight ahead between tall larch and fir trees before reaching a few scattered houses and cottages at Cleddon. The sound of rushing water heralds Cleddon Falls, an attractive feature worth investigating, and especially impressive after heavy rain.

Leave the Wye Valley Walk, cross the stream by a stone bridge, and follow the Cleddon Falls sign along a rustic path, steeply descending wooden steps alongside the falls. Then briefly climb to join a wider track to the right which is the start of a leisurely leafy path which zigzags down the mossy wooded ravine. The Cleddon rises in a peat bog 700ft above the River Wye, which it joins at Llandogo after a fast and furious journey through a scenic gorge. The lengthy zigzag path, partly disturbed by forestry work at present, is part of a nearly forgotten 19th-century tourist route used by the Victorians.

The twisting leaf-strewn path soon returns to the banks of the falls after crossing a number of small rivulets through this boulder-strewn valley. Here keep right to cross the stream by a stone bridge. The path continues to the left, then bears right leading out of the woods to pass cottages with enviable views of the Wye Valley. Immediately turn left along a narrow signed footpath which crosses a lane and continues, descending steeply, between cottage gardens. Turn right at the tarmac lane and follow it for ¾ mile, gently climbing back to Bargain Wood. Catch superb views of the river and Llandogo before a spinney of tall spindly firs blocks the scene.

Where the lane bears right rejoin the Wye Valley Walk, which leads to the right along a pleasant leafy path back to the car park.

Llandogo, birthplace of Bertrand Russell, is scattered among trees on the steep side of the valley

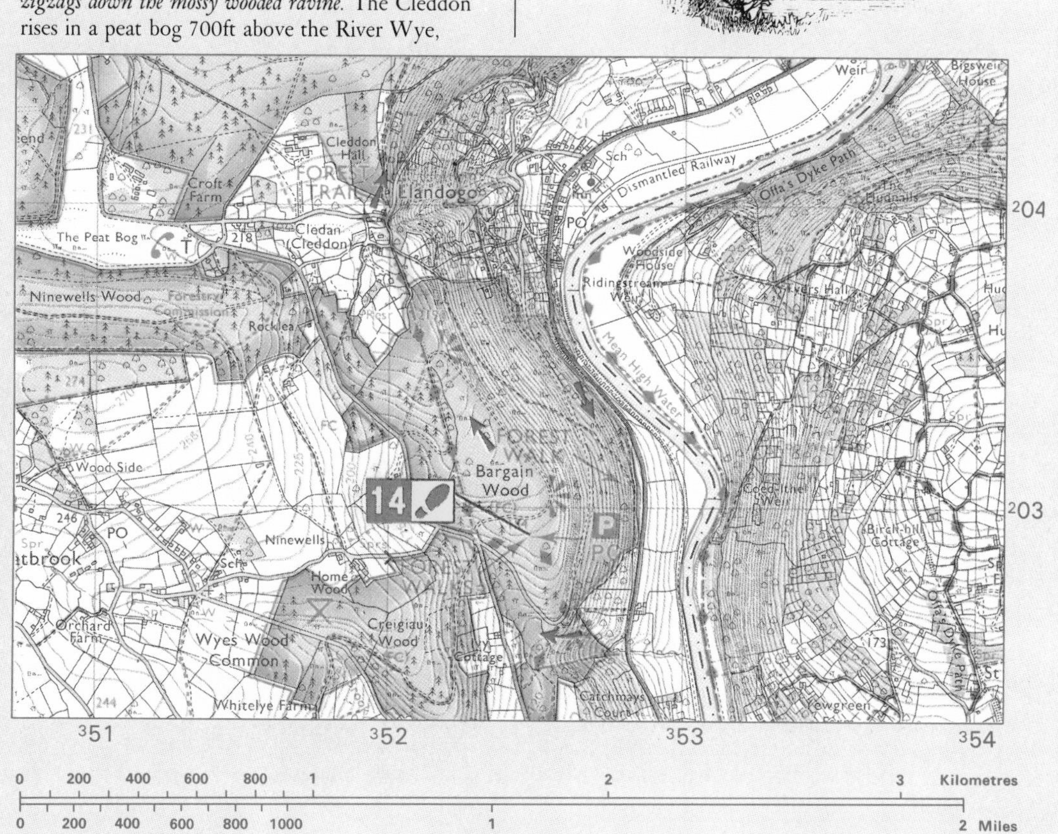

WALK 15

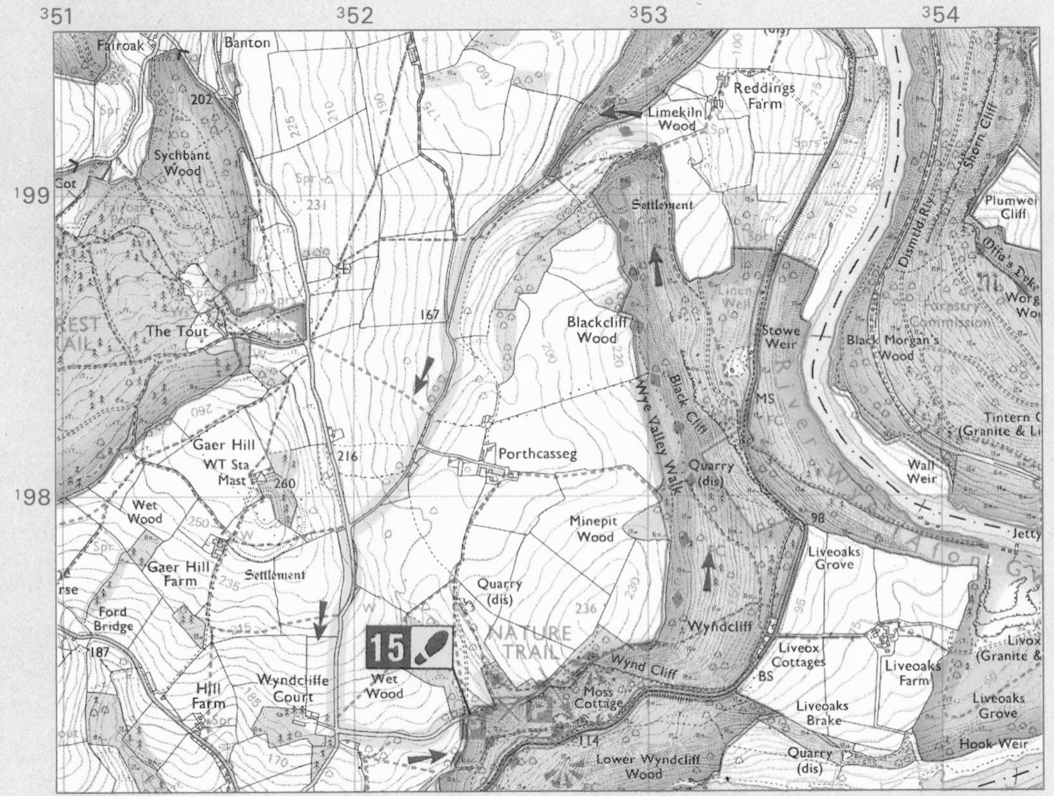

Wynd Cliff

Allow 2½ hours

There are spectacular views of the lower Wye Valley from the steep limestone crags of the Wynd Cliff, which rise to over 700ft. From here the walk continues along the cliff top through attractive beech woods. Ancient cart tracks and quiet lanes lead back amid a serene landscape of gentle undulating fields dotted with mature hardwoods.

Begin from the Upper Wynd Cliff car park (ST524973), which is on a minor road 3 miles north of Chepstow. Follow the yellow arrows of the Wye Valley Walk, winding along the top of the Wynd Cliff towards the fascinating 365 steps and the Eagle's Nest viewpoint. The path follows the footsteps of 18th- and 19th-century poets, writers and artists who toured the Wye Valley during the Romantic period when it was fashionable to discover places of 'untamed beauty'. The 365 steps leading down the Wynd Cliff were constructed in 1828 as a tourist attraction and were renovated in 1971 by the Beachley Army College Apprentices. The lookout known as the Eagle's Nest is set 700ft above the River Wye where there is a famous and magnificent view of the Wye Valley. The stone seat commemorates a Wye Valley warden who was involved with the planning and construction of the Wye Valley Walk.

Continue along the waymarked path through a variety of woodland where scenic views can be glimpsed between the beech, oak, holly, yew and ash trees. Young children should be carefully supervised along this stretch, where the cliffs fall dramatically and steeply to the river.

After Blackcliff Wood the uneven path rises over an enchanting outcrop of mossy boulders, the site of an ancient settlement. After a steep and rocky descent the Wye Valley Walk turns right then left before leaving these attractive cliff-top woods.

Wye Tourers on the Chepstow road at the Wynd Cliff

Yellow arrows direct the way over a solid stile and across a sloping field to another stile leading into the dark Limekiln Woods, where a steep and narrow path joins an old cobbled track. Leave the Wye Valley Walk by turning left up this old forgotten byway. This track has been described as a pack-horse road, but it was probably widened to accommodate iron-shod traffic carrying lime and iron ore down to the barges at the riverside and to the iron furnaces at Tintern. This village became an important industrial centre in the 17th century, with wire works, furnaces and forges which gradually ceased production during the latter part of the last century. Today Tintern is famous for its ruined Cistercian abbey standing romantically by the banks of the Wye.

Rough and uneven, the track rises and continues between hedges which enclose undulating fields offering a more comforting landscape. On meeting a tarmac lane turn left where a steeper climb passes one or two isolated cottages. At a T-junction keep to the left, and left again at Wyndcliffe Court where the lane returns to the car park.

WALK 16

Devil's Pulpit

Allow 2½ hours

An invigorating ramble over mixed terrain including peaty forest tracks and level pastures leading to a magnificent view of the Wye Valley and Tintern Abbey from the Devil's Pulpit. After a magical woodland stroll along a short stretch of Offa's Dyke Path, pleasant footpaths lead back across farmland and along old lanes.

This walk starts from the Forestry Commission car park at Tidenham (ST559993) a few miles north of Chepstow on the Gloucestershire side of the River Wye. From the car park a footpath sign to the Devil's Pulpit directs the way along a spongy waymarked path through thick conifer plantations known as The Park. On reaching a narrow lane turn right and after about 300yd turn left over an unusual stone and wood stile. Tidenham Chase is a large area of woodland in the parish of Tidenham managed by the Forestry Commission. Opposite the Tidenham car park visitors can admire a panoramic view of the Severn Estuary. It is hard to believe that in 1445 the vicar of Tidenham was allowed to leave because of the danger of wolves.

From here a clearly marked footpath leads across pleasant level pastures to the steep wooded slopes of the Wye, then follows the Offa's Dyke Path to the right alongside a substantial section of the ancient earthwork. To reach the rocky outcrop known as the Devil's Pulpit, detour for 100yd to the left. The Devil's Pulpit offers a memorable view of the Wye Valley and Tintern Abbey below. Legend relates that from this eminence the devil preached to the monks working in the abbey grounds, hoping to take their minds off their work. Offa's Dyke was constructed in the 8th century by a king of Mercia, to form the boundary between Wales and Mercia.

From the Devil's Pulpit walk north for about 1½ miles along the waymarked Offa's Dyke Path. The rough, uneven, but well-trodden path winding under trees of beech, holly and yew indicates an ancient, arcadian woodland.

At a wooden barrier leave the Dyke Path by turning right over a stile beside a huge boulder. The right of way is followed along the left-hand side of the field to a gate. Here by a fence turn sharp right up the slope to Beeches Farm where yellow arrows direct the way around the farmyard to join a lane ahead. This wide grassy byway known as Miss Grace's Lane narrows and continues along a pleasant stretch before returning to the conifer plantations of The Park.

Follow the first wide track on the left which leads past the triangulation point where the way is easily retraced back to the car park.

Majestic arches, fine doorways and elegant windows combine in Tintern Abbey's superb West Front

Index

Page numbers in bold type indicate main entries. See also Directory, page 73.